"May and Perry bring rare methodological skill and grounded political insights to demonstrate that it is possible to shift the urban knowledge economy to work for all citizens. Theirs is a creative partnership that foregrounds the transformative potential of universities (and scholars) as knowledge brokers and agents of economic change." — *Professor Susan Parnell, African Centre for Cities, University of Cape Town, South Africa*

"May and Perry go digging into today's dominant notions about what is good for a city, especially the much admired advances coming from the sciences and technology. They re-emerge with facts and possibilities that often run against 'what we know', to the delight of some and horror of others." — *Saskia Sassen, Columbia University, USA, author of* Expulsions

CITIES AND THE KNOWLEDGE ECONOMY

Cities and the Knowledge Economy is an in-depth, interdisciplinary, international and comparative examination of the relationship between knowledge and urban development in the contemporary era. Through the lenses of promise, politics and possibility, it examines how the knowledge economy has arisen, how different cities have sought to realise its potential, how universities play a role in its realisation and, overall, what this reveals about the relationship between politics, capitalism, space, place and knowledge in cities.

The book argues that the 21st century city has been predicated on particular circuits of knowledge that constitute expertise as residing in elite and professional epistemic communities. In contrast, alternative conceptions of the knowledge society are founded on assumptions which take analysis, deliberation, democracy and the role of the citizen and communities of practice seriously. Drawing on a range of examples from cities around the world, the book reflects on these possibilities and asks what roles the practice of 'active intermediation', the university and a critical and engaged social scientific practice can all play in this process.

The book is aimed at researchers and students from different disciplines – geography, politics, sociology, business studies, economics and planning – with interests in contemporary urbanism and the role of knowledge in understanding development, as well as urban policymakers, politicians and practitioners who are concerned with the future of our cities and seek to create coalitions of different communities oriented towards more just and sustainable futures.

Tim May is Professor of Social Science Methodology and Director of Research in the Sheffield Methods Institute, University of Sheffield. He has authored and edited sixteen books, including new editions, which have been translated into fifteen languages, as well as over one hundred and eighty articles, book chapters, research reports and policy briefings.

Beth Perry is Professorial Fellow in the Urban Institute, University of Sheffield. She focuses on the potential of research to interrogate and support pathways to more just and sustainable urban futures. She leads the UK's participation in the *Realising Just Cities* programme, and two major ESRC grants, *Jam and Justice: Coproducing Governance for Social Innovation* and *Whose Knowledge Matters: Competing and Contesting Knowledge Claims in 21st Century Cities.*

Science in Society Series

Series Editor: Steve Rayner
Institute for Science, Innovation and Society, University of Oxford

The Earthscan Science in Society Series aims to publish new high-quality research, teaching, practical and policy-related books on topics that address the complex and vitally important interface between science and society.

Experiment Earth
Responsible innovation in geoengineering
Jack Stilgoe

Rethinking Greenland and the Arctic in the Era of Climate Change
New Northern Horizons
Frank Sejersen

International Science and Technology Education
Exploring Culture, Economy and Social Perceptions
Edited by Ortwin Renn, Nicole C. Karafyllis, Andreas Hohlt and Dorothea Taube

Policy Legitimacy, Science and Political Authority
Knowledge and action in liberal democracies
Edited by Michael Heazle and John Kane

Systems Thinking for Geoengineering Policy
How to reduce the threat of dangerous climate change by embracing uncertainty and failure
Robert Chris

Assessing the Societal Implications of Emerging Technologies
Anticipatory governance in practice
Evan Michelson

Aid, Technology and Development
The lessons from Nepal
Edited by Dipak Gyawali, Michael Thompson and Marco Verweij

Climate Adaptation Policy and Evidence
Understanding the Tensions between Politics and Expertise in Public Policy
Peter Tangney

Cities and the Knowledge Economy
Promise, Politics and Possibilities
Tim May and Beth Perry

CITIES AND THE KNOWLEDGE ECONOMY

Promise, Politics and Possibilities

Tim May and Beth Perry

Routledge
Taylor & Francis Group
LONDON AND NEW YORK

from Routledge

First published 2018
by Routledge
2 Park Square, Milton Park, Abingdon, Oxon OX14 4RN

and by Routledge
711 Third Avenue, New York, NY 10017

Routledge is an imprint of the Taylor & Francis Group, an informa business

© 2018 Tim May and Beth Perry

British Library Cataloguing-in-Publication Data
A catalogue record for this book is available from the British Library

Library of Congress Cataloging-in-Publication Data
A catalog record for this book has been requested

ISBN: 978-1-138-81038-9 (hbk)
ISBN: 978-1-138-81039-6 (pbk)
ISBN: 978-1-315-74953-2 (ebk)

Typeset in Bembo
by Servis Filmsetting Ltd, Stockport, Cheshire

CONTENTS

TABLES

ACKNOWLEDGEMENTS

Whilst writing this book, Beth and I were authoring other works. Like all processes of writing, often contained outside of the written pages, these represent a reflexive journey forged through experiences, interactions, contexts and directions. This is not surprising, for we have spent over fifteen years working in and for cities and universities and during this time encountered the knowledge economy in its various manifestations. So we decided we needed to write this book. For this and other reasons, I would like to thank Beth for sharing this journey and in the process being a supportive colleague and a good friend.

I would like to record my thanks to those who have been supportive of my endeavours now and in the past, including the late Zygmunt Bauman, Carole Sutton, Davydd Greenwood, Morten Levin, Bev Skeggs and Dorothy Smith. My thanks to the Institute of Advanced Study, University of Durham, where I spent the Spring Term of 2016 as a fellow and wrote a part of this book and met and discussed ideas with a group of scholars from varying disciplines, as well as my new colleagues in the Realising Just Cities research programme and the Methods Institute, both at the University of Sheffield. Thanks to Ken Parsons for our frequent chats over the years; to the 'Kalkan 7' for the fun, sharing of experiences and the holidays; to Vicky Simpson for her support; to Catherine Barlow for compiling the bibliography and index and to the editorial and production teams at Routledge for enabling this book to be published. My love and gratitude to Vikki for her support and encouragement in her own busy life and to Cian, Alex, Calum, Nick and Lewis, my sons and stepsons, for demonstrating that the world can be a better place through a care and concern for others.

Tim and I have been working together for many years on projects and writings informing this book. It has been a productive and supportive relationship, underpinned by a shared orientation to critique and possibility – from which this book has sprung. I thank Tim for his friendship, wisdom and advice in all our endeavours. I would like to thank other colleagues who have supported me in my career in different ways: Steve Fuller, Davydd Greenwood, Simon Marvin, Steve Rayner and Alan Scott. Past and current colleagues – Catherine Barlow, Victoria Habermehl, Sophie King, Bert Russell, Vicky Simpson and Nick Taylor Buck – have witnessed the slow production of this work and for their patience and support I offer my thanks. I would also like to recognise newer colleagues at the Urban Institute, University of Sheffield and my academic collaborators in UK and international universities for their collegiality and encouragement. To the Watts clan, thank you for your warm wishes, helpful chats and all round support. And to the Perry posse, my love and solidarity in all that we face together.

We would like to thank Steve Rayner for including this book in his series. We also acknowledge the support of the funders of the Realising Just Cities programme. They are: the Mistra Foundation for Strategic Environmental Research which enables our participation in the Mistra Urban Futures Centre (http://www.mistraurbanfutures.org/en); the Arts and Humanities Research Council for 'Cultural Intermediation: Connecting Communities in the Creative Urban Economy' (Grant number: AH/J005320/1); the Economic and Social Research Council for 'Jam and Justice: Co-producing Urban Governance for Social Innovation' (Grant number: ES/N005945/1) and 'Whose Knowledge Matters? Competing and Contesting Knowledge Claims in 21st Century Cities' (Grant number: ES/N018818/1). Responsibility for the arguments in the book remains our own.

The book itself is both an elaboration and development of our writings on this subject to date. Whilst we have referenced these in the text, we would like to acknowledge the following journals, publishers and editors:

May, T. (2017), 'Urban crisis: bonfire of vanities to find opportunity in the ashes', *Urban Studies*. Available at: http://journalsx.sagepub.com/eprint/sgcNiC9nzUTeAJrGGxch/full

May, T. (2011), 'Urban knowledge arenas: dynamics, tensions and potentials'. *International Journal of Knowledge-Based Development*, 2 (2): 132–147.

May, T. and Perry, B. (2016), 'Knowledge for Just Urban Sustainability', *Local Environment*, available at: http://www.tandfonline.com/eprint/iE9gQiruc4ahFAzFcnFF/full

May, T. and Perry, B. (2016), 'Cities, experiments and the logics of the knowledge economy?', in Evans, J., Karvonen, A. and Raven, R. (eds.) *The Experimental City*, London: Routledge

May, T. and Perry, B. (2013), 'Universities, reflexivity and critique: uneasy parallels in practice', *Policy Futures in Education*, 11 (5): 505–514.

May, T. and Perry, B. (2011), 'Contours and conflicts in scale: science, knowledge and urban development', *Local Economy*, 26 (8): 715–720.

May, T. and Perry, B. (eds.) (2006), 'Universities in the knowledge economy: places of expectation/spaces for reflection?', *Social Epistemology*, 20 (3–4).

May, T. and Perry, B. (eds.) (2005), 'The future of urban sociology', *Sociology*, 39 (2): 343–370.

Perry, B. and May, T. (2015), 'Context matters: the english science cities and visions for knowledge-based urbanism', in Tian Miao, J., Benneworth, P. and Phelps, N. (eds.)

Making 21st Century Knowledge Complexes: Technopoles of the World 20 Years After, London: Routledge.

Perry, B. and May, T. (2015), 'Lessons on the research-practice relationship: from critique to co-production in greater manchester', in Polk, M. (ed.) *Co-Producing Knowledge for Sustainable Cities: Joining Forces for Change*, London: Routledge.

Perry, B. and May, T. (eds.) (2011), 'Building knowledge cities: the roles of universities', *Built Environment*, 37 (3).

Perry, B. and May, T. (2010), 'Urban knowledge exchange: devilish dichotomies and active intermediation', *International Journal of Knowledge-Based Development*, 1 (1/2): 6–24.

INTRODUCTION

Cities matter. Some 54 per cent of the world's population live in cities, with this number expected to increase to 66 per cent by 2050. Accompanying this is a growth in 'mega-cities' that have populations of ten million or more. There are twenty-eight across the world, with an anticipated further rise to forty-one by 2020 (United Nations 2014). Urban areas possess a density of population which has positive and negative consequences. They exhibit the effects of agglomeration: that is, the production and exchange of goods and services and housing within particular areas which is said to provide location-specific advantages to firms. Cities also create pollution and are sites of huge inequalities in income, wealth and health.

Concentration and connectivity are accompanied by hope, fear, opportunity and anxiety. Some cities operate at a supra-national level by being major sites into which capital has invested and is located. Finance centres, for example, exist in London, New York, Shanghai, Hong Kong and Tokyo. Others are left behind in the global race for success, characterised as lagging and dragging on national economies. Whilst some places have prospered in the shift from manufacturing to service economies, others have fared less well. As the flows of global finance continue to dominate the fates and fortunes of cities, such inequalities are reinforced. The assets held by UK banks in 2013, for example, were four times the value of its GDP. The result is a sector that pervades economic activity and concentrates power within a small group of countries (Newfield 2016).

A financial system exists across the globe, which has been characterised as resembling: "nothing as much as a vast casino. Everyday games are played in this casino that involve sums of money so large that they cannot be imagined. At night, the games go on at the other side of the world" (Strange 2016: 1). This is assumed to be informed by rational calculation with little concern for places, only global flows. In the process, attempts by liberal democratic nation-states to regulate practices for the benefit of their citizens can be undermined; the former variably lacking in political will, or else concerned about the mobility of capital, given its enormous power and influence over democratically elected governments. The global economic system is based on and perpetuates specific systems of value and exchange. Forces of globalisation shape the focus and direction of cities. They produce a 'global consciousness' in which we see: "the compression of the world and the intensification of consciousness of the world as a whole" (Robertson 1992: 8). Fear of the 'other' mixes with the intensification of economic aspirations and the manifestation of environmental degradation. Urban strategies are unavoidably saturated by these dynamics, raising questions of what to embrace, for what reasons, according to which values and for whose benefit.

Structural inequalities, the power of mobile capital, the intensification of economic activity and inactivity, financial crashes and global recession: these are the essential backdrops to our exploration of cities and the knowledge economy. The knowledge economy is not separate from the global economic system, but is part of that system – actively produced and reproduced to enable globalisation, economic liberalisation and the movement of financial capital. The key shift is the movement from knowledge *about* the economy to knowledge *for* the economy as part of a broader set of processes designed to reify all possible resources as objects amenable to commodification and control. For Cornelius Castoriadis, reification is an essential tendency of capitalism which: "can never be wholly realized. If it were, if the system were actually able to change individuals into things moved only by economic 'forces', it would collapse not in the long run, but immediately... Capitalism can function only by continually drawing upon the genuinely *human* activity of those subject to it, while at the same time trying to level and dehumanize them as much as possible" (1997: 16. Original italics).

The knowledge economy is a powerful aspirational device in the face of the ambivalence created by global change. It can encompass many activities that depend on generating and deploying knowledge to reach their goals. The knowledge economy provides evidence for urban policy that seeks to shape the city and enables a critical evaluation of existing conditions in terms of their causes and effects and thus, possible solutions. It is held to be dispassionate in its content and removed from the realm of values. Neutrality thereby works to provide a distance from the realm of political strategy through clearly bounded relations between knowledge, value and choice. However, the idea that the knowledge economy remains neutral and disinterested in the face of the intensification of aspirations, or that it is separate from political and economic spheres, is difficult to maintain. After all, those who produce knowledge have a sense of what will, and will not, be acceptable to those for whom it is produced and for what reasons. Those who receive that knowledge will, in turn, consider some forms of knowledge more relevant and useful than others. Knowledge is therefore poured into the mix of ambivalence between aspiration, expectation and use.

Against the backdrop of a movement from manufacturing to service economies in the West, the knowledge economy is a mobilising image for cities to create opportunities for their futures. In so doing, its promise rests upon the concentrations of services and economies of scale through generating a critical mass of expertise intended to lead to innovation and wealth creation. Can the promise of the knowledge economy provide a recipe for success in an uncertain world which, despite the effects of global forces, remains reliant for its success upon location? What are the expectations placed upon knowledge and how are these mediated in different spatial contexts? What is the overall purpose of the knowledge-based economy? Is it to enhance democratic aspirations by bringing political control closer to urban citizens, or a technocratic fix to enhance the efficiency of urban political apparatuses to pursue particular economic agendas? What does this mean for the strategies cities pursue, in terms of who is setting the agenda, according to what kinds of rationales and mobilising whose knowledge? Most importantly, what are the mediating factors that shape the outcomes of knowledge-based change? Who wins and who loses?

These are the central questions that underpin this examination of cities and the knowledge economy. Our distinctive contribution is to take these issues into the heart of the traditional knowledge-producing establishment. As major sites for knowledge-producing activities, universities cannot simply remain insulated and privileged from the obligations which follow in terms of contributing to urban economic vibrancy and growth. As a result: "the chill winds of economic necessity that is the encompassing weather of most people's lives blow a little more searchingly into the too-protected groves of academe" (Collini 2017: 32). Hence, we are also centrally concerned with how universities are implicated in the knowledge-based economy and with what consequences for social scientific knowledge production.

Promise, politics and possibilities

This book is our response to these issues. It offers a critique of how the dynamics of the knowledge economy have unfolded to embrace so few and exclude so many. It is about where, what and whose knowledge matters in this latest stage of capitalist development, about who gains and who loses. If expectations outstrip what can be delivered, what is the result? Is disappointment inevitable as knowledge falls short of expectations to solve policy dilemmas? Or are such failures pre-emptively avoided through the mobilisation of particular forms of knowledge? Overall, this is a book concerning what happens when expectations of knowledge, forged to realise images of the future in an uncertain world, become blurred and divorced from the realm of public, political deliberation. Circuits of knowledge are created in which analysis feeds aspiration and the desire for recognition based on forms of expertise, but is separated from public deliberations concerning the desirability, direction and consequence of urban futures. Yet this book is also about how things might be different if we move from politics to possibility through engaging with, and moving beyond, our current conditions.

The arguments in this book are based on over fifteen years' experience working in and for cities and universities which have sought to embrace the knowledge economy promise. We have analysed these experiences elsewhere (May and Perry 2017). In this book, we outline how the promise of the urban knowledge economy (Part I) is mediated by key factors – scale, institutions and expertise. We argue that it is the politics of these factors which both delimits the promise (Part II) and raises hopes of alternative possibilities and practices (Part III). Our argument navigates between promise, politics and possibilities and weaves key themes throughout the book: convergence and divergence, capitulation and resistance, control and freedom, certainty and doubt. In contrast to easy pronouncements about its form and character, we illustrate the Janus-faced character and nebulous quality of the knowledge economy. It is restless, contradictory, weightless and laden with heavy and variable expectations that can be populated from different sources.

The distinctiveness of the book lies in its recognition of this ambiguity alongside identification of lines of tension and difference. Our critique is positioned against the backdrop of accelerations in capitalist development which shapes our interest in illustrating how forces are mediated through scalar relations, institutions of knowledge production and values attributed to different forms of knowledge and expertise. For this purpose, we draw upon our national and international work and experiences to illustrate our argument, along with studies from varying disciplines – geography, economics, sociology, political science, anthropology, social epistemology and management and organisation studies. The literature on knowledge and urban development is frequently fragmented across disciplines and has hitherto not been made accessible in a single book.

In moving into analysis of universities as sites of knowledge production and the values attributed to different forms of expertise, the book also extends beyond the usual boundaries – into reflexive territory that may be uncomfortable for some. This is not to irresponsibly lay bare institutional complicities, nor to tar academics with labels based on simplistic self-interest. Rather, we believe that universities and social scientific knowledge have more positive roles to play in sustainable urban transformations that can only be realised through deep reflection and alterations in the social organisation of knowledge production. In an era marked by supposed 'post-truth' politics, a questioning of expertise and an apparent revolt against globalisation whilst voting for those who have benefited from it, ours is not a relativist position. Expertise and social science matter, but we contend we need to be more attentive to the conditions of knowledge production and practices of research if we are to contribute to an economy for the many not the few.

The structure of the book

To chart these dynamics, we examine their international manifestations and urban contexts through an investigation in three parts. The first part of the book, *Promise*, has two chapters, each summarising, analysing and illustrating literatures on knowledge and urban development. In the first chapter, we chart the rise of the knowledge economy. We examine its origins in more detail against the backdrop of global forces and the general shift from industrial to post-industrial societies.

As part of this discussion, we look at the changing expectations that are placed upon knowledge and the key factors that frame the potential of knowledge *for* the economy: spatial developments, universities and expertise. We briefly outline how these have become the targets of policy, reified into objects to be managed for economic success.

Cities around the globe are seeking to harness the power of knowledge in creating science cities and urban innovation platforms to develop new visions upon which to base their strategies. Chapter two therefore examines how cities have embraced the promise of the knowledge economy. For this purpose, we consider the urban strategies that have emerged to harness knowledge through the acquisition of talent, promotion of research expertise, marketing and image management. We seek to further understand the relations between knowledge and the city in terms of its attributed value informed by uncertain and uneven development, dancing between convergent and divergent pressures.

The second part of the book, *Politics*, examines the political reproduction of the idea of the knowledge economy and its consequences for cities. Continuing our interdisciplinary understanding and comparative analysis of cities, we look at how political-economic imperatives limit or constrain the realisation of different visions of knowledge-based development. Part II comprises three essays elaborating in turn the politics of spatial development (chapter three), universities (chapter four) and expertise (chapter five) in order to construct an explanatory framework for how the knowledge-based economy is mediated to produce diverse outcomes for different groups. Our argument here is that in order to construct alternative trajectories, there is a need for a critical urban practice to understand how the promise of the knowledge economy is reproduced across different sites and scales of action and for varying reasons. We examine the forces that inform and sustain particular techno-centric views of knowledge and urban development, identifying ideas and practices that find institutional and cultural expression in government, business and universities.

Despite differences between the Global North and South, globalisation can work to constitute interdependencies manifest in claims to the exceptionality of world cities that act as exemplars for best practice. How contemporary pressures on cities in relation to globalisation and the development of capitalism shape aspirations and expectations of urban development is of central importance for understanding and building alternatives. This, therefore, is the focus of chapter three. Whilst global flows seem to favour the content of the knowledge economy over the contexts of its application, places remain vital to realise its potential. Hence, we see how context both matters and has been simultaneously devalued in the search for knowledge-based advantage. As ideas circulate around the globe, this creates ambivalence between the exogenous influences of the promise of the knowledge economy and its endogenous realisation manifest in a game of scales. In the process, "new spaces of knowledge, such as universities, science parks and cultural quarters ... are created side by side with the new spaces of consumption and new patterns of social inequality" (Madanipour 2011: 1–2).

In our journey to understand the politics of reproduction, we continue our analysis of universities in the knowledge economy in chapter four. As throughout the book, we note the differences in political economy between universities and cities, but note a general aspiration they have in common: that is, to become global and participate in the generation of competitive advantage. Those who are concerned to recover the time for contemplation within universities have observed: "Concerns about the future of the university may vary by stakeholder. While some may be shared across continents, others are nationally specific. But they nevertheless emerge from a common set of pressures, and lead to some common organizational responses" (Popp Berman and Paradeise 2016: 3). The knowledge economy challenges the idea that universities are distinctive because of their distance from the economy; instead, they are centred in its potential and must participate in its reproduction as a condition of survival. At an organisational and cultural level, we see a movement from a public service to a performance and audit-based ethos in which success can be measured by particular sets of indicators and ideas of urban development. What emerges, we argue, is a missing middle between expectations, organisational structures and cultures with particular consequences for the recognition and production of different forms of knowledge: "A system with so few 'winners' and so many 'losers' is toxic for democratic society and should not be allowed to persist" (Levin and Greenwood 2016: 196).

In chapter five, we turn to questions of expertise and the relationships between the justification and application of knowledge. We particularly focus on the geographies of knowledge production and how particular ideas of expertise and knowledge are reproduced within certain groups. To examine this in detail and the relations between the content and context of knowledge, we present a typology for the spatial dimension of expertise in terms of the relations between excellence, relevance and scale. Our investigations are about what happens when the boundaries between values, knowledge, action and the present and future start to move and blend for particular purposes. We then see popular examples of success that hold an exemplary status as cities and universities seek to replicate the same outcome to achieve global recognition. However, what of those who are left out of this race? Whose knowledge matters?

Having highlighted the politics of reproduction that inform the practices of knowledge-based urban development, we move into Part III of the book, *Possibilities*, to understand the consequences for urban communities and the formulation of alternatives for the future. What alternatives might exist to the frenetic pace of change in the pursuit of growth? What kinds of knowledge and expertise are required for more sustainable and just urban futures? How can we create new and value existing knowledge in cities for the many and not the few? Part III therefore considers the relations between knowledge, control, participation and coproduction. We examine the sources and dynamics of potential alternatives to city trajectories and university futures and ask what we can learn from them. In the process we emphasise the possibilities to transcend, transmute and disrupt dominant relations between knowledge and the urban and open these up to different forms of experience, justification and application in the pursuit of urban justice.

Chapter six starts by considering alternative knowledge-based urbanisms that may be emerging from within the shadows of the knowledge economy. Grassroots initiatives, experiences, struggles and experiments aim to produce social, cultural and ecological knowledge outside of the narrow constitution of the economic, which has sought to colonise their differences. We ask how knowledge can be opened up as a common good and challenge the narrow and destructive individualism that pervades the contemporary landscape. For this to happen, the focus needs to be on deliberation within civil society rather than analysis and justification being the preserve of defined political groupings. Chapter six opens up the possibility that alternative ways of knowing and seeing might challenge hegemonic rationalities.

The urban, as with all phenomena, is not amenable to study through the gaze of those whose training refuses to see the limits, as well as strengths, of their modes of analysis. Despite this, the 'silo' mentality within universities prevails within departments and faculties and there is often little thought given to the organisational cultures needed for interdisciplinary working. Administrative control over bounded units, as an end in itself, is antithetical to imaginative and innovative ways of working that are a precondition for the sustainable futures of institutions of higher education, as well as imaginative responses to contemporary urban problems. Thus, in chapter seven, we focus on alternative institutional designs and go in search of the 'real' university. Of course, our title is ironic, but as with urban development, we see possibility in drawing out progressive ideals and actions that also easily unsettle any sideswipes at notion of the 'ivory tower'.

In drawing attention to possibilities in chapters six and seven, we do not claim that alternatives have been realised, nor do we downplay the power of the forces we have examined. We do argue, however, that it is only by recognising, actively confronting and exploring and learning from efforts to transform current trajectories that change can be brought about. There is no quick fix and dangers lurk in the long shadows of the knowledge economy which threaten potential alternatives through cooptation and control, bolstering the status quo or bracketing politics through creating delusive bubbles that apparently keep economic forces at bay. Chapters six and seven ask how things might be different if the politics of scale, institutional power and transformative knowledge can be harnessed in pursuit of more sustainable urban futures.

We have not been content in this book to just chart the 'what' and 'where' of the knowledge economy, but to also illuminate the 'how', 'why' and for 'whom'? We find changes indicative of an excess of expectations going hand in hand with the abdication of any general – or indeed specific governmental – responsibility for mediating change, harnessing inclusive potentials and distributing opportunity. Instead, time and power are implicated in global flows of ideas where quick fixes, short cuts or technical solutions, rather than the work of understanding and learning, is assumed appropriate to urban development. In the process, knowledge is expected to produce something it cannot possibly deliver. A narrow deployment of concepts of scientific expertise and its relationship to place means knowledge is configured to transform the nature of democracy from a politics of sovereign citizens to circuits of epistemic privilege.

This is why our final chapter turns squarely to social scientific practice and what it might contribute in the face of contemporary forces. In chapter eight, we reprise our critique and the key themes we have examined. We explore the conditions of uncertainty, doubt and complexity and the 'wickedness' of urban problems. We then consider what different outcomes we might envisage and how social scientific knowledge production might be placed in service to a different kind of society. Deliberative spaces, exchange between groups and the fostering and upscaling of learning are all central aspects in realising this alternative promise. If we take seriously the 'devilish dichotomies' that beset relations between knowledge and action and focus on the knowledge needed for more sustainable and just urban futures, then we must also create spaces of mediation and participation to examine whose knowledge matters and what implications that has for research practice. We argue that what we term 'active intermediation' plays a key role in developing the civic university as a distinctive institution in which the integration of forms of knowledge for deliberation on urban futures might take place.

The search for just, sustainable futures requires organising cities in such a way as to connect knowledge about an area to the capacities and capabilities to make desired changes. Our experiences have taught us that conceptions of knowledge and the economy exert pressures upon expectations that cannot be downplayed through simple dismissal. The knowledge economy discourse has become "so pervasive that it has assumed the status of truth, to the extent of denying that alternatives exist" (Kenway et al. 2006: 4). We deal here with tendencies, the outcomes of which can be real in their effects. Economists often introduce knowledge as a commodity, "rendering invisible the social nature of knowledge and its fabrication" (Stehr 2002: 7). This book is a corrective to this oversight. We argue that ideas of the future are a spur to the present and what we examine is not all determining. We thus examine the practices of those who seek alternatives and so open up the future to other possibilities. This is not the triumph of hope over experience. Rather, it is recognition that between the past, the present and the future, we find ambivalence. This should not paralyse us, nor foreclose the making of better futures. Our book is a contribution to that endeavour.

References

Castoriadis, C. (1997 [1975]), *The Imaginary Institution of Society*, translated by Blamey, K. Cambridge: Polity.

Collini, S. (2017), *Speaking of Universities,* London: Verso.

Kenway, J., Bullen, E., Fahey, J. and Robb, S. (2006), *Haunting the Knowledge Economy* (Vol. 6), New York: Routledge.

Levin, M. and Greenwood, D. (2016), *Creating a New Public University and Reviving Democracy: Action Research in Higher Education*, Oxford: Berghahn.

Madanipour, A. (2011), *Knowledge Economy and the City: Spaces of Knowledge*, London: Routledge.

May, T. and Perry, B. (2017), *Reflexivity: The Essential Guide*, London: Sage.

Newfield, C. (2016), *The Great Mistake: How We Wrecked Public Universities and How We Can Fix Them*, Baltimore: John Hopkins University Press.

Popp Berman, E. and Paradeise, C. (eds.) (2016), *The University Under Pressure*, Bingley: Emerald.

Robertson, R. (1992), *Globalization: Social Theory and Global Culture*, London: Sage.

Stehr, N. (2002), *Knowledge and Economic Conduct: The Social Foundations of the Modern Economy*, Toronto: University of Toronto Press.

Strange, S. (2016) [1986]), *Casino Capitalism*, Manchester: Manchester University Press.

United Nations (2014), *Concise Report on the World Population Situation in 2014, Department of Economic and Social Affairs Population Division*. http://www.un.org/en/development/desa/population/publications/trends/concise-report2014.shtml (accessed May 2017).

PART I
Promise

1

THE KNOWLEDGE ECONOMY

Introduction

The emergence of the knowledge economy is part of an historical process. It is not a sudden event. Texts have been devoted to charting its origins in the proliferation of information technologies, increases in high value goods and services and the changing nature of the workforce in response to post-industrialisation. As a promise of the future, it arose largely in the context of Western liberal democracies through the late 20th and early 21st centuries. Yet it has also become a rallying call for economic development across the world. Whilst described as 'immaterial' or 'weightless' (Quah 2002), the knowledge economy is laden with expectations and assumptions, which place a heavy burden on those who are excluded from its promise.

This chapter charts the history of the knowledge economy by looking at the changing relationship between knowledge and economic development and seeing how knowledge *about* the economy moves into becoming knowledge *for* the economy. The narratives, drivers and manifestations of the knowledge economy and range of influences – exogenous and endogenous – are examined to see how they have shaped the development of responses, including the idea of universities as 'engines' of growth. Matters of scale, institutions and expertise mediate and frame the promise of the knowledge economy, so we consider each of these during the course of our investigations.

The promise emerges

There has always been a relationship between knowledge and economic development. The philosopher David Hume (1711–1776), for instance, was described by Friedrich von Hayek as: 'the founder of the modern theory of knowledge, but also one of the founders of economic theory' (1968: 339). In the writings of Adam

Smith (1723–1790), in whose work we find the origins of political economy, we can see that knowledge and skills were essential to the functioning of the market. As Smith put it: "the most dissimilar geniuses are of use to one another; the different produces of their respective talents, by the general disposition to truck, barter, and exchange, being brought, as it were, into a common stock, where every man may purchase whatever part of the produce of other men's talents he has occasion for" (Smith in Parsons et al. 1965: 105).

Since the latter part of the 20th century, we have witnessed the consolidation and pursuit of the principles of competition and the free market. Deregulation and the removal of barriers to trade signalled globalisation and liberalisation on a previously unprecedented scale. What become known as neoliberalism is: "a theory of political economic practices that proposes that human well-being can be best advanced by liberating individual entrepreneurial freedoms and skills within an institutional framework characterized by strong private property rights, free markets, and free trade" (Harvey 2007: 2). Here was a view that came not only to influence, but penetrate into middle-ground European social democratic thought (Marquand 2004). In extending the insights of Karl Polanyi (2001) into the changes that took place in the 1970s, it is possible to see how the ideas of monetarist, classical macroeconomist and public choice devotees were mobilised to mould existing institutions in the name of its promise (Blyth 2002). Particular desires were emphasised, informed by a combination of values and power, which became more public and were then reflected in institutionalised constructions of the economy (Graeber 2012). For this reason, it has been seen less as an ideology or economic policy, but a rationality that: "tends to structure and organize not only the action of rulers, but also the conduct of the ruled" (Dardot and Laval 2013: 4).

During this time, we see how Western liberal democracies became concerned with the limits to their abilities to expand their manufacturing bases under the weight of competition from abroad and cheap goods and services. A combination of the predominance of neoliberal ideas and these manifestations of globalisation led to concerns about competition from developing economies, such as Brazil, Russia, India and China. Global capital has little affiliation in its search for profit and so manufacturing began to move to developing countries, leading to questions over new forms of production and consumption. As the forces of globalisation increased, finance capital became more prominent with a resulting internationalisation and concentration of power in a few countries (Norfield 2016), whilst manufacturing moved around the globe and transnational companies emerged to take advantage of new markets and cheaper labour. Deregulation and a lessening of control of markets within nation-state boundaries led to a separation of industrial capital and the circulation of private, money-capital within a process that has been termed 'deterritorialization' (Lash and Urry 1987; Harvey 2012).

The idea of the knowledge economy took hold in this context. Knowledge became emphasised over physical and tangible assets as the foundation for wealth creation and economic growth. Accounts of this change and its consequences can be found across a wide range of disciplines (see, for example, Allen 2000; Bowring

2002; Burton-Jones 1999; Delanty 2001; Fuller 2000; Gibbons et al. 1994; Hellström and Raman 2001; May 2001). Several thinkers are credited with contributing to the idea, exemplified in the works of those such as Peter Drucker and Daniel Bell (see Castells 2010; Drennan 2002; Scarborough 2001). By the end of the 1970s, many governments around the world had adopted information society policies, including Japan, France and Canada (Kenway et al. 2006).

The promise of knowledge moving us beyond physical and more tangible assets permeated policy discourses and possessed a power of continual economic possibility through new forms of growth. Evidence was mobilised to suggest that the main mechanism for economic convergence at domestic and international levels was the diffusion of knowledge and further, that depends on: "a country's ability to mobilize financing as well as institutions that encourage large-scale investment in education and training of the population while guaranteeing a stable legal framework that various economic actors can reliably count on" (Piketty 2014: 71). A shift from industrialism to 'informationalism' heralded a new mode of production in which 'knowledge capitalism' characterised the contemporary economic, social and institutional world (Jessop 2002; Gibbons et al. 1994). The primary importance of knowledge as *the* resource, rather than *a* resource, heralded a post-capitalist society, which was to fundamentally change the structure of society, the economy and political worlds (Drucker 1998).

The singular driving feature of this economy is knowledge and, in particular, codified abstract knowledge (Allen 2000). A 'new' post-industrial economy is one based on creating, doing things to or with knowledge (Castells 2010). Some of those who were influenced by Bell saw this new dawning as possessing nothing less than an end to war, the enhancement of democracy, an age of plenty and the introduction of new opportunities for leisure (see Kumar 1995). Evidence of these shifts in the economy included an increase in the volume of workers involved in distributing, processing and producing knowledge, along with the percentage of Gross National Product (GNP) and salaries related to specific business sectors; all of which signified the final coming of the 'information age' (Bell 1979). The new age was characterised by the proliferation of high-tech industries; expansion of the scientific base; a movement from manufacturing to a service-based economy; new information technologies and accelerated technological changes in general (Neef 1998). Knowledge was the source of competitive advantage and the search was on for: "new ways of producing, using and combining diverse knowledges; the same ingredients … rearranged in new and better recipes" (Bryson et al. 2000: 1).

The promise of knowledge for the economy was embodied in building 'high value-added' economies characterised by increased wages, employment and skills. It is not that land and labour were no longer important; rather the primary focus is upon the role of knowledge in wealth creation. This alteration has been characterised as an economic shift from 'action centred' to 'intellectual' skills, or from 'brawn' to 'brains' and 'natural' to 'tangible and intangible created assets' (Bryson et al. 2000). Aside from the set of key characteristics highlighted above as evidence for the knowledge economy, an emphasis also emerges upon the growth of symbolic goods, demassification and the so-called firm without boundaries (Burton-Jones 1999: 13). Information communication technologies (ICTs) become a central catalyst, with growing recognition of the economic value of tacit knowledge and 'extra-economic' resources in creating competitiveness. Although the ICT revolution is not synonymous with the advent of the knowledge-based economy it gave: "the knowledge-based economy a new and different technological basis which radically changes the conditions for the production and distribution of knowledge as well as its coupling to the production system" (Lundvall and Foray 1996: 14).

Knowledge, strategy and policy

Common to these accounts is a view that there is something inherently different about the dynamics of the knowledge economy that represents both a qualitative and quantitative shift from previous phases of capitalist development. Whilst recognising that knowledge has always played an important role in human activities (Stehr 1994), it is the quantity, complexity and speed which characterises this phase in economic development (de Weert 1999: 5). Seen as part of a 'new spirit of capitalism', it leads to the realms of meaning and the imaginary being explicitly drawn upon to promote growth and opportunity: "Faced with a demand for justification, capitalism mobilizes 'already-existing' things whose legitimacy is guaranteed, to which it is going to give a new twist by combining them with the exigency of capitalist accumulation" (Boltanski and Chiapello 2005: 20). That spirit can be seen in the rise of brand marketing, an emphasis upon corporate culture, the entrepreneurial self, the use of social media and knowledge management in an overall combination of emerging relations between what were once more bounded areas of activity: the economy, values and affect (Arvidsson 2012; du Gay 2007; Lazzarato 2014; Little, Quintas and Ray 2002). Indeed, increasing concerns with happiness and well-being is symptomatic of these trends (Davies 2015).

In the process, knowledge is viewed not as means to inform decisions, but often as a panacea to specific problems and so is given a more instrumental and strategic role. Science, for example, is not just about interest-free explanation, but bound up with the reproduction of the economy. Knowledge is a 'tool' which can be appropriately wielded to produce advantage and for this purpose, it needs to be harnessed, codified, managed and stored. The translation of knowledge into economic advantage becomes a key goal, as is the ability to measure, define and demonstrate success in hierarchies between places and institutions through metrics and league tables of indicators and outputs in ever-increasing 'rituals of verification' (Power 1999). New terms emerge to provide impetus and justification for policy interventions based upon the realisation of the promise. They include the need to attract a 'creative class' (Florida 2002) within the growth of a 'cognitive capitalism' (Boutang 2011) and new instruments of intervention, such as clusters, technological districts and innovation poles. It is a combination of these elements that informs the promise of the knowledge economy through different forms of knowledge; the role of technology in socio-economic relations and changing forms of the organisation of knowledge production and knowledge products (Madanipour 2011). It draws upon what were distinct domains for its reproduction: "The knowledge society – and therefore, necessarily, the third capitalism that draws its substance from its specific exploitation – revolves around the creation of new knowledges within the three-fold modalities of science, art and language" (Boutang 2011: 151).

Knowledge became identified as a legitimate policy focus in the pursuit of economic goals. As we have moved further towards a global knowledge-based economy, differences within and between countries are often assumed to be equal-ised within a process of convergence for collective benefit. Yet this is not economic manna from heaven: it was part of strategic public policy in countries that moved their focus to the role of science, technology and innovation (STI) as key to eco-nomic competitiveness and wealth creation. Whilst Bell's observations were rooted in the logics of a Fordist-based mixed economy, this does not detract from the need for states to invest in knowledge. It should be noted, however, that different states are: "situated differently in this regard. They tend to polarize, first, around interests in projecting or enclosing the commons (for example, North–South) and, second, around the most appropriate forms of intellectual property rights and regimes on different scales from local to global" (Jessop 2002: 129).

In respect to policy, the Organisation for Economic Cooperation and Development's (OECD) 1996 report on the knowledge-based economy was based on the idea of a 'new growth theory' which captured the role of knowl-edge and technology in driving productivity and economic growth. It cited the rising high-technology share of OECD manufacturing production, the growth of knowledge-intensive service sectors and estimated that more than 50 per cent of Gross Domestic Product (GDP) in the major OECD economies was knowledge-based. Science and technology were then placed at the heart of eco-nomic development processes with considerable investments made in the science base to attract key scientific personnel and exploit scientific outputs (OECD 2004). Similarly, the World Bank identified four pillars of the knowledge economy: edu-cation and training; information infrastructure; economic incentives and institu-tional regimes; and innovation systems. Variables were developed into a Knowledge Assessment Methodology (KAM) in 2013 to assess and benchmark the performance of countries according to these pillars.

In the European context, the Lisbon Strategy for Growth and Jobs of March 2000 committed the Union to making Europe the most dynamic and competitive knowledge-based economy in the world, with the original aim of investing 3 per cent of GDP in research and development by 2010 (European Commission 2000). National and regional governments competed to attract major science infrastruc-tures, such as the International Thermonuclear Experimental Reactor, European Spallation Sources or Synchrotron Radiation Sources (Perry 2008) as if such facilities were linked to economic futures. In 2000, there was a European Council Resolution 'to turn the EU into the most competitive knowledge-based society by 2010' with a programme which focussed broadly on knowledge for innovation and growth, making Europe a more attractive place to invest and work, creating more and better jobs. Then, the 'Europe 2020' strategy was developed as a ten-year plan to create the conditions for "smart, sustainable and inclusive growth" by "creating value by basing growth on knowledge" (European Commission 2009: 5). The five headline targets to measure this achievement were: employment, research and development, climate/energy, education, social inclusion/poverty reduction.

Outside Europe and through the actions of international organisations, there was a consistent effort to export a westernised view of the knowledge-based economy to the Global South and other developing contexts. Programmes of economic change have been embedded within organisations such as the World Trade Organization and International Monetary Fund (IMF). As we discuss in chapter 6, the ways in which the discourses of the knowledge economy – with its reliance on data, technology and particular kinds of skills and expertise – have been recast into and through a development agenda requires greater analysis, in so far as they potentially offer insights into how the needs of the poorest in society might be met through rethinking the relationship between knowledge and action. Countries such as South Korea, Malaysia, China and Chile have pursued a coherent strategy to create, access and use knowledge and absorb Westernised concepts of the knowledge economy – and so are seen as ones that have made rapid progress (World Bank 2007).

The knowledge economy is rolling off the policy mass-production line. Flexible accumulation, new technologies, the production of signs and images, just-in-time delivery and a constant process of re-skilling and de-skilling of the workforce are travelling around the world. Geographically distant events and decisions can impact on 'glocal' education (Loader 2001). Thus, the insistence by powerful political leaders that the IMF requires countries to commit themselves to particular economic policies, or innovations in information technology in one country might affect practices in another. These changes brought with them new opportunities in relation to cosmopolitanism (Delanty 2006) and economic growth (Smart 2007). They can be seen to integrate countries in a global economy that is assumed to enhance living standards (Giddens 1991) with those developing nations that seek to isolate themselves from trade liberalisation doing less well than those who are prepared to not only embrace, but fully engage with its promise (Legrain 2006).

Policy targets for knowledge-based success

An entire industry has sprung up around the idea that knowledge is now the source of competitive advantage in a globally competitive market (Scarborough 2001). In seeking to realise the promise we can identify three distinct pillars around which public and private interventions have focussed. First, there is a spatial pillar informed by the increasing recognition that proximity and agglomeration matter in the creation of innovative 'milieu' in which tacit knowledge and skills can be exchanged. The second forms around universities through the efforts to harness their knowledge production capacities for economic gain, whilst the third relates to skills and forms of expertise, which can be commodified in order to commercialise and market new products and processes.

In terms of space and place, contextual negotiations, discussions and interpretations remain of importance in the dynamics between socio-economic development and urban spaces (Sassen 2012). Since human activities still remain influenced by geographical locations, the more decisive facet of globalisation concerns the manner in which distant events, cities and forces impact on local or 'glocal' spaces and relations (Tomlinson 1999). Here, the state, as both the source and enforcer of the law, remains important not only in terms of having a clear framework for economic development, but also in terms of political demands for accountability (Hirst, Thompson and Bromley 2009). Calls to constitute the promise are linked not simply to macroeconomic policy, but the embedding of economic and social developments in the behaviour of local firms and communities (Storper 1997). Providing opportunity through the building of good relations between sectors and effective business support become central to success in the pursuit of 'competitive advantage' (Porter 1998).

Having the right skills, attracting those to particular places, identifying knowledge needs and knowing how to build those into practice represent the challenges. Most often cited in this context and certainly best known in policy circles, is the work of the business economist, the 'godfather' of clusters, Michael Porter, whose 1990 thesis on the Competitive Advantage of Nations stressed that firms draw on location-specific factors for competitive success and on resources inherent within local environments. 'Clusters' to deliver success became more and more popular and were defined as: "a geographically proximate group of interconnected companies and associated institutions in a particular field, linked by commonalities and complementaries" (Porter 2000: 254). Porter, along with others from very different theoretical orientations, made the case that regions are increasingly becoming important locations for the competitive activities of mobile investors and as 'engines' of national growth (Dunning 2000).

Writers referred to a shift from mass production to flexible specialisation or from Fordism to post-Fordism to describe how proximity matters in offering more appropriate economies of scale to avoid complex externalities (Newlands 1995). In the most dynamic locales, face-to-face relations remain important, particularly given the divide between different kinds of knowledges and their relationship to space (Amin and Graham 1997; Bryson et al. 2000). On the one hand, the knowledge economy is characterised by 'explicit' cognitive knowledge, or information, which can be easily stored and codified, often through the use of information technology. In principle, therefore, it is globally accessible (Allen 2000). However, when we introduce place and context, the emphasis moves to 'tacit' knowledge – most commonly referred to as 'know-how'. As tacit knowledge is hard to codify, it is less easily transferred across wide distances (Bryson et al. 2000). This form of knowledge is specialised, frequently specific to a firm, network or locality and so can offer a unique competitive advantage compared with more widely networked knowledge.

The importance of locality for the development, exploitation and diffusion of tacit knowledge is widely recognised, giving rise to a plethora of studies on 'learning by doing' and knowledge accumulation within firms, other organisations and regions (Malecki 2000; Evangelista et al. 2002. Simmie et al. 2002). Whilst the significance of local networking and clustering for competitiveness is not securely established in academic circles (Gordon and McCann 2000; Martin and Sunley 2001; Simmie et al. 2002), that has not prevented national and subnational governments and agencies from adopting clusters and networks as articles of faith and as the basis for competitiveness and economic development policies. So we find evidence that the subnational level acquired greater significance and this is manifest in the idea that innovative 'milieus' foster high-tech industries and it is in the financial districts of 'global cities' where control of the global financial system is concentrated (Sassen 2012; Norfield 2016). We also find diverse geographies of power where issues associated with the binary of centralised and decentralised appear inadequate to the task of understanding the landscape (Allen 2003).

Theories of agglomeration and the importance of economic processes as embedded in localised networks are said to offer the prime explanation for these outcomes (Fujita and Krugman 1995; Soja 2000). This has spawned a range of efforts to harness locational specific advantage such as industrial districts, innovative milieu and learning regions (Uyarra 2009). The concept of the 'technopole' fits neatly into this conceptualisation, in which particular forms of public-private partnerships are developed to build university-industry partnerships through new 'growth machines' (Logan and Molotch 2007; Miao, Benneworth and Phelps 2015). Many of these ideas were supported by the success of the Silicon Valley model which has given rise to a series of cloning efforts for the next generation 'high tech hotspots' (Rosenburg 2002; Karlsson 2008). European countries, such as Germany, have embraced the development of clusters nationwide, but especially in areas struggling with post-industrialisation and the reinvigoration of their economic base. Bavaria, for instance, is a region in which clusters in 'sunrise sectors', such as mobility, materials engineering, biotechnologies and electronics, are intended to make it a leader in economic and scientific change and enable state companies to compete in globalised markets.

In Asia, clusters and technology hotspots are spreading. In 1998, Bangalore gained the accolade of one of the world's hottest tech cities from *Newsweek* magazine, in recognition of its assemblage of nearly 1000 ICT companies in innovation clusters. According to the UN Human Development Report, Bangalore now stands fourth amongst leading 'Global Hubs of Technological Innovation' and is recognised by the World Economic Forum. Other examples include: Taipei High Tech Corridor, created by the Taipei Government with Nankang Software Industrial Park and the Beitou-Shilin Technology Park and Hsinchu Science Park in Taiwan and Daedeok Innopolis in South Korea. Siliconmania has spread not only across Asia but also the Middle East. Offenhauer (2008) suggests that 'Silicon Wadi' in Tel Aviv is one of the most successful clusters outside the United States that is 'second only' to Silicon Valley. The cluster emerged in the 1990s led by the predominant development of ICTs and focussed around academic institutions. As one report, 'Global Cities', notes of China, clustering is: "the latest trend in China's urbanisation process, in which nearby cities utilise each other's comparative advantage to maximise their economic gain. The famous examples are the rise of the Yangtze River Delta (YRD) led by Shanghai, and the Pearl River Delta (PRD) bordering Hong Kong. These are powerhouses of the global economy" (Knight Frank 2016: 57).

In focussing upon the concentration of skills and knowledge in place, universities are increasingly centred in economic and social development processes (Castells and Hall 1994; Goddard and Chatterton 2001). Taking the supra-national level of the European Union as an example, we see an increase in concerns with the roles and diverse functions of the university designed to realise the knowledge economy at particular scales of activity. This is of no surprise for, as the author of a study of higher education policy in Europe over a period of fifty years put it, they are central to the development of the knowledge economy: "They are characterised by their mass of intellectual resource and their functional involvement in all the processes on which a knowledge economy depends. Through research and teaching and various types of partnership to exploit research, they participate in the production of new knowledge. They provide highly skilled manpower through teaching students, and training them in techniques of learning and research. They are usually a stimulus to local and regional economies" (Corbett 2005: 6).

In recognition of the movement towards a knowledge society, the European Commission set up initiatives to ensure that innovation, research, education and training became core to the EU's internal policies. An initial broad focus on education, training and employment is evident in 'Towards a Europe of Knowledge' which sought to 'promote the highest level of knowledge for its people through broad access to education and its permanent updating' (European Commission 1997). Subsequent developments have concentrated more specifically on higher education. Building on the Sorbonne Declaration of 1998, the Bologna Process committed signatory member states to a process of coordination towards the creation of a European Higher Education Area (EHEA), which became a reality with the Budapest-Vienna Declaration in March 2010. The EHEA focusses on co-ordinating member state policies to achieve goals on comparable degree structures, system cycles, credit systems, mobility, quality assurance and European dimensions in higher education (Joint Declaration of European Education Ministers 1999).

European higher education ministers met in 2003 to reaffirm commitment to the EHEA and to review progress on meeting the original objectives (Communiqué of the Conference of Ministers Responsible for Higher Education 2003). The Yerevan Ministerial Communiqué (2015: 1) then noted: "progress has been made in enabling students and graduates to move within the EHEA with recognition of their qualifications and periods of study; study programmes provide graduates with the knowledge, skills and competences either to continue their studies or to enter the European labour market; institutions are becoming increasingly active in an international context; and academics cooperate in joint teaching and research programmes. The EHEA has opened a dialogue with other regions of the world and is considered a model of structured cooperation" (available at: https://www.hrk.de/ fileadmin/redaktion/hrk/02-Dokumente/02-03-Studium/02-03-01-Studium-Studienreform/Bologna_Dokumente/Yerevan_Communique.pdf). Alongside the EHEA, the Lisbon Strategy focussed on agreement to create a European Research Area to lay the foundation for a common science policy across the EU and coordinating national research policies.

European responses are part of a more general trend to accelerate and integrate universities into the promise of the knowledge economy. Universities are seen as unique in their contributions to the core functions of the knowledge society in producing new knowledge, knowledge transfer and transmission and in new industrial processes or services (European Commission 2003). Yet core issues remain, relating to the global lack of competitiveness of the European university system, the sustainability of university research funding, questions of autonomy and professionalism, the achievement and maintenance of research excellence and the contribution more generally of universities towards the sets of initiatives that comprise the 'Europe of Knowledge'.

These trends reflect a more general recognition that the potential realisation of the knowledge economy rests fundamentally on the extent to which institutions, including local and regional government and universities, can adapt to the challenges placed upon them. Universities have become subjects of policy designed to influence their behaviours, programmes and marketability, reflected in a number of means that include: the adoption of quasi-market systems and processes depending on the sources of funding, legal status and cultures; a shift from public service to a performance and audit-based ethos; responses to commercialisation of activities in teaching and research; ability to respond to the varying needs of government, industry and 'customers'; ability to link research to demands for societal and economic relevance; adaptation to pressures on traditional methods of management and governance; revised systems of remuneration and reward linked to revisions in evaluations of worth and what action is taken in terms of increased contestability of their knowledge claims and possible accompanying de-legitimation of the university (Harloe and Perry 2004). Such adaptive capabilities are informed by the interactions between the global and local and between the content of knowledge and the context of its production. These are issues to which we will return in chapter 4.

Universities have become central in ideas about 'knowledge capitals', 'silicon alleys', 'smart' and 'digital' cities. The preexisting strengths of the knowledge base, of which the university is a prime institution, have become part of broader strategies aimed at competitive success. In the process, there is an argument that universities have moved under pressures of globalisation towards a single institutional model of the type that exists among private universities in the United States. An increasing process of marketisation has seen students becoming 'customers' accompanied by changes in regulatory environments and the proliferation of new information technology for the widespread delivery of curricula. New providers have moved into markets for the provision of higher education (Margolis 2004). A greater emphasis upon academics being entrepreneurial and engaging with industry can also be detected, and with that, we find changing expectations of what constitutes a successful academic career.

With these changing expectations we have seen the emergence of what has become known as the 'third mission of universities' which lies beyond the normal focus on teaching and research. It is mediated through an emphasis on universities being core to the knowledge economy through not only the provision of skills and knowledge, but also industrial restructuring, consultancy, partnerships with different sectors and the commercialisation of research. Although universities have a long history of application-driven research and industrial partnerships, one study notes: "engagement in commercialization activities such as patenting and spin-off companies seems to have increased by academics and academic institutions, which might be conceptualized as a development towards more *science-directed commercialization*" (Gulbrandsen and Slipersaeter 2007: 137. Original italics).

It is these activities that increasingly dominate universities' participation in the knowledge economy. Building on the Silicon Valley example and the centrality of the Massachusetts Institute of Technology in transmitting its success, universities have developed their own science parks to support their intellectual exploitation for economic gain. The Cambridge Science Park is one the largest and most established high-tech clusters and is driven by the university. Established in the 1970s, there are around 1,500 high-tech firms there, which aim to bring together industry and academia in partnership. Operating as a commercial research centre the Cambridge Science Park works in a range of sectors, including biomedical, computing, consulting, energy, environment, finance and industrial technologies. It is supported by a host of other incubators and knowledge exchange units designed to support academic entrepreneurialism and bolster knowledge-based growth, such as IdeaSpace and Cambridge Enterprise. Outside of the so-called Golden Triangle of Oxford, Cambridge and London, other universities are also organising themselves into alliances for science-based economic growth. The Science City Research Alliance, for instance, represents collaboration between the universities of Warwick and Birmingham in areas that include Advanced Materials, Energy Futures and Translational Medicine. The group works with regional companies and businesses, including small and medium sized enterprises and multinational organisations. In Sheffield, the Advanced Manufacturing Research Centre aims to be a world-class centre for advanced machining and materials research for high-value manufacturing sectors, including aerospace. The aim, as with Cambridge, is to commercialise expertise through providing 'solutions' to technological challenges and contribute to knowledge-based growth.

Codified, commodified and tacit expertise

The knowledge economy relies on knowledge, skills, innovation and creativity, but rests on "whatever passes as knowledge, as a new form of capital ... being converted into money" (Madanipour 2011: 2–3). Skills require continual updating and technological change, another core component of the infrastructure, produces a further differentiation through a requirement to meet varied needs. Abramowitz and David argue: "perhaps the single most salient characteristic of recent economic growth has been the secularly rising reliance on codified knowledge as a basis for the organisation and conduct of economic activities" (1996: 35). Within firms this translated into a range of knowledge management techniques (Drucker 1993; Little, Quintas and Ray 2002). The knowledge management industry is based on the idea that knowledge can be codified and extracted to produce economic value.

As the importance of tacit knowledge for competitive advantage is recognised, efforts to commodify it are amplified in order to achieve 'smart' technological developments (Perry and May 2015; May and Perry 2016). As a result, it becomes: "ironic to find the socialisation of theories of knowledge being faced with its own reification in the form of veritable social epistemological principles developed and sold in the market for management consultants" (Hellström and Raman 2001: 139). The production of knowledge about knowledge practices informs the very things that they are supposed to reflect through representation. In this way, they feed back and inform actions. Accompanying this is the attribution of value to scientific work. Where science was to manipulate objects in the desire for control over a world of objects, we now have a science that is increasingly framed within the promise of the knowledge economy. Here is an activity where science is expected to resolve issues, without raising any problems! In this way it is: "released from the need for questioning as well as from any burden of responsibility". It thereby possesses: "A divine innocence … a marvellous form of extraterritoriality" (Castoriadis 1991: 263).

The extent of these changes has been characterised as signalling a fundamental alteration in knowledge production (Gibbons et al. 1994; Nowotny et al. 2001). The traditional cognitive and social norms that inform the boundaries around the production, legitimation and diffusion of knowledge – what is termed 'Mode 1' – are argued to have been changed by alternative modes of conceptualising knowledge in terms of its organisation, systems of reward and resulting quality. What is a new 'Mode 2' is characterised by the following: knowledge is produced in the context of application; knowledge is transdisciplinary and non-hierarchical; it is heterogeneous and has a transience of organisational form outside of traditional university structures; multiple actors are involved in the research process; it is socially accountable and reflexivity, and wider criteria for quality control beyond those implied by peer review, are apparent. These changes are bound to vary in different contexts and are informed by interactions with the content of knowledge. To that extent, what is being presented is less an account that may be tested in particular localities, but an indicative paradigm shift in modes of knowledge production, deployment and attribution. Thus, whilst it has been subjected to critical evaluation (May with Perry 2011), the articulation of Mode 1/Mode 2 has resonance in the context of discourses on knowledge-based economies, rather than because it represents individual change factors as such.

In respect to changes in the loci of knowledge production, we can see the changing role of expertise in the knowledge economy, with opportunities for taking exemplars of success from one place to another as each seeks to fulfil the promise based on models of success. That is part of the changing role of knowledge, evidence and expertise in policymaking itself (Fischer 2000; Noveck 2015; Turner 2003). In the process boundaries change and the knowledge economy becomes something that is not simply about a separate realm of the 'economic' in terms of the value of knowledge – as if such a thing could ever be simply separated from social, political and cultural issues. Indeed, it also has a component whereby persuasion and the fulfilment of needs to meet the demands of new environments informs and shapes the very desires it seeks to supply. To this extent, the promise of the knowledge economy goes further than previous developments in capitalism because it is concerned, as we noted earlier, with the role of affect and value and there are now armies of experts who have filled the chasm opened up by the promise.

Accompanying this shift is the greater integration of 'experts' into governance systems across a range of policy-fields – though whether this is seen as the result of an increasing recognition of the importance of accurate evidence-based policy, or the result of processes of depoliticisation and technocratisation of decision-making is varied. What we can say is that science is integrated into the fabric of modern economies (de la Mothe 2001) and is a core part of decisions made about the environment, health, welfare and security (Stehr 2004). In this way, knowledge societies run on expert processes and systems, informed by science, but also structured into ever-increasing areas of social life (Knorr-Cetina 1999). Science is interacting with democracy in a process of change that runs from a politics of sovereign citizens to a politics of diffused experts. For some, electoral struggle is replaced by expert bodies and the growth of specialised technical discourse is threatening the life blood of democratic discussion (Turner 2003).

Such is the value attributed to knowledge, it adds to the idea that the fulfilment of the promise may arrive in unambiguous and disinterested technocratic 'solutions' to multiple areas of policy, including the realisation of the knowledge economy. As an ever-increasing number of expert actors become involved, expectations of science shift towards ideas of application, relevance and use, and away from public discussion of justification. At one level, this is not new. Indeed, the notion of relevance dates back as far as Francis Bacon in the 16th century, who believed that knowledge of nature should be turned to the benefit of mankind by exploiting new discoveries and inventions in a practical way (Henry 2002). Others have noted the role of science and technology in economic and social life, from the industrial revolution to the military applications of the 20th century. What has changed, however, is an increase in attempts to regulate, manage, control and direct science into a new form of 'knowledge politics' (Stehr 1994). In so doing, the link between science and economic development has led to a blurring of policy domains. Science is linked to innovation and processes of wealth creation to such an extent that science, research and innovation policies are often regarded as one and the same.

Summary: Mediating the knowledge economy

Analysis of the validity of a paradigm shift in capitalist development is divided. The knowledge economy has been subject to critical appraisal in terms of being spin or substance and whether it is fundamentally 'new' (Weingart 1997). From a historical viewpoint, authors have seen the knowledge economy as a new phase of economic development on a parallel with the agricultural or Industrial Revolution. 'Informationalism', as the latest stage of development (Jessop 2000), brings with it the idea that we are at the limits of the productivity revolution (Drucker 1998). Now, it seems, it is the application of knowledge to the production of knowledge that is new (Castells 2010).

Capitalism has not been rivalled by the knowledge economy, insofar as the fundamental tenets of capitalism remain in place. We still see massive efforts directed towards capital accumulation, open market competition, free trade, the power of the individual based on ideas of negative liberty and a 'survival of the fittest' mentality. In this sense, it may be said that it is the 'equipment' which is deployed that alters the game, whilst the rules remain in place. Knowledge capitalism is a generic form of capitalism based on the accumulation of knowledge, not just monetary and physical forms of wealth. Towards this end, spatial clusters, universities and expertise were noted as three main pillars constituting the knowledge economy and which underpinned public policy interventions at multiple scales. Yet these are not matters that are simply amenable to control in the name of global economic forces or state management. The dynamics of the knowledge economy are not just *implemented* through them, but *mediated* by them and informed through particular circuits of knowledge. It is the politics of these processes that concerns Part II of this book. First we consider how nation-states and local administrations in cities and municipalities are interacting with the promise of the knowledge economy.

References

Abramovitz, M. and David, P.A. (1996), 'Technological change and the rise of intangible investments: the US economy's growth-path in the twentieth century', in Foray, D. and Lundvall, B.A. (eds.) *Employment and Growth in the Knowledge-based Economy*, Paris: Organisation for Economic Co-operation and Development.

Adkins, L. and Lury, C. (eds.) (2012), *Measure and Value*, Oxford: Wiley-Blackwell.

Allen, J. (2000), 'Power/economic knowledge: symbolic and spatial formations', in Bryson, J., Daniels, P., Henry, N. and Pollard, J. (eds.) *Knowledge, Space, Economy*, London: Routledge.

Allen, J. (2003), *Lost Geographies of Power*, Oxford: Blackwell.

Amin, A. and Graham, S. (1997), 'The ordinary city', *Transactions of the Institute of British Geographers, New Series* 22, 411–429.

Arvidsson, A. (2012), 'General sentiment: how value and affect converge in the information economy', in Adkins, L. and Lury, C. (eds.) *Measure and Value*, Oxford: Wiley-Blackwell.

Bell, D. (1979), 'The social framework of the information society', in Dertouzos, M. and Moses, J. (eds.) *The Computer Age: A 20 Year View*, Cambridge, MA: MIT Press, pp. 500–549.

Blyth, M. (2002), *Great Transformations: Economic Ideas and Institutional Change in the Twentieth Century*, Cambridge: Cambridge University Press.

Boltanski, L. and Chiapello, E. (2005), *The New Spirit of Capitalism*, translated by Elliott, G., London: Verso.

Bonaccorsi, A. and Daraio, C. (eds.) (2007), *Universities and Strategic Knowledge Creation: Specialization and Performance in Europe*, Cheltenham, UK: Edward Elgar.

Boutang, Y.M. (2011), *Cognitive Capitalism*, translated by Emery, E. with a foreword by Thrift, N., Cambridge: Polity.

Bowring, F. (2002), 'Post-Fordism and the end of work', *Futures*, 34 (2): 59–172.

Bryson, J., Daniels, P., Henry, N. and Pollard, J. (eds.) (2000), *Knowledge, Space, Economy*, London: Routledge.

Burton-Jones, A. (1999), *Knowledge Capitalism. Business, Work and Learning in the New Economy*, Oxford: Oxford University Press.

Castells, M. (2010), *The Rise of the Network Society. The Information Age: Economy, Society and Culture, Volume 1*, 2nd edition, Oxford: Blackwell.

Castells, M. and Hall, P. (1994), *Technopoles of the World*, London: Routledge.

Castoriadis, C. (1991), *Philosophy, Politics, Autonomy: Essays in Political Philosophy*, edited by Curtis, D.A., Oxford: Oxford University Press.

Chappell, V.C. (ed.) (1968), *Hume*, London: Macmillan.

Clark, G.I., Feldman, M.P. and Geertler, M.S. (eds.) (2000), *The Oxford Handbook of Economic Geography*, Oxford: Oxford University Press.

Communiqué of the Conference of Ministers Responsible for Higher Education 2003, http://www.enqa.eu/wp-content/uploads/2013/03/BerlinCommunique1.pdf (accessed May 2017).

Corbett, A. (2005), *Universities and the Europe of Knowledge: Ideas, Institutions and Policy Entrepreneurship in European Higher Education Policy, 1955–2005*, Basingstoke, Hampshire: Palgrave Macmillan.

Dardot, P. and Laval, C. (2013), *The New Way of the World: On Neo-Liberal Society*, translated by Elliott, G., London: Verso.

Davies, W. (2015), *The Happiness Industry: How the Government and Big Business Sold Us Well-Being*, London: Verso.

de la Mothe, J. (2001), 'Knowledge, politics and governance', in de la Mothe, J. (ed.) *Science, Technology and Governance*, London and New York: Continuum.

de la Mothe, J. (ed.) (2001), *Science, Technology and Governance*, London and New York: Continuum.

de Weert, E. (1999), 'Contours of the emergent knowledge society: theoretical debate and implications for higher education research', *Higher Education*, 38: 49–69.

Delanty, G. (2001), *Challenging Knowledge: The University in the Knowledge Society*, Buckingham: Open University Press.

Delanty, G. (2006), 'The cosmopolitan imagination: critical cosmopolitanism and social theory', *British Journal of Sociology*, 57 (1): 25–47.

Drennan, M.P. (2002), *Information Economy and American Cities*, Baltimore: John Hopkins University Press.

Drucker, P. (1998), 'From capitalism to knowledge society', in Neef, D. (ed.) *The Knowledge Economy*, Boston: Butterworth-Heinemann.

Drucker, P. (2011 [1993]), *Post-Capitalist Society*, Oxford: Routledge.

du Gay, P. (2007), *Organizing Identity*, London: Sage.

Dunning, J. (2000), 'Regions, globalisation and the knowledge economy', in Dunning, J. (ed.) *Regions, Globalisation and the Knowledge Economy*, Oxford: Oxford University Press.

Dunning, J. (ed.) (2000), *Regions, Globalisation and the Knowledge Economy*, Oxford: Oxford University Press.

European Commission (1997), *Towards a Europe of Knowledge: Communication from the Commission*, COM (1997), 563 final, Brussels.

European Commission (2000), *Communication from the Commission: The Lisbon Strategy*, Luxembourg: Commission of the European Communities.

European Commission (2003), *Communication from the Commission on The Role of the Universities in the Europe of Knowledge*, COM (2003), 58 final, Luxembourg: Commission of the European Communities.

European Commission (2009), *Europe 2020: A European Strategy for Smart, Sustainable and Inclusive Growth*, Luxembourg: Commission of the European Communities.

Evangelista, R., Iammarino, S., Mastrostefano, V. and Silvani, A. (2002), 'Looking for regional systems of innovation: evidence from the Italian innovation survey', *Regional Studies*, 36(2): 173–186.

Evans, J., Karvonen, A. and Raven, R. (eds.) (2016), *The Experimental City*, Oxford: Routledge.

Fischer, F. (2000), *Citizens, Experts, and the Environment: The Politics of Local Knowledge*, Durham: Duke University.

Florida, R. (2002), *The Rise of the Creative Class – And How It's Transforming Work, Leisure, Community and Everyday Life*, New York: Basic Books.

Foray, D. and Lundvall, B.A. (eds.) (1996), *Employment and Growth in the Knowledge-based Economy*, Paris: Organisation for Economic Co-operation and Development.

Fujita, M. and Krugman, P. (1995), 'When is the economy monocentric? von Thünen and Chamberlin unified', *Regional Science and Urban Economics*, 25(4): 505–528.

Fuller, S. (2000), *The Governance of Science: Ideology and the Future of the Open Society*, Buckingham: Open University Press.

Gibbons, M., Limoges, C., Nowotny, H., Schwartaman, S., Scott, P. and Trow, M. (1994), *The New Production of Knowledge: The Dynamics of Science and Research in Contemporary Societies*, London: Sage.

Giddens, A. (1991), *Modernity and Self-Identity*, Cambridge: Polity.

Goddard, J. and Chatterton, P. (2001), 'The response of HEIs to regional needs', paper given at *Universities and Regional Development in the Knowledge Society*, 12–14 November 2001, Barcelona.

Gordon, I. and McCann, P. (2000), 'Industrial clusters: complexes, agglomeration and/or social network', *Urban Studies*, 373.

Graeber, D. (2012), *Debt: The First 5000 Years*, London: Melville House.

Gulbrandsen, M. and Slipersaeter, S. (2007), 'The third mission and the entrepreneurial university model', in Bonaccorsi, A. and Daraio, C. (eds.) *Universities and Strategic Knowledge Creation: Specialization and Performance in Europe*, Cheltenham, UK: Edward Elgar.

Hardy, S., Hart, M., Albrechts, L. and Katos, A. (eds.) (1995), *An Enlarged Europe, Regions in Competition?* London: Regional Studies Association.

Harloe, M. and Perry, B. (2004), 'Universities, localities and regional development: the emergence of the mode 2 university?', *International Journal of Urban and Regional Research*, 28 (1): 212–223.

Harvey, D. (2007), *A Brief History of Neoliberalism*, Oxford: Oxford University Press.

Harvey, D. (2012), *Rebel Cities: From the Right to the City to the Urban Revolution*, London: Verso.

Hayek, F.A. (1968), 'The legal and political philosophy of David Hume', in Chappell, V.C. (ed.) *Hume*, London: Macmillan.

Hellström, T. and Raman, S. (2001), 'The commodification of knowledge about knowledge: knowledge management and the reification of epistemology', *Social Epistemology*, 15 (3), 139–154.

Henry, J. (2002), *Knowledge is Power: How Magic, the Government and an Apocalyptic Vision Inspired Francis Bacon to Create Modern Science*, Cambridge: Icon Books.

Hirst, P., Thompson, G. and Bromley, S. (2009), *Globalization in Question*, 3rd edition, Cambridge: Polity.

Jessop, B. (2000), 'The crisis of the national spatio-temporal fix and the ecological dominance of globalizing capitalism', *International Journal of Urban and Regional Research*, 24 (2): 323–360.

Jessop, B. (2002), *The Future of the Capitalist State in its Place*, Cambridge: Polity.

Joint Declaration of European Education Ministers 1999 (The Bologna Declaration), https://www.eurashe.eu/library/bologna_1999_bologna-declaration-pdf/ (accessed May 2017),

Karlsson, C. (ed.) (2008), *Handbook of Research on Innovation and Clusters: Cases and Policies* (Vol. 2), Cheltenham, UK: Edward Elgar.

Kenway, J., Bullen, E., Fahey, J. and Robb, S. (2006), *Haunting the Knowledge Economy* (Vol. 6), New York: Routledge.

Knight Frank (2016), *Global Cities*, http://www.knightfrank.com/resources/global-cities/2016/all/global-cities-the-2016-report.pdf (accessed May 2017).

Knorr-Cetina, K. (1999), *Epistemic Cultures: How the Sciences Make Knowledge*, Harvard: Harvard University Press.

Kumar, K. (1995), *From Post-Industrial to Post-Modern Society: New Theories of the Contemporary World*, Oxford: Blackwell.

Lash, S. and Urry, J. (1987), *The End of Organized Capitalism*, Cambridge: Polity.

Lazzarato, M. (2014), *Signs and Machines: Capitalism and the Production of Subjectivity*, Los Angeles, CA: Semiotext(e).

Legrain, P. (2006), 'Why NAMA liberalisation is good for developing countries', *The World Economy*, 29(10): 1349–1362.

Little, S., Quintas, P. and Ray, T. (eds.) (2002), *Managing Knowledge: An Essential Reader*, London: Sage.

Loader, B. (2001), *Community Informatics: Shaping Computer-Mediated Social Networks*, London: Routledge.

Logan, J. and Molotch, H. (2007 [1987]), *Urban Fortunes: The Political Economy of Place*, Berkeley: University of California Press.

Lundvall, & Foray, D. B.-A. (1996). The Knowledge-Based Economy: From the Economics of Knowledge to the Learning Economy. In *Oecd Documents: Employment and Growth in the Knowledge-Based Economy* (pp. 11–32). Paris: OECD.

Madanipour, A. (2011), *Knowledge Economy and the City: Spaces of Knowledge*, London: Routledge.

Malecki, J. (2000), 'Creating and sustaining competitiveness: local knowledge and economic geography', in Bryson, J., Daniels, P., Henry, N. and Pollard, J. (eds.) *Knowledge, Space, Economy*, London: Routledge, pp. 103–119.

Margolis, M. (2004), 'The withering of the professoriate: corporate universities and the internet', in Odin, J.K. and Manicas, P.T. (eds.) *Globalization and Higher Education*, Honolulu: University of Hawaii Press.

Marquand, D. (2004), *Decline of the Public: The Hollowing out of Citizenship*, Cambridge: Polity.

Martin, R. and Sunley, P. (2001), 'Rethinking the "economic" in economic geography: broadening our vision or losing our focus?', *Antipode*, 33(2): 148–161.

May, T. (2001), 'Power, knowledge and organizational transformation: administration as depoliticisation', Special Issue 'Social Epistemology and Knowledge Management', *Social Epistemology*, 15(3): 171–186.

May, T. with Perry, B. (2011), *Social Research and Reflexivity: Content, Consequences and Context*, London: Sage.

May, T. and Perry, B. (2016), 'Cities, experiments and the logics of the knowledge economy', in Evans, J., Karvonen, A., and Raven, R. (eds.) *The Experimental City*, Oxford: Routledge.

Miao, J.T., Benneworth, P. and Phelps, N. (eds.) (2015), *Making 21st Century Knowledge Complexes: Technopoles of the World 20 Years After*, London: Routledge.

Neef, D. (ed.) (1998), *The Knowledge Economy*, Boston: Butterworth-Heinemann.

Newlands, D. (1995), 'The economic role of regional governments in the European Community', in Hardy, S., Hart, M., Albrechts, L. and Katos, A. (eds.) *An Enlarged Europe, Regions in Competition?*, London: Regional Studies Association, pp. 70–80.

Norfield, T. (2016), *The City: London and the Global Power of Finance*, London: Verso.

Noveck, B.S. (2015), *Smart Citizens, Smarter State: The Technologies of Expertise and the Future of Governing*, Cambridge, Mass: Harvard University Press.

Nowotny, H., Scott, P., and Gibbons, M. (2001), *Re-thinking Science: Knowledge and the Public in an Age of Uncertainty*, Cambridge: Polity.

Odin, J.K. and Manicas, P.T. (eds.) (2004), *Globalization and Higher Education*, Honolulu: University of Hawaii Press.

Offenhauer, P. (2008), *Israel's Technology Sector*, Washington DC: Library of Congress Federal Research Division.

Organisation for Economic Co-operation and Development (OECD) (2004), *Innovation in the Knowledge Economy: Implications for Education and Learning*, Paris: Centre for Educational Research and Innovation.

Parsons, T., Shils, E., Naegele, K.D. and Pitts, J.R. (eds.) (1965), *Theories of Society: Foundations of Modern Sociological Theory*, New York: Free Press.

Perry, B. (2008), 'Academic knowledge and urban development: theory, policy and practice', in Yigitcanlar, T., Velibeyoglu, K. and Baum, S. (eds.) *Knowledge-Based Urban Development: Planning and Applications in the Information Era*, London: IGI Global, pp. 21–41.

Perry, B. and May, T. (2015), 'Context matters: the English science cities and visions for knowledge-based urbanism', in Miao, J., Benneworth, P. and Phelps, N. (eds.) *Making 21st Century Knowledge Complexes: Technopoles of the World Revisited*, London: Routledge, pp.105–127.

Piketty, T. (2014), *Capital in the Twenty-First Century*, translated by Goldhammer, A., Cambridge, Mass: Harvard University Press.

Polanyi, K. (2001 [1994]), *The Great Transformation: The Political and Economic Origins of our Time*, Boston, Mass: Beacon Press.

Porter, M.E. (1998), *Competitive Advantage: Creating and Sustaining Superior Performance*, with a New Introduction, New York: Free Press.

Porter, M.E. (2000), 'Locations, clusters, company strategy', in Clark, G.I., Feldman, M.P. and Geertler, M.S. (eds.) *The Oxford Handbook of Economic Geography*, Oxford: Oxford University Press.

Powell, J.L. and Owen T. (eds.) (2007), *Reconstructing Postmodernism*, New York: Nova Science

Power, M. (1999), *The Audit Society: Rituals of Verification*, Oxford: Oxford University Press.

Quah, D. (2002), 'Matching Demand and Supply in a Weightless Economy: Market-Driven Creativity With and Without IPRs', Centre for Economic Performance, London: London School of Economics and Political Science. Available at: http://cep.lse.ac.uk/pubs/download/DP0534.pdf

Rosenberg, D. (2002), *Cloning Silicon Valley: The Next Generation High-Tech Hotspots*, London: Pearson Education.

Sassen, S. (2012), *Cities in a World Economy*, 4th edition, Thousand Oaks, California: Sage.

Scarborough, H. (2001), 'Knowledge a la mode: the rise of knowledge management and its implications for views of knowledge production', *Social Epistemology*, 15 (3): 201–213.

Simmie, J., Sennett, J., Wood, P. and Hart, D. (2002), 'Innovation in Europe: a tale of networks, knowledge and trade in five cities', *Regional Studies*, 36, 47–64.

Smart, B. (2007), '(Dis)interring postmodernism or a critique of the political economy of consumer choice', in Powell, J.L. and Owen T. (eds.) *Reconstructing Postmodernism*, New York: Nova Science.

Soja, E.W. (2000), *Postmetropolis: Critical Studies of Cities and Regions*, Oxford: Blackwell.

Stehr, N. (1994), *Knowledge Societies*, London: Sage.

Stehr, N. (ed.) (2004), *The Governance of Knowledge*, London: Transaction.

Storper, M. (1997), *The Regional World: Territorial Development in a Global Economy*, New York: Guildford Press.

Tomlinson, J. (1999), *Globalization and Culture*, Cambridge: Polity.

Turner, S. (2003), *Liberal Democracy 3.0: Civil Society in an Age of Expert*, London: Sage.

Uyarra, E. (2009), 'What is evolutionary about "regional systems of innovation"? Implications for regional policy', *Journal of Evolutionary Economics*, 20, 115–137.

Weingart, P. (1997), 'From "Finalization" to "Mode 2": old wine in new bottles?', *Social Science Information*, 36 (4): 591–613.

World Bank Institute (2007), 'Building Knowledge Economies Advanced Strategies for Development', Washington: World Bank. Available at: http://siteresources.worldbank.org/KFDLP/Resources/461197-1199907090464/BuildingKEbook.pdf

Yigitcanlar, T., Velibeyoglu, K. and Baum, S. (eds.) (2008), *Knowledge-Based Urban Development: Planning and Applications in the Information Era*, London: IGI Global.

2

CITIES AS SITES OF INTERVENTION

Introduction

Cities are critical places where social, political, economic and ecological challenges in the 21st century will fall. 54 per cent of the world's population live in cities with estimates that this number will increase to 70 per cent by 2050 (United Nations 2014). In these sites, knowledge is accorded a central role in aspirations for economic growth and competitiveness. Policy frameworks at international, national and subnational levels position cities, in different ways, to play a key role in harnessing science, technology and innovation towards particular ends. The consequences are hat urban areas benefit from density and agglomeration for the purpose of economic growth, whilst also being sites of heightened social injustice (Fainstein 2014).

The promise of the knowledge economy is transforming urban strategies. This chapter examines how the discourses of the knowledge economy have influenced urban development strategies. It focusses on these dynamics in different cities and, for this purpose, it is divided into three sections. First, we explore the increasing importance of cities as sites of intervention and governance in the knowledge-based economy. We then look at different ways in which cities have embraced the promise of a high-tech, knowledge-based future. The promissory nature of capitalism is examined through different lenses, including smart, experimental, creative cities, urban living labs or technopoles. The aim is to show the sheer scale, breadth and scope of ambition to build the knowledge economy at the urban level. We then examine the drivers and rationalities behind some of these initiatives through a number of common themes, particularly in terms of how issues of scale frame expectations and the role of universities in the knowledge economy. That discussion then leads into Part II of the book where we explore the politics of these processes in more detail.

Embracing the urban promise

In parallel with the promise of the knowledge-based economy, the nation-state was being characterised as 'hollowed out' (Ohmae 1995). The processes producing this outcome came from above and below through regional demands for greater autonomy and processes of supra-nationalism and regional bloc formation. Trading blocs, such as the Southern Common Market ('Mercosur') or the North American Free Trade Agreement, whose futures are in doubt following the election of a new US President, forged economic relations which began to first replace and then constitute new political ones. The concept of a 'borderless world' epitomised the enthusiasm for free markets and the promise of improvements in human conditions (Ohmae 2005). Ohmae's 'invisible continent' may be seen in the first version of Microsoft's Windows, 24-hour news channels and the making and distribution of computers into the mass market. There is also the rise of transnational corporations whose powers move over and through nation-states (Crouch 2011). What we see is the global fluidity of capital in pursuit of its own reproduction (Harvey 2010; Jessop 2002). Accompanying this were processes of liberalisation, deregulation, privatisation and alterations in institutional arrangements to underwrite individualism (Harvey 2007).

Globalisation encapsulated a wider ideological shift away from the state towards the primacy of market forces moving across boundaries and the increasing involvement of non-state actors in policy design, formulation and governance (Majone 1999). Debates around the rise of the post-industrial or post-Fordist economy were accompanied by a concern with the emergence of new networked and distributed forms of governance and multi-level arrangements which highlighted the relevance of the 'city' – and then 'city-regions' – as appropriate units of analysis and action in both political and economic terms (Bache and Flinders 2004; Brenner 2004; Perry and May 2007; Neuman and Hull 2009). In Europe, there has been a strong move towards top-down devolution and decentralisation accompanied by bottom-up demand and subnational mobilisation, particularly in the context of debates over the democratic deficit and the Single European Market project (Newlands 1995; Cooke et al. 1997). In the 1996 Constitution of South Africa, forms of government saw the introduction of 'spheres' rather than 'tiers' with a corresponding emphasis upon distinction, interrelations and interdependency (Schmidt 2010). The emphasis in these developments was upon reproducibility within the realm of the political whose parameters became informed by the 'imagined economies of globalization' (Cameron and Palan 2004).

The idea of the city-region can be viewed against this backdrop. It does, after all, draw attention away from what are static geographies to the role of cities in promoting regional and national growth. The development of regions in this process is sporadic. Some regions are constituted as a means to intervene in new systems of production and distribution, whilst large cities can also play the same role (Keating 2003). This will vary in those conditions where the nation-state sees its role as a facilitator of national development based on attracting global capital. Overall, however, the economic arguments for city-regions seem less contested than those made on the grounds of political or administrative/technocratic reasons. The debate seems to focus not on whether the concept makes economic sense, but on the need for greater understanding in relation to *how* it should translate into actions within given areas and corresponding measures of their success. City-regions may seem appropriate for many large metropolitan areas, whilst others will seek to move beyond their historical boundaries to encompass new spaces in an attempt to demonstrate their economic vibrancy, reach and attraction.

The relationship between cities and knowledge is often understood through studies of 'innovation' and the city (Marceau 2009). As we noted in the last chapter, rather than seeing economic activities as seemingly disembedded from territory via globalising processes existing in a space of flows, writers stress that the subnational level is crucial in building national economic competitiveness and developing the knowledge economy (Storper 1995). Knowledge-based wealth creation requires economies of scale, clusters and a critical mass of complementary expertise within a particular location such that spillover leads to innovation and productivity (Florida 2002). Firms draw on location-specific factors to ensure competitive success and thus upon the resources within local environments (Simmie et al. 2002). Equally, one of the main aims of corporations which exist in different contexts is: "to hold varied knowledge architectures in place and establish knowledge coherence across different spatial scales" (Amin and Cohendet 2004: 96). To this extent, control, space and place exist in a dynamic tension and the varying emphases that may be found on global cities and medium size cities and their relationship to their regions reflect these issues. Yet it is also a part of what we discussed in the last chapter in terms of the relations between promise and a new form of capitalism moving into terrains that were not previously felt to be a part of the 'economic' realm of activity.

In a world of fluidity and unpredictability, cities constitute the places in which such possibilities can emerge. Whilst in centralised democracies urban policies have been characterised as 'space-blind' (May and Marvin 2009), with neoliberalism's naturalisation of competition comes the importance of communicating that particular places are essential for global success. Paradoxically, in the face of economic 'flows' and 'connections', strategies of attraction are in fact needed to underpin a disembedded idea of globalisation which is not assumed to discriminate on the grounds of place. The results are sets of urban strategies that inform, drive, fund, shape and validate particular forms of work. As such, contexts of enactment still count: they not only inform what outcomes are sought, what actions are taken and the organisational processes to capture value, but also shape the conditions in which judgements concerning ultimate worth are made. In the face of global promise, context becomes a conduit in which political, social and economic issues become tangible.

Forging the knowledge city

Under these circumstances, the city becomes a site of promise that mediates between place and global opportunity. As the knowledge economy moved into cultural terrains in seeking its realisation in spheres of activity that were previously regarded as peripheral, so the city came to position itself as an attractor by being an agent of persuasion. This concerns not simply representing what exists, but is part of an advertising process where places are positioned as desirable for capital invest-ment and the mobile knowledge worker. In that way, it seeks to influence those who might consume its benefits in terms of the offer of a cultural 'quality of life', as well as economic vibrancy in terms of concentration of sectors and networks. Despite the evident concerns of the Chinese authorities concerning what is termed the 'Bible of capitalism', by the end of 2012 China had 377,800 advertising agen-cies, employing 2.18 million people with revenues of $75.52 billion (Puppin 2014).

Moving into the terrain of urban marketing may be seen as part of a set of changes that include waves of economic activity in terms of boom and depres-sion. We can see in these developments, albeit in diverse cities across the globe, underlying class interests, but ones that lie deep: "like the fault lines under urban California" (Hall 1998: 935). However, how they manifest themselves in particu-lar places is mediated by a myriad of factors leading to cities choosing different responses over time. If there is a generalisation to be made then, to use a char-acterisation from Peter Hall (1998: 938), it comes in terms of globally persuasive movements with particular geographical manifestations. Those movements can be divided into the following four elements (Scott 2008: 133–135). First, there are ever-increasing amounts of cross-border economic activities that, in turn, lead to political responses, new coalitions of interests and decisions by the UN, G8, OECD and World Bank. Second, as noted earlier, we see the formation of trading blocs which seek to obtain benefit and reduce negative effects. Third, as we have dis-cussed, the idea that the nation-state is in retreat in the face of globalisation is an exaggeration that omits the extent to which nations accelerate and mitigate its effects. What we do see is regulatory functions moving at different scales from the supranational to subnational. Finally, city-regions obtain more prominence as 'staging posts' from which: "Much of the contemporary global system of trade in cognitive-cultural products and services is managed" (Scott 2008: 135).

Place, economically speaking, matters (Sassen 2012). Case studies show how dif-ferent cities approach the challenges of knowledge-based growth from Manchester and Eindhoven, to Barcelona, Holon and Singapore (Wong et al. 2006; Clua and Albet 2008; Fernandez-Maldono and Romein 2010; May and Perry 2011a). Emphasis is placed on different pathways to development, critical success factors, historical trajectories and the consequences and limitations of various approaches. In the process, an increased relevance attached to knowledge has led to a plethora of actors focussing upon and positioning themselves within a sphere of activity characterised by the promise of possibility. Efforts to reshape regional and local identities through harnessing the 'brand' power of science and technology have been charted (Brenner 2004; Perry and May 2007). Place is rebranded as knowl-edge capitals, silicon alleys, Bio-Valleys, digital cities or, more broadly, capitals of culture. These become emblematic of preexisting strengths within the knowledge base, acting as a magnetic foundation for broader strategies of competitive success in a desire to create exclusive, entrepreneurial environments (O'Mara 2005). In the words of George Osborne, former UK Chancellor of the Exchequer, in a speech in 2014 concerning the generation of a 'Northern powerhouse' in the UK: "A great global city has many things. Great jobs and businesses. Fast and effective transport connections. Strong universities and hospitals, colleges and schools for aspirational families. It will have the entertainment, the green spaces, the housing, culture and sport that makes for a good lifestyle" (available at: https://www.gov.uk/government/speeches/chancellor-we-need-a-northern-powerhouse).

There are a vast range of approaches and tools city authorities adopt to embrace the knowledge economy. These range from economic-technological cluster development, to experimental projects, strategic partnerships and brand marketing (see Table 2.1). Often these might be used at the same time. Thus, in the Greater Manchester, UK context, developments in knowledge-based urban development in the 2000s including strategic partnerships between local authorities, universities and organisations such as the health sector or transport agencies; data-driven smart city projects; science park and creative cluster development and efforts to rebrand the city-region as a 'Knowledge Capital' (May and Perry 2006; 2011b; Perry and May 2015). What is reflected is a global phenomenon which encompasses examples from Europe, Asia, the Middle East and America.

Caught up in the demands of global capital and the flows of knowledge and skills from one creative city to another, we witness a rush to embrace science and knowledge for urban development. Cities such as Amsterdam began to brand themselves as smart cities, entering competitions to prove their knowledge-based credentials. Experimental projects around mobility or infrastructure sprung up, such as the Vehicle2Grid project in Amsterdam and Lochem around locally produced energy, serious gaming or smart grids. Initiatives position cities as test-beds for demonstrator projects such as urban living labs to test new products and services. Such

TABLE 2.1 Making the knowledge city

Strategies and tools	Description	Examples
Ecological-technological clusters	Place-based clusters for economic and high-tech growth; emphasis on university-firm relationships in a specific location to increase spillover effects	Silicon Valley, technopoles, science parks, high-tech clusters, creative districts
Smart urban experiments	Bounded digitally enabled experiments to reshape urban infrastructures	Smart city initiatives and projects, Urban Living Labs
Strategic partnerships	Alliances between local authorities, universities and public-private providers	Triple Helix partnerships, Knowledge Capital, 'ideopolis'
Brand marketing	Marketing campaigns around the knowledge-based offer of the city, appealing to grand urban themes	EcoCity, Media City, Creative Capital, Green Cities

developments are not new. In the US, Athelstan Spillhaus developed the concept of the 'experimental city' in 1967 and then worked with local state officials on the Minnesota Experimental City, a proposed 'test tube' city, intended to act as a laboratory to solve urban crises of the time (May and Perry 2016).

Cities around the world have pinned their hopes on knowledge-based growth to reinvent their economic fortunes, a strategy which many proclaim as a success. Boston is heralded as a city that successfully reinvented itself as a high wage, low unemployment and highly educated metropolitan economy. An emphasis upon the development of human capital leads to recommendations such as an increase in spending on education: "the best single policy … to enhance economic growth for the information sector is improvement in the quality of and access to higher education" (Drennan 2002: 134). Specialisation in the information sector becomes linked to metropolitan growth: "metropolitan economies that are specialised in some parts of the information sector are more likely to have higher per capita income and stronger growth than metropolitan economies with traditional specialisations in manufacturing or distribution" (Drennan 2002: 8). The rise and fall of metropolitan economies – San Francisco, New York, Chicago and Philadelphia among others – is cited as evidence of this outcome.

In Australia, Charles (2011) examined the ways in which Queensland and Victoria state governments have sought to foster knowledge city developments. Innovation-based economic development strategies focussed on universities and featured the emergence of knowledge precincts. The universities of Brisbane and Melbourne are described as prestigious elements of major property developments as well as stimulating wider knowledge-based economic development. Melbourne, along with Greater Manchester, is particularly well respected for its knowledge-based growth (Yigitcanlar, O'Connor and Westerman 2008), on account of its fundamental 'knowledge cities' components: that is, technology and communication, creativity and cultural infrastructure, human capital, knowledge workers and urban development clusters. 'Knowledge Melbourne' is an initiative that saw the city winning the 'Most Admired City' award in 2010 (see chapter 3) with its focus on biotechnology, advanced manufacturing, creative industries, events management, financial services, health, higher education, ICT, sustainability, social enterprise and micro businesses. Such activity is underpinned by the city's knowledge strategy (2014) based on knowledge-intensive activities, retention and attraction of knowledge, talent, firms and investment and local, national and international recognition.

The discourse of smart cities has been particularly mobile. The winner of the World Smart City award in 2014 was Tel Aviv, with a strategy to both develop technologically enhanced solutions for urban administration and increase citizen engagement and participation. Elsewhere, brand new cities are being constructed to deliver on the knowledge-based promise. The Malaysian city of *Bandar Seri Iskandar* was physically developed from scratch on a greenfield site as a cornerstone of Malaysian knowledge-development policies (Yigitcanlar and Sarimin 2011). It required creating not only capacity and infrastructure, in terms of public universities in the 1990s, but also city structures and forms. Whilst these examples suggest a wholesale embrace of the knowledge economy, evidence also points to the difficulties of translating theory into practice. Such examples include the translation of the 'triple helix' model (Etzkowitz 2008) into developing contexts and the difficulties in sustaining clusters. We shall return to these issues in the next chapter.

The value placed in science, knowledge and innovation to secure economic growth is placed at the heart of global knowledge competitiveness. As this is done, so the city enters into a terrain of attraction to realise global promise through presenting particular images. This is not lost on knowledge-intensive firms who, in seeking to turn knowledge into a commodity, realise that it is ambiguous in its operation with the result that: "'knowledge', 'expertise', and 'solving problems' to a large degree become matters of belief, impressions, and negotiations of meaning. Institutionalized assumptions, expectations, recognitions, reputation, images, etc. matter strongly for how the products of knowledge-intensive organizations and workers are perceived" (Alvesson 2004: 72). In the face of such ambiguity, there is a turn to particular forms of language expressed in terms such as 'drivers', 'opportunities', 'pillars', 'initiatives' and 'solutions' (see, for example, Dresner 2001). We also see an emphasis on physical development in terms of 'hubs', 'incubators' and 'science parks' (Youtie and Shapira 2008). These are reflected in national and urban initiatives whereby science and innovation come to lie at the heart of economic growth and competitiveness.

A dominant view of the relationship between knowledge and cities emphasises an instrumentally driven, econo-centric perspective on their contributions to national wealth and competitiveness. Many developments focus on technology as a key driver and enabler, creating 'Invented Edens' with the result that: "the techno-city represents an experiment in integrating modern technology into the world of ideal life" (Kargon and Molella 2008: 12). However, there are differences in cities' responses to the promise which are dependent on a series of different drivers which, in turn, relate to systems of spatial governance and higher education systems. These influence different types of knowledge-based urban development and their manifestations in practice.

Convergence and divergence in knowledge-based development

We can identify four different drivers behind cities' embrace of the knowledge economy promise which blend at different points in time: economic, political, cultural and scientific. First, an economic perspective emphasises the relationship between knowledge and place in the context of globalisation, localisation, the knowledge economy and the relative importance of different factors in the process of production. In many countries, the promise of convergence met with a rationale for balanced growth and the potential of science, technology and innovation (STI) to address regional disparities. In France, Germany and Italy examples could be seen of national policies with strong subnational dimensions (Crespy et al. 2007; Koschatzky and Kroll 2007). These include initiatives to target specific regions and to build capacity, such in East Germany or Southern Italy, as well as open competitions to build excellence, in which all regions can participate. This contrasts with situations in places such as England where regional economic development arguments have not traditionally been accepted at national level as legitimate rationales for influencing the contours of national policy. Here we see a requirement on subnational actors to link STI and socio-economic development goals (Charles and Benneworth 2001; Perry 2007).

Second, there is another rationale that relates to urban growth coalitions and entrepreneurialism (Macleod 2002; Salet et al. 2003). The roles of local governments and authorities have been recast in light of discourses of competitiveness and economic development with the result that city governance has become increasingly characterised by a focus on entrepreneurial activities and issues of production, rather than social welfare or consumption (Boddy and Parkinson 2004; Wilks-Heeg et al. 2003). Barcelona's '22@bcn' project, seen as a 'top-down redevelopment strategy to capture high-tech activities', has been held up as a central exemplar of urban policy strategy as an exercise in economic 'boosterism' (Casellas and Palleres-Barbera 2009: 1151). Cities have become more concerned with marketing, branding and global success and position, emphasising the roles of creativity, innovation and knowledge in city futures (Hospers 2008). Here, 'science' is a label, utilised and valued for its ability to conjure up territorial images of the new, engaged, cutting-edge city. Through this focus, it tends to be the promulgation of vision that is seen to change urban fortunes.

Third, there is the 'creative city' or 'city of ideas'. In the UK, this has found particular resonance with policy and practitioner communities through the concept of the 'ideopolis' as a means to capture the essential ingredients of a post-industrial city (Work Foundation 2006). The ideopolis was initially seen to have three key elements: a set of key physical and economic features; a particular social and demographic mix; and a specific cultural climate and set of commonly held values (Canon et al. 2003). From a socio-cultural perspective the 'creative city' links clearly to Florida's (2002) notion of the 'creative class', concerned with attracting the right kind of knowledge workers, cultural feel and 'buzz', physical regeneration and connectivity as well as the support networks necessary to develop as a smart and modern city. Human capital and the social, cultural and institutional conditions for growth take central stage (Archibugi and Lundvall 2001). On the other hand, a more economic-cultural perspective emphasises the creative industries and the development of the creative economy (Collinge and Musterd 2009). Here, a hybridised discourse can be seen that links economic competitiveness with branding and positioning in the search for cultural capital at the urban level (Christopherson and Rightor 2009). Science, knowledge, culture and creativity are collapsed to produce particular ways of seeing the urban knowledge economy (Hutton 2009).

Fourth, there are also large-scale changes in knowledge production. A paradigmatic shift in how knowledge is produced, for what reasons, by whom, for whom and how it is subsequently judged is said to be occurring. New modes of knowledge production emphasise interdisciplinarity, heterogeneity, distributed expertise, the need for user relevance, collaboration and an interactive process between research and practice and implicitly bring issues of scale into focus (Gibbons et al. 1994; Nowotny et al. 2001; May 2006; May with Perry 2011). Local and regional stakeholders become important not only in assessing impact and demonstrating engagement, but also in defining and co-funding research. This is reflected in increasing emphasis placed on impact assessment and innovative methodologies and action research approaches, based on the aspiration that excellence comes together with relevance through place to build localised systems for knowledge exchange (Perry and May 2010). Knowledge management literatures, drawing on business, critical management and organisational studies are also reflected through this window in their focus upon tacit and embodied knowledge, codification and knowledge sharing (Amin and Cohendet 2004).

Each of these dimensions – economic, political, socio-cultural and scientific – are not exclusive and may be in tension or even contradictory in terms of their spatial implications vis-à-vis, concentration or distribution of resources and capacities (Edler, Kuhlmann and Behrens 2003; Perry and May 2007). In multiple countries within Western Europe, Australasia, Asia and North America, an increasing percentage of national programmes were delivered by regional and local actors in centralised, decentralised and federal contexts (Kitagawa 2007; Salazar and Holbrook 2007; Sotarauta and Kautonen 2007). National programmes may have varied subnational dimensions as regional actors become stages for the implementation of national policies; they may be partners or co-funders in national/ regional infrastructures, or develop independent subnational policies for STI or knowledge-based growth.

The context for the growth of knowledge-based urban development, including the opportunities for commercialisation, is informed by patterns of intergovernmental interaction and existing governance structures between national and subnational actors. A widespread, albeit often unintentional, regionalisation of policy for science, research and higher education has taken place within Europe. The UK provides an extreme example of this, moving in the late 1990s from a centralised system towards an asymmetrically devolved governance structure for higher education in Scotland and Wales. Even in the absence of formal devolution to the English regions, regional science policy governance emerged. What were the nine English Regional Development Agencies (RDAs) established Science and Industry Councils from 2004 to bring together academic, industry and governmental actors, with the aim of linking science and research to wider regional socio-economic objectives. Following that, six Science Cities were nominated by the Treasury to drive the UK forward in terms of innovation and economic competitiveness. These included 'Science City York' (1998) and 'Manchester: Knowledge Capital' (2002). National government then became involved, with the first three Science Cities – Manchester, Newcastle and York – being announced in December 2004 by the then Chancellor of the Exchequer, Gordon Brown, in his pre-budget report. This was further followed in 2005 by three cities, Birmingham, Bristol and Nottingham. The RDAs were disbanded in 2012 under conditions of reducing the national budget deficit due to the financial crisis of 2008. They were replaced by voluntary local enterprise partnerships that are charged with the promotion of economic growth.

In France, the centralised or Colbertist system of research and innovation underwent profound changes (Mustar and Larédo 2002). Here, the *collectivités* were increasingly important actors in the financing and shaping of policy priorities through the state-regional planning process, the *Contrat de Projet État-Région*. The German situation, with sixteen regional governments, the *Länder*, traditionally had the greatest responsibility over higher education through the financing of universities, sharing responsibility with the federal government in certain areas of science policy and research funding. In reforms of the federal state, however, the responsibilities of the *Länder* in relation to higher education were increased. In both France and Germany, cluster-based policies had strong spatial effects aiming to create agglomerations of critical mass bridging between the research and industrial base. Given the asymmetrical nature of the Spanish system, competences for science and technology vary between regions (Sanz-Menéndez and Cruz-Castro 2005). An oft-cited example of developing regional competencies could be seen in the actions of the Catalonian government with the creation of the Inter-Ministerial Commission for Research, Innovation and Technology and series of regional research plans (Charles, Perry and Benneworth 2004; Dresner 2001).

In federal countries, such as Germany or Australia, the involvement of regional authorities in funding higher education and formulating science and innovation policies were well established (Charles 2006; Koschatzky and Kroll 2007). In France, reform of the contractual relationship between the state and subnational levels strengthened the institutional arena for intergovernmental bargaining in research and higher education (Crespy, Heraud and Perry 2007). The UK case is substantially different with highly centralised research resources distributed through a dual support system comprised of Research Council project funding and quality-related recurrent institutional support through the Research Assessment Exercise (RAE) and latterly, the Research Exercise Framework (REF). Devolution in Scotland and Wales since 1997 introduced a partially devolved system of higher education, science and research with clear differences emerging in the charging of tuition fees to students.

National and regional responses to the demands of the regional science paradigm are intrinsically linked to the wider debate on governance and devolution. The challenge is for a greater consideration of how specific national/regional responses are addressing the demands of a multi-scalar knowledge economy within particular governance structures. Multiple actors at multiple levels are involved in science policy and knowledge-based development (KBD). Differences have been identified in what 'regionalisation' means in practice, as mediated through national economic and scientific systems (Fristch and Stephan 2005). What matters is how pre-reflexive understandings about knowledge and space, informed implicitly or explicitly through different theoretical lenses, interrelate with multi-scalar governance arrangements. As the quantity and quality of interactions across levels of governance increase, so too does the potential for differences in terms of the relationships between knowledge, space and place, with important effects on the capacities and capabilities of subnational actors to build sustainable knowledge-based futures (Van Winden et al. 2007).

City strategies in the knowledge economy

Theoretically grounded justifications for considering the relationship between knowledge and place are varied. Rationales are both exogenous and endogenous, stemming from within and outside epistemic communities (May with Perry 2011). At the same time, urban strategies are mediated through systems of territorial governance and higher education. These differences account for the ways in which cities variously develop approaches in response to the knowledge economy. We can distinguish three types of knowledge-based development: acquisition, product and process (see Table 2.2).

Embodied within each mode of knowledge-based urban development are differing conceptualisations of knowledge, the urban and the roles of different actors (Perry 2008). In an *acquisition-driven knowledge-based urban development,* the attraction of talent, research expertise, the development of assets and external symbols of success or marketing and image are critical as it is the symbolic value, rather than actual content, of knowledge that matters. It is large 'scientific emblems' and facilities, or stellar 'world class' academics that have the greatest potential for these kinds of representational effects. Universities are seen as tools, instruments, assets and status symbols to be acquired, harnessed and their benefits extracted. In an acquisition-driven view, universities are one among many participants, operating on an institutional basis within strategic alliances with little engagement with individual academics. In the context of the knowledge-economy, universities may be part of urban growth coalitions, yet they may alternatively be absent – as it is their existence that is deemed important as assets, rather than the knowledge they produce. Alternatively, what is counted as 'knowledge' may be broader, taking in the sciences, social sciences, humanities and arts through the idea of the 'creative economy'. The urban may be important through partnership between different actors within a locality in the definition of research priorities, or the involvement of institutional interests, including local authorities, business interests and city partners as potential users of, or participants in, research processes. On the other hand, it may be absent, as proximity and localised relationships are seen to take place without according any agency to the 'city' itself.

As we have seen, cities have become more concerned with marketing, branding and global success and position. The concept of the 'ideopolis', outlined above, is one example concerning the ingredients that need to be acquired within cities as the basis for competitive success, rather than how knowledge itself can be harnessed for wider social benefit. Knowledge itself as a process or product has a role, but this is within a broader vision in which the acquisition of talent, research expertise, the development of assets and external symbols of success or marketing and

TABLE 2.2 Three types of knowledge-based development: acquisition, product and process

	Influences	Knowledge	Urban	University
Acquisition-driven knowledge-based urban development	Urban growth theory; urban entrepreneurialism; the 'ideopolis'.	Emphasis on the ingredients for success to be acquired; 'what' rather than the 'how' or 'why'.	City governments at centre of new urban strategies. Emphasis on branding and position.	Universities as one among many partners. Strategic institutional engagement more than individual academic.
Product-driven knowledge-based urban development	Economics and innovation studies.	Knowledge as a product to be exploited by 'end-users'.	A passive, facilitative role in terms of creating an environment for innovation. Indirect benefits to locality seen to accrue.	Universities as providers of knowledge; emphasis on business–university interactions. No necessary strategic engagement.
Process-driven knowledge-based urban development	Science and technology studies.	Knowledge as a process; new modes of knowledge production, ways of working, user engagement and knowledge exchange.	An active role. Range of local stakeholders, including city governments, involved in research processes. Varied political, economic and social benefits.	Universities as critical. Engagement with academics at all levels of university hierarchy. Fluid and diverse interactions, difficult to map. Universities providing strategic intelligence.

image are equally, if not more, important – as tools in global positioning. In an acquisition-driven view, universities are one among many participants, operating on an institutional basis within strategic alliances with little engagement with individual academics. In the context of the knowledge-economy, universities may be part of urban growth coalitions that have, certainly in the case of Manchester, been attributed with delivering urban renaissance. Yet they may alternatively be absent – as it is their existence that is deemed important as assets, rather than the knowledge they produce. 'Knowledge' as academic research is only a secondary concern; at the forefront, is an understanding of the 'knowledge city' as being clever, smart, skilful, creative, networked, connected and competitive. All too often, however, acquisition is seen as a goal in its own right, without due consideration of the factors which lead to positive knowledge-based outcomes: "there are plenty of large cities containing good universities, numerous firms and business services between which knowledge spillovers could take place that, nevertheless, do not develop strong virtuous circles of innovation and economic growth" (Simmie 2002: 899)

Second, we can identify *product-driven knowledge-based urban development*, in terms of the exploitation of particular knowledge products, with processes of knowledge production hermetically sealed from 'outside' interference. An econocentric perspective emphasises products, outputs and particular forms of knowledge more amenable to codification with a focus on linkages between universities and businesses as a precursor for commercialisation and spin-offs, rather than the redefinition of academics' research agendas and ways of working. The urban is framed as facilitating 'innovation' with a reliance on trickle-down to achieve objectives of increased Gross Value Added (GVA). Knowledge may alternatively be seen as a central element in the rebranding of places – again, as a tool in global positioning.

This is more consistent with a 'Mode 1' of knowledge production in which the process of research is detached from the subsequent harnessing of knowledge for socio-economic benefit. The emphasis is on a more linear model of innovation and knowledge transfer or on the mechanisms through which knowledge is managed and communicated, such as networks or ICTs. Knowledge-based development relates more to the changing nature of the industrial fabric, for instance, in terms of knowledge-based industries and the linkages between universities and businesses as a precursor for commercialisation and spin-offs. A particular conception of the 'urban' is inherent in this view of knowledge-based development. As we saw, there is an emphasis on innovation systems and the importance of spatial proximity, agglomeration economies and knowledge spillovers (Cooke and Piccaluga 2006; Krätke 2011).

Here, the 'urban' is generally conceived either as a container in which innovation takes place, with few inherent properties or agency, or as a location factor in the attraction of knowledge-based assets and creation of particular environments. In other words, cities are where innovation or knowledge transfer happens to take place, rather than agents that actively seek to foster knowledge-based urban development or direct beneficiaries. The interactions between universities and businesses may take place within particular locations (particularly if incentives are tied to spatial boundaries) but are not driven by specific place-based factors. We once again enter the terrain of a 'managed' view of knowledge where we see the growth of technology transfer offices, business departments and academic-linked science parks or business incubators. Individual academics are implicated in terms of intellectual property, but relationships can be mediated or brokered through specific liaison offices at the institutional level. The extent to which this is encouraged depends on the relative importance at strategic level that is attached to income generation and spin-out activities.

What is counted as 'knowledge' tends to be broader in *a process-driven view* of knowledge-based development. What is taken on board are the physical sciences, social sciences, humanities and arts. A product-driven view tends to be more technologically driven and focussed on the exploitable products of the physical sciences, in terms of new companies, patents and intellectual property. There are of course exceptions to this tendency: for instance, as we saw in the idea of the cultural economy and marketing the city, there is an increasing emphasis on the cultural. Here we also find the idea of creative industries and transmission of knowledge to pupils, students and the public more broadly. Thus, the social sciences and humanities can operate at the reception end of physical science knowledge in terms of being concerned with transmission and application for enhancing public understanding of science.

Responding to the changes we have charted has led to the rise of disciplinary combinations and new creativity in fields such as health care, informatics, biomedical research and the creative arts. Thus, another way to characterise university-knowledge-urban relations concerns newer processes of knowledge production. This view draws on the Mode 2 thesis (Gibbons et al. 1994) and the distinction between codified and tacit (or embedded) knowledge (Polanyi 1958; 1966; Collins 2010) and the shift towards 'knowing how' as opposed to 'knowing that' (Schön 1991; Ryle 2000; Sternberg and Horvath 1999). Core to a process-driven view of KBD are fundamental questions relating to how knowledge is produced, for what reasons, by whom, for whom and how it is subsequently judged. In relation to research, this involves multiple stakeholders in the definition of priorities, research questions and the conduct of the research itself. Action research, coproduction and policy-oriented work become more commonplace, with a linear model of knowledge transfer replaced by the concept of 'exchange' through active and constant communication between stakeholders throughout the research process. Such concepts apply equally to pedagogy in terms of new working patterns and modes of engagement between academics, students and/or local partners, such as new curricula to meet the skills needs of industry, placements or continuing professional development.

An 'urban' dimension is implicit in these relationships. The Mode 2 thesis makes no explicit reference to space or scale, seeing 'contexts of application' as largely relating to the interstices between public and private sectors, rather than geographical locations. However, a 'process-driven' conceptualisation of knowledge-based urban development involves partnership between different actors within a locality in the definition of research priorities and draws attention to the importance of institutional interests, including local authorities, business interests and city partners as potential users of, or participants in, research processes. To take advantage of tacit and embedded knowledge through new modes of academic engagement requires spatial proximity over time. Of course, this may be afforded through short bursts of concentrated activity such as placements, but continuous interaction through well-established networks of communication is desirable to create the kinds of productive flows between knowledge-producing institutions, particularly universities, and knowledge users seen as necessary for competitive economic and social advantage. This is particularly the case given the interdisciplinary nature of urban studies, with traditionally strong connections to policy and practice, which is evidenced in the increasing emphasis on the notion of the 'urban knowledge arena' (May 2011; May and Perry 2005).

In terms of university-urban relations, the significance of a process-driven view of knowledge-based urban development is threefold: first, it involves new ways of working that finally break the illusion of the ivory tower; second, it requires engagement with academic staff at different levels of the university hierarchy outside senior management; third, it is characterised by multiple, fluid, informal and formal external interactions that are difficult to map, let alone manage. While some commentators have posited the demise of the institutional authority of the university as a result of the rise of alternative sites of knowledge production (Gibbons et al. 1994), others have emphasised instead the continued pivotal role of universities within contemporary innovation processes (Etzkowitz 2008).

Whilst these modes of cities' engagement with knowledge-based urban development are not mutually exclusive, they point to the relative importance of how relations between knowledge and space alter. In the first, knowledge is central and subject to change as a result of external pressures, whilst in the last, knowledge production in recognised formal institutions is itself only a small part of knowledge-based urban development processes, embedded in a wider set of economic, social and cultural processes. Similarly, while the 'urban' is only implied and peripheral in process- or product-driven knowledge-based urban development, 'place' is central to the realisation, particularly when local authorities themselves take a central role. This is a distinction of emphasis rather than an inherent tension, between knowledge-based development that takes place within particular city contexts and urban development, some of which is knowledge-based. Acquisition-driven knowledge-based urban development may be necessary, but is not sufficient to harness knowledge as a factor in growth and development. Indeed, it is only through a combination of all three dimensions into a more holistic knowledge-based urban development vision can the expected benefits of the knowledge economy be delivered. Again these are themes we shall return to later in the book.

Summary: Mediating knowledge-based urban development

When it comes to the promise of the knowledge economy in cities, the assumption is often that 'doing something' about innovation and the knowledge economy is enough to result in transformation. Rationales for action in practice may relate to theoretical frameworks, but more commonly they have developed in policy and practice born of experience or justified by necessity through pressures of convergence, with post hoc justifications deployed to legitimise prior courses of action. Equally, urban responses may vary according to divergent rationalities, mediated through national-regional systems of urban governance and higher education. Dynamics have been illuminated in relation to the conflation between creative, digital and knowledge economies, a narrow preferencing of particular forms of knowledge and the socio-cultural implications of dominant approaches (Chapain et al. 2009).

A desire to market the city in the face of increasing globalisation comes from a push, or lack of ability or unwillingness of national governments to act, along with greater disaggregation that results from the same pressures that lead to internal divisions between cities and city-regions for competitive advantage. As the economic increasingly blends with the social and cultural, a new reflexive relation comes into being requiring different responses from cities themselves. A positive relation, constituted through urban efforts aimed at realising the promise, was expressed by Michael Storper. He took as his target mechanical, economic views of cities, expressed in ideas of agglomeration, resource concentration and allusion to flows of information. These all tell us a story that: "does not add up to the living result of the urban economies which are before us" (Storper 1997b: 1). What is held out here is a possibility for cities to shape the economic through groups of actors coming together in 'reflexive human action': "the nature of the contemporary city is as a local or regional 'socio-economy', whose very usefulness to the forces of global capitalism is precisely as an ensemble of specific, differentiated and localised social relations. These consist of concrete relations between persons and organisations which are necessary to the economic functioning of those entities. Cities are sites where these relations are routinised through rules, institutions and, most importantly, conventions, many of which are localised and are different from one city to another" (Storper 1997b: 2).

What is missing is a specific emphasis on the overall framing of debates and how the interplay between conceptualisation and governance frameworks delimits the capacities and capabilities of city-regions to work towards alternative knowledge-based futures. Greater attention is needed not only on the governance of the knowledge economy, but on the alignment between national policies and local priorities (Van Winden et al. 2007). This is an issue which tended to be underplayed in Castells and Hall's (1994) original work. What is clear is a movement from the representation of what exists, through to an intensification of efforts directed towards the presentation of place in the name of promise. Here, global forces may align and round which clusters and networks of individuals and small and medium sized enterprises may establish themselves and flourish in a milieu of creativity, innovation and knowledge. Cities are investing because they believe it will transform their fortunes and universities are responding accordingly as they become embedded in these ambitions. These are mediated through scale, governance and institutions. Despite mediated differences, there are similarities in urban responses, views on universities in the knowledge economy and the framing of expertise in urban environments. It is to an examination of the politics of these processes that we now turn.

References

Alvesson, M. (2004), *Knowledge Work and Knowledge-Intensive Firms*, Oxford: Oxford University Press.

Amin, A. and Cohendet, P. (2004), *Architectures of Knowledge: Firms, Capabilities, and Communities*, Oxford: Oxford University Press.

Archibugi, D. and Lundvall, B. (eds.) (2001), *The Globalising Learning Economy*, Oxford: Oxford University Press.

Bache, I. and Flinders, M. (eds.) (2004), *Multi-Level Governance*, Oxford: Oxford University Press.

Beynon, H. and Nichols, T. (eds.) (2006), *Patterns of Work in the Post-Fordist Era: Volume 2*, Cheltenham: Edward Elgar.

Boddy, M. and Parkinson, M. (eds.) (2004), *City Matters. Competitiveness, Cohesion and Urban Governance*, Bristol: The Policy Press.

Brenner, N. (2004), *New State Spaces: Urban Governance and the Rescaling of Statehood*, Oxford: Oxford University Press.

Brenner, N. and Theodore, N. (eds.) (2002), *Spaces of Neoliberalism: Urban Restructuring in North America and Western Europe*, Oxford: Blackwell.

Brenner, N., Jessop, B., Jones, M. and MacLeod, G. (eds.) (2003), *State/Space: A Reader*, Oxford: Blackwell.

Cameron, A. and Palan, R. (2004), *The Imagined Economies of Globalization*, London: Sage.

Canon, T., Nathan, M. and Westwood, A. (2003), *Welcome to the Ideopolis*, London: Work Foundation Working Paper.

Carillo, F. (ed.) (2006), *Knowledge Cities: Approaches, Experiences and Perspectives*, Oxford: Butterworth-Heinemann.

Casellas, A. and Pallares-Barbera, M. (2009), 'Public sector intervention in embodying the new economy in inner urban areas: the Barcelona experience', *Urban Studies*, 46 (5 and 6): 1137–1155.

Castells, M. and Hall, P. (1994), *Technopoles of the World,* London: Routledge.

Chapain, C., Collinge, C., Lee, P. and Musterd, S. (eds.) (2009), 'Can we plan the creative knowledge city?' *Special Edition, Built Environment*, 32 (2): 292.

Charles, D. (2006), 'Universities as key knowledge infrastructures in regional innovation systems', *Innovation: The European Journal of Social Science Research*, 19: 117–130.

Charles, D. (2011), 'The role of universities in building knowledge cities in Australia', *Built Environment*, 37 (3): 281–298.

Charles, D. and Benneworth, P. (2001) 'Are we realising our potential? joining up science and technology policy in the English regions', *Regional Studies*, 35 (1): 76.

Charles, D., Perry, B. and Benneworth, P. (2004), *Towards a Multi-level Science Policy: Regional Science Policy in a European Context*, Regional Studies Association.

Christopherson, S. and Rightor, N. (2009), 'The creative economy as "big business": evaluating state strategies to lure filmmakers', *Journal of Planning Education and Research*, 29 (3): 336–352.

Clua, A. and Albet, A. (2008), '22@bcn: bringing Barcelona forward in the information era', in Yigitcanlar, T., Velibeyoglu, K. and Baum, S. (eds.) *Knowledge-Based Urban Development: Planning and Applications in the Information Era*, London: IGI Global, pp. 132–148.

Collinge, C. and Musterd, S. (2009), 'Deepening social divisions and the discourses of knowledge and creativity across the cities of Europe', *Built Environment*, 35 (2): 281–285.

Collins, H. (2010), *Tacit and Explicit Knowledge*, Chicago: University of Chicago Press.

Cooke, P. and Piccaluga, A. (eds.) (2006), *Regional Development in the Knowledge Economy*, London: Routledge.

Cooke, P., Gomez Uranga, M. and Etxebarria, G. (1997), 'Regional innovation systems: institutional and organisational dimensions,' *Research Policy*, 26: 475–491.

Crespy, C., Heraud, J-A. and Perry, B. (2007), 'Multi-level governance, regions and science in France: between competition and equality', *Regional Studies*, 41 (8): 1069–1084.

Crouch, C. (2011), *The Strange Non-Death of Neoliberalism*, Cambridge: Polity.

Drennan, M.P. (2002), *Information Economy and American Cities*, Baltimore: John Hopkins University Press.

Dresner, S. (2001), 'A comparison of RTD structures in EU member states' in Dresner, S. and Gilbert, N. (eds.) *The Dynamics of European Science and Technology Policies*, Aldershot: Ashgate, pp. 109–135.

Dresner, S. and Gilbert, N. (eds.) (2001), *The Dynamics of European Science and Technology Policies*, Aldershot: Ashgate.

Edler, J., Kuhlmann S. and Behrens, M. (2003), *Changing Governance of Research and Technology Policy: The European Research Area*, Cheltenham: Edward Elgar.

Etzkowitz, H. (2008), *The Triple Helix: University-Industry-Government Innovation in Action*, Oxford: Routledge.

Evans, J., Karvonen, A. and Raven, R. (eds.) (2016), *The Experimental City*, Oxford: Routledge.

Fainstein, S.S. (2014), 'The just city', *International Journal of Urban Sciences*, 18 (1): 1–18.

Fernandez-Maldono, A. and Romein, A. (2010), 'The role of organisational capacity and knowledge-based development: the reinvention of eindhoven', *International Journal of Knowledge-Based Development*, 1 (1/2): 79–97.

Florida, R. (2002), *The Rise of the Creative Class and How It's Transforming Work, Leisure, Community and Everyday Life,* New York: Basic Books.

Fritsch, M. and Stephan, A. (2005), 'Regionalisation of innovation policy – introduction to the special issue', *Research Policy*, (34): 1123–1127.

Gibbons, M., Limoges, C., Nowotny, H., Schwartaman, S., Scott, P. and Trow, M. (1994), *The New Production of Knowledge: The Dynamics of Science and Research in Contemporary Societies*, London: Sage.

Hall, P. (1998), *Cities in Civilization: Culture, Innovation, and Urban Order*, London: Phoenix.

Hardy, S., Hart, M., Albrechts, L. and Katos, A. (eds.) (1995), *An Enlarged Europe, Regions in Competition?*, London: Regional Studies Association.

Harvey, D. (2007), *A Brief History of Neoliberalism*, Oxford: Oxford University Press.

Harvey, D. (2010), *The Enigma of Capital and the Crisis of Capitalism*, London: Profile Books.

Hospers, G-J. (2008), 'Governance in innovative cities and the importance of branding', *Innovation: Management, Policy and Practice*, 10 (2–3): 224–234.

Hulme, A. (ed.) (2014), *The Changing Landscape of China's Consumerism*, Oxford: Elsevier

Hutton, T. (2009), 'Trajectories of the new economy: regeneration and dislocation in the inner city', *Urban Studies*, 46 (5–6): 987–1001.

Jessop, B. (2002), *The Future of the Capitalist State in its Place*, Cambridge: Polity.

Kargon, R.H. and Molella, A.P. (2008), *Invented Edens: Techno-Cities of the Twentieth Century*, Cambridge, Mass: MIT Press.

Keating, M. (2003), 'The invention of regions: political restructuring and territorial government in Western Europe', in Brenner, N., Jessop, B., Jones, M. and MacLeod, G. (eds.) *State/Space: A Reader*, Oxford: Blackwell.

Kitagawa, F. (2007), 'Regionalisation of science and innovation governance in Japan?' in Perry, B. and May, T. (eds.) *Special Edition 'Regional Governance and Science Policy'*, *Regional Studies*, 41 (8): 1099–1114.

Koschatzky, K. and Kroll, H. (2007) 'Which side of the coin? The regional governance of science and innovation', *Regional Studies*, 41 (8): 1115–1128.

Krätke, S. (2011), *The Creative Capital of Cities*, Oxford: Wiley Blackwell.

Macleod, G. (2002), 'From urban entrepreneurialism to a "revanchist city"? On the spatial injustices of Glasgow's renaissance' in Brenner, N. and Theodore, N. (eds.) *Spaces of Neoliberalism: Urban Restructuring in North America and Western Europe*, Oxford: Blackwell.

Majone, G. (1999), 'The regulatory state and its legitimacy problems', *West European Politics*, 22 (1): 1–24.

Marceau, J. (ed.) (2009), 'Innovation in the city and innovative cities', Special Edition, 'Innovation Management', *Policy and Practice*, (10): 2–3.

May, T. (2006), 'Transformative power: a study in a human service organization', in Beynon, H. and Nichols, T. (eds.) *Patterns of Work in the Post-Fordist Era: Volume 2*, Cheltenham: Edward Elgar.

May, T. (2011), 'Urban knowledge arenas: dynamics, tensions and potentials', *International Journal of Knowledge-Based Development*, 2 (2):132–147.

May, T. and Marvin, S. (2009), 'Elected regional assemblies: lessons for better policy making', in Sandford, M. (ed.) *The Northern Veto*, Manchester: Manchester University Press.

May, T. and Perry, B. (2005), 'Urban sociology: into the future', *Sociology*, Vol. 39 (2), pp. 361–365.

May, T. and Perry, B. (2006), 'Cities, knowledge and universities: transformations in the image of the intangible' *Social Epistemology*, 20 (3–4): 259–282.

May, T. and Perry, B. (2011a), 'Contours and conflicts in scale: science, knowledge and urban development', *Local Economy* 26 (8): 715–720.

May, T. and Perry, B. (2011b), 'Urban research in the knowledge economy: content, context and outlook', *Built Environment*, 37 (3): 352–368.

May, T. and Perry, B. (2016), 'Cities, experiments and the logics of the knowledge economy', in Evans, J., Karvonen, A. and Raven, R. (eds.), *The Experimental City*, Oxford: Routledge.

May, T. with Perry, B. (2011), *Social Research and Reflexivity: Content, Consequences and Context*, London: Sage.

Miao, J.T., Benneworth, P. and Phelps, N. (eds.) (2015), *Making 21st Century Knowledge Complexes: Technopoles of the World 20 Years After*, London: Routledge.

Mustar, P. and Larédo, P. (2002), 'Innovation and research policy in France (1980–2000) or the disappearance of the Colbertist state', *Research Policy* 31 (1): 55–72.

Neuman, M. and Hull, A. (2009), 'The futures of the city region', *Regional Studies* 43 (6): 777–787.

Newlands, D. (1995), 'The economic role of regional governments in the European Community', in Hardy, S., Hart, M., Albrechts, L. and Katos, A. (eds.) *An Enlarged Europe, Regions in Competition?*, London: Regional Studies Association, pp. 70–80.

Nowotny, H., Scott, P. and Gibbons, M. (2001), *Re-thinking Science: Knowledge and the Public in an Age of Uncertainty*, Cambridge: Polity.

O'Mara, M.P. (2005), *Cities of Knowledge: Cold War Science and the Search for the Next Silicon Valley*, Princeton: Princeton University Press.

Ohmae, K. (1995), *The End of the Nation State*, New York: Free Press.

Ohmae, K. (2005), *The Next Global Stage: Challenges and Opportunities in Our Borderless World*, New Jersey: Wharton.

Osborne, G. (2014), 'We need a northern powerhouse', speech available at https://www. gov.uk/government/speeches/chancellor-we-need-a-northern-powerhouse (accessed May 2017).

Perry, B. (2007), 'The multi-level governance of science policy in England', *Regional Studies*, 41 (8): 1051–1067.

Perry, B. (2008), 'Academic knowledge and urban development: theory, policy and practice', in Yigitcanlar, T., Velibeyoglu, K. and Baum, S. (eds.) *Knowledge-Based Urban Development: Planning and Applications in the Information Era*, London: IGI Global, pp. 21–41.

Perry, B. and May, T. (eds.) (2007), 'Governance, science policy and regions', *Special Edition, Regional Studies*, 41 (8).

Perry, B. and May, T. (2010), 'Urban knowledge exchange: devilish dichotomies and active intermediation', *International Journal of Knowledge-Based Development*, 1 (1–2): 6–24.

Perry, B. and May, T. (2015), 'Context matters: the English science cities and visions for knowledge-based urbanism', in Miao, J., Benneworth, P. and Phelps, N. (eds.) *Making 21st Century Knowledge Complexes: Technopoles of the World Revisited*, London: Routledge, pp.105–127.

Pieterse, E. (ed.) (2010), *Counter-Currents: Experiments in Sustainability in the Cape Town Region*, Auckland Park, South Africa: Jacana Media.

Polanyi, M. (1958), *Personal Knowledge: Towards a Post-Critical Philosophy*, University of Chicago Press: Chicago.

Polanyi, M. (1983 [1966]), *The Tactic Dimension*, Gloucester, Mass: Peter Smith.

Puppin, G. (2014), 'Advertising and China: How does a love/hate relationship work?', in Hulme, A. (ed.) *The Changing Landscape of China's Consumerism*, Oxford: Elsevier.

Ryle, G. (2000 [1949]), *The Concept of Mind*, Penguin: Harmondsworth.

Salazar, M. and Holbrook, A. (2007), 'Canadian science, technology and innovation policy: the product of regional networking?' *Regional Studies*, 41: 1129–1141.

Salet, W., Kreukels, A. and Thornley, A. (eds.) (2003), *Metropolitan Governance and Spatial Planning: Comparative Case Studies of European City-regions*, Aldershot: E and FN Spon.

Sandford, M. (ed.) (2009), *The Northern Veto*, Manchester: Manchester University Press.

Sanz-Menéndez, L. and Cruz-Castro, L. (2005), 'Explaining the science and technology policies of regional governments', *Regional Studies – Cambridge and New York*, 39 (7): 939.

Sassen, S. (2012), *Cities in a World Economy*, 4th edition, Thousand Oaks, California: Sage.

Schmidt, D. (2010), 'The Dynamics of Leadership in Cape Town', in Pieterse, E. (ed), *Counter-Currents: Experiments in Sustainability in the Cape Town Region*, Auckland Park, South Africa: Jacana Media.

Schön, D. (1991 [1983]), *The Reflective Practitioner*. London: Ashgate.

Scott, A.J. (2008), *Social Economy of the Metropolis: Cognitive-Cultural Capitalism and the Global Resurgence of Cities*, Oxford: Oxford University Press.

Simmie, J. (2002), Trading places: competitive cities in the global economy, *European Planning Studies*, 10 (2).

Simmie, J., Sennett, J., Wood, P. and Hart, D. (2002), 'Innovation in Europe: a tale of networks, knowledge and trade in five cities', *Regional Studies*, 36: 47–64.

Sotarauta, M. and Kautonen, M. (2007), 'Co-evolution of the Finnish national and local innovation and science arenas: towards a dynamic understanding of multi-level governance', *Regional Studies*, 41: 1085–1098.

Sternberg, R.J. and Horvath, J.A. (1999), *Tacit Knowledge in Professional Practice*, London: Lawrence Erlbaum.

Storper, M. (1995), 'The resurgence of regional economies, ten years later: the region as a nexus of untraded interdependencies', *European Urban and Regional Studies* 2 (2): 191–221.

Storper, M. (1997a), *The Regional World: Territorial Development in a Global Economy*, New York: Guildford Press.

Storper, M. (1997b), 'The city: centre of economic reflexivity', *The Service Industries Journal*, 17 (1):1–27.

United Nations (2014), *World Urbanization Prospects, 2014 Revision*, https://esa.un.org/unpd/wup/publications/files/wup2014-report.pdf (accessed May 2017).

Van Winden, W., Van Den Berg, L. and Pol, P. (2007), 'European cities in the knowledge economy: towards a typology', *Urban Studies*, 44 (3): 525–549.

Wilks-Heeg, S., Perry, B. and Harding, A. (2003), 'Metropolitan regions in Europe: regimes, rescaling or repositioning?', in Salet, W., Kreukels, A. and Thornley, A. (eds.), *Metropolitan Governance and Spatial Planning: Comparative Case Studies of European City-regions*, Aldershot: E and FN Spon.

Wong, C., Choi, C-J. and Millar, C. (2006), 'The case of Singapore as a knowledge-based city', in Carillo, F. (ed.) *Knowledge Cities: Approaches, Experiences and Perspectives*, Burlington and Oxford: Butterworth-Heinemann, pp. 87–96.

Work Foundation (2006), *Ideopolis: Knowledge City-Regions*, London: The Work Foundation.

Yigitcanlar, T. and Sarimin, M. (2011), 'The role of universities in building prosperous knowledge cities: the Malaysian experience', *Built Environment*, 37 (3): 260–280.

Yigitcanlar, T., O'Connor, K. and Westerman, C. (2008), 'The making of knowledge cities: Melbourne's knowledge-based urban development experience', *Cities*, 25 (2): 63–72.

Yigitcanlar, T., Velibeyoglu, K. and Baum, S. (eds.) (2008), *Knowledge-Based Urban Development. Planning and Applications in the Information Era*, London: IGI Global.

Youtie, J. and Shapira, P. (2008), 'Building an innovation hub: a case study of the transformation of university roles in regional technological and economic development', *Research Policy*, 37 (8): 1188–1204.

PART II
Politics

3
GAME OF SCALES

Introduction

The idea of the knowledge economy is driven by a globalised, ideological framing of a future filled with promise. The process is characterised by a continual search for competitive advantage through the utilisation of knowledge and the reconfiguring of institutions, including those which were once public, in its name. Space appears to become a passive entity in which things are expected to occur, but the practical efforts to make it happen seem of secondary consideration to the power of the imaginary that dwells in and animates this programme of change. Places do not speak back, but are presented as ripe for the fulfilment of the promise in whose name they are represented and reconfigured. Contexts which are viewed as an impediment to its realisation lack voice in a process that often exhibits an indifference to consequence.

Why not take context more seriously? Because to do so is to undermine the pursuit of universal growth patterns, replicated in a narrow economic orthodoxy that 'sees' space as absolute, rather than relational and constitutes social relations according to the pursuit of individual preferences abstracted from context. Entrepreneurial government, the persistence and power of those defending an outdated neoclassical economics, a movement from the rights of universal welfare systems to a construction of personhood in terms of rational calculation, explain some of the means through which this is perpetuated (Dardot and Laval 2013; Mirowski 2014). The politics of this reproduction are of central importance for understanding how knowledge becomes caught in these discourses. Whilst we will argue that such processes do not saturate the social, political and economic spheres, they inform the possibilities for our lives to be otherwise. Therefore, we need to understand how the politics of the field of the knowledge economy produces its effects through representations in cities that: "claim to be grounded in a 'reality' endowed with all the means of imposing its verdict through the arsenal of methods, instruments and experimental techniques collectively accumulated and implemented" (Bourdieu 2000: 113).

With this in mind, this chapter examines how the promise of the knowledge economy is mediated through the politics of global capitalism. We examine the global race for success and how knowledge has become implicated in the economy. Those relations are underpinned by a particular idea of what constitutes 'success' within the dynamics of competition. Following this discussion, we consider these dynamics in term of cities positioning themselves in relation to varying scales of action and the consequences for those that win and lose in the game of scales.

The global race for success

If we take our historical perspective on change over time, it tends to reduce the propensity to talk of breaks, or ruptures in socio-economic development. From this point of view, the commodification of knowledge can be seen as old as capitalism itself and historical studies demonstrate the changing relations emerging over time without reference to ideas of either revolution or continuity (Burke 2000; Mokyr 2002). At the same time, commentary about economic development in terms of the compression of territorial space comes from that most incisive of analysts of capitalism who wrote about the imperatives that drove the bourgeoisie to: "nestle everywhere, settle everywhere, and establish connections everywhere. The juggernaut of industrial capitalism constituted the most basic source of technologies resulting in the annihilation of space, helping to pave the way for intercourse in every direction" (Marx 1980: 476). Karl Marx identified spatio-temporal integration as core to the 'laws of motion' of capitalist development.

When it comes to an understanding of the role of the urban, we have witnessed the emergence of global cities that serve the economic system through a concentration of command functions that serve as sites for finance, as well as marketplaces and nodes in the knowledge economy. These are places where exogenous global processes become activated through participation, anticipation and the busy process of sense-making which seek to reduce ambiguity in complex environments. These processes and practices constitute what is admissible as context expressed in terms of the: "endogenizing of the key dynamics and conditionalities of the global economy" (Sassen 2001: 347).

Despite the varying possibilities for knowledge in society, we have seen knowledge become the object, not subject, of aspirations for economic growth. The reasons we have given for this state of affairs include: an increase in information in terms of volume and speed, combined with connectivity through information and communication technologies that shrink space and time; a drive for innovation to seek advantage in the face of a greater number of competitors; proliferation of small and medium businesses involved in the process of information gathering, knowledge formulation and innovation; an enhanced reflexive emphasis on learning and knowledge management in order to reduce the levels of uncertainty associated with margins of errors and contextual factors in interpretation; the actions of large corporations seeking competitive advantage through sets of activities that are often aimed at securing a monopoly position in the marketplace and an increasing emphasis upon partnerships between, for example, universities and cities through a recognition of mutuality of interest. All of this takes place within a general orientation of decontextualisation which, as Stefan Krätke puts it at the end of his study on the 'creative city' takes place within a framework of a capitalist economy in which: "the unfolding of creativity and innovation activity takes place 'under the command of capital'"(2011: 198).

We have seen a change in the relations between science and society within a particular construction of the economic realm and with that, the attribution of value to types of knowledge whose effects are real in their consequences for the urban form. Take the Mode 1 and Mode 2 thesis. When applied to the political economy of knowledge, it may be seen as problematic due to the continued importance of institutions in the production of knowledge (May with Perry 2011). Yet its attraction can be seen in terms of a migration from social democratic possibilities to being harnessed to a neoliberal imaginary. Knowledge is characterised, on the one hand, as being concerned with 'pure inquiry' within bounded communities of expertise according to the pursuit of things which are interesting for their own sake and on the other, being subject to the need to 'open it up' to a more inclusive idea of 'relevance' through the participation of a greater number of 'stakeholders' (people) who represent varying interests. To harness knowledge in terms of the notion of relevance is diffuse and as Steve Fuller (2005) characterises it, might be better understood as a 'market attractor'. Relevance is not something one can be against because it encapsulates a very broad aspiration within the idea that knowledge is also a public good. Yet here is the tension between the public realm of social democratic deliberation according to effective communication and access against the aspiration for competitive advantage through knowledge acquisition for private gain. We are seeing particular views of analysis in the name of the economy being separated from deliberation in terms of the implications of its content for contexts and its consequences for where people live. That creates an ambivalence which is captured in the idea of Mode 2 which: "resonates of a Habermasian 'ideal speech situation' for establishing consensus and a Hayekian 'clearing house' for setting prices ... Mode 2 discourse conceals some recognizably capitalist, and even pre-capitalist, forms of domination within a pluralist rhetoric that disperses power and responsibility" (Fuller 2005: 71).

These forces combine to induce greater permeability of boundaries between differing domains of activity: for example, the worlds of business, urban governance and universities. A process of de-differentiation is underway through the need to move from information to knowledge and to have adaptable structures to changing worlds in the name of particular patterns of economic growth. In the search for place-based advantage this process heightens the value of knowledge which cannot be commodified in the relations between value and affect as captured by 'practice' or 'tacit' knowledge. We can see this in terms of concerns with the 'culture' of organisations and the constitution of 'knowledge spaces' where particular ideas can be generated and captured; all of which adds up to what has been termed 'soft capitalism' (Thrift 2005). The purpose, function and form of knowledge-producing institutions and modes of production themselves are then subject to alteration and with that, issues concerned with justification, application and the relations between reflexivity, knowledge and the present and future (May and Perry 2017).

These trends form cities into strategic sites for the investment and acceleration of capital and information flows with the potential to increase their power relative to nation-state boundaries which appeals to those seeking political recognition and control. These conditions inform the innovative activity that is said to typify the knowledge economy in which global spaces of flows are continuously in the process of 'becoming'. As a result, we see a focus upon mediation, rather than recognising and enhancing endogenous assets (Doel and Hubbard 2002). As Peter Hall writes at the end of his historical study of cities: "No place has a monopoly, whether large metropolis or small emerging city, old European capital or new West Coast upstart; any city can play. Time and chance happeneth to them all; it is a question of finding the moment and seizing the hour" (1998: 939).

Finding the moment and seizing the hour have become a permanent search. In this process, we are witnessing altering relationships between knowledge, economy and society that are manifest in particular places with varying consequences. Despite differences between cities across the world and various preexisting conditions, general trends in the circulation of urban ideas have tended to flatten distinctive approaches. A predominant set of collaborative practices between state and market has emerged, underpinned by elite, entrepreneurial forms of urban partnership and legitimised by consensus around the nature of urban problems and their solutions. Examples include the rise of public-private partnerships, 'triple helix' initiatives, creative city quarters or green city brands. What city would not want to be world-class, demonstrate close relationships between universities and industries, lead the way in cultural regeneration, attract international sporting events, host Nobel Prize winners or achieve global recognition for their achievements in innovation?

City elites and those with interests in urban growth coalitions share common aspirations: a search for symbolic and material advantage to be attractive to inward investment by global capital. The promise of the knowledge economy is reflected in rhetorical flourishes accompanied by geological imagery: corridors, clusters, capitals and valleys to alleys, glens and fens. Expectations in these contexts are high; knowledge is attributed with the power to remake places, accompanied by significant improvement in economic, social, cultural, educational, health and environmental outcomes. Cities seek recipes for growth whose origins and perpetuation lie not just in the practices of consultancies, but also in academia (O'Mara 2005; May and Perry 2011b). Aspiring cities frequently see their universities as strategic actors moving towards common goals, which, by virtue of their estates or specific engagement activities and similar aspirations to be global, become part of the aspirational mix (May and Perry 2006).

Cities that aspire to be global in their aspirations want global universities and together they form part of the clamour for symbolic advantage. Whilst 'place matters', it is an absolute sense of space that continues to exist in which global ambitions cannot be held back by context. Efforts to reshape regional and local identities through harnessing the 'brand' power of science and technology abound (Brenner 2004; Perry and May 2007). So we have knowledge capitals, digital and smart cities as the apparent foundation for strategic, competitive success, in a desire to create exclusive environments. In this context the 'Experimental City' becomes little more than the new sub-brand, a world-class accolade sought to differentiate and position cities in global knowledge hierarchies. Greater Lyon, France, is a case in point that proclaims itself to be a 'Smart City – Experimenting Today for Better City Living Tomorrow' (Only Lyon 2014). Whilst embracing ecological and technological innovation, such a strategy is for the few not the many, led by business interests and clearly positioned to attract international capital investment. Such is the power of the global knowledge economy that awards have been developed to reward cities creating knowledge-based wealth (May and Perry 2016).

The Most Admired Knowledge City Awards is one example, set up in 2007 as an "international consulting process to recognise cities engaging in formal and systematic knowledge-based development processes", with Vienna being the recipient in 2015 (see: http://www.km-a.net/english/kcws2016/). Policies towards these ends are then transferred like commodities. Yet any importation of policies from one context to another is highly problematic, particularly in the case of 'inner city' initiatives where we find different urban spatial configurations. Despite this, we have a marketplace of ideas in a competitive arena where transfer appears as a spectacular conflation of the model of reality with the reality of the model. Both cities in search of global status and academics in search of recognition from their peers through contributory global expertise according to the perpetuations of particular ideas may then be aligned.

If we take the knowledge economy as being concerned with 'knowledge about knowledge' and ask how particular forms are constructed as being more relevant than others for urban attraction and growth, we might remember that economics had historical roots in providing an academic respectability to the practical knowledge of merchants (Burke 2000). We may take the same dynamic into contemporary urban development with respect to the preconceptions of elites and the circulation of policy formulations according to the exemplary politics that constitute global city hierarchies of success. Aligned here is a politics of recognition framed around urban vitality and attraction mixing with a knowledge-economic view of distribution. The desire to be seen as a city that is at the forefront of the knowledge economy and so engaging in the indicators race of its proof is ably assisted by a kind of flat-earth view of knowledge that circulates across an apparently smooth surface of flows. This is in direct contrast to a sociology and geography of knowledge in which places, groups, time, interests and institutions play their role. However, to start to think in these terms is to introduce the messy business of contextual reality into the clamour for advantage. What, therefore, are the trends that enable the continuation of a tendency towards decontextualisation?

Context or content? Ambivalence in action

Issues associated with objectivism and relativism in relation to knowledge have been the subject of prior investigation (Bernstein 1983; May and Perry 2017; May and Williams 1998). If the content of knowledge is to work in context, it requires inter-action, interpretation and effort between groups. A process of interpretation can introduce contestability in terms of both the content of knowledge and its antici-pated consequences. Once the context of knowledge is taken to be of importance, then its universality and generalisability is placed in question. Differing forms of knowledge come into play, question the idea knowledge informs particular actions, including those associated with ethnoscience: that is, the means local groups use to navigate their ways through their environments, including indigenous forms of classification. At a policy level, conception can find itself placed in question through a focus upon its applicability, or execution, in a context that requires 'sense-making' (Weick 2009). Policy studies thus focus upon the idea of an 'implementation gap' with studies in that genre examining discretionary elements associated with front-line workers (May 1991) following Lipsky's (1980) earlier studies.

For discretionary elements to work in translation, there needs to be recognition of the relations between the content of knowledge informing the promise of the knowledge economy and knowledges concerning the contexts of its execution. However, as argued at the beginning of the chapter, whilst a great deal of insight and learning is to be gained in the dialectical relations existing between context and content, what characterises discourses of the knowledge economy is the ten-dency to sideline context in the power of an imaginary that resides in a future given over to growth via the acquisition of and justification for, particular forms of knowledge. Yet the control of content over context is never final as discretion, contextual factors and unanticipated consequences all play their role. Thus, we end up with a situation in which there is a desire to manage knowledge about knowl-edge at the urban level, whilst having to acknowledge that knowledge itself cannot be managed in advance if it is to be a source of innovative activity. To tackle this tension, the literature on knowledge management: "turns knowledge into infor-mation or social relations or turns management into administration, networking, or organizational culture" (Alvesson 2004: 187). In other words, there is work to do in order to render it 'manageable'. That effort, in turn, leads to a paradoxical result for it becomes a: "rhetorical appeal to a broad and differentiated field of theory and practice that on the whole deals specifically neither with knowledge nor with management, and even less with the two together" (Alvesson 2004: 187).

To tackle this paradox at an institutional level, we see the production of admin-istrative criteria that are assumed to be 'objective': that is, not being context-sensitive and so lying beyond the supposed particularity of contextual experiences. The resulting tactics employed in the process of urban change aim at outcome measures of performance with the expectation that they will inform and control the processes of practice. Built into this is the presupposition that the determination of performance lies in the realm of contextual discretion which itself is the target of transformation. This assumes a model of action shared by professionals (who regard the social and economic conditions under and through which they work as separate from the knowledge base in order to maintain the idea of neutrality) and managers (who target 'values' in terms of professional culture as if those informed, as opposed to interacted with, those conditions). The result is a whole series of attempts to determine the 'how' of knowledge through audit and the feedback of outcome measures into practice. The desire for uniformity is ubiquitous and bolstered by states in the desire for control: "The aspiration to such uniformity and order alerts us to the fact that modern statecraft is largely a product of internal colonization, often glossed, as it is in imperial rhetoric, as a 'civilizing mission'. The builders of the modern nation-state do not merely describe, observe and map; they strive to shape a people and landscape that will fit their techniques of observation" (Scott 1998: 82).

In the content of these practices, we see an accompanying move towards concerns with what were once regarded as being 'outside' of the remit of 'economic reason' through a focus on matters of affect. Ideas regarding employee emotions, values and motivations, along with attention to urban culture and the presence of particular corporations as a means of economic attraction, all feature as dynamics in this process. Culture is then 'woven into the fabric of capitalism': "In the continued battle against the irrationalities of capitalism, cultural concerns – by which I mean the clash between culture as an instrument of self-realisation (whatever specific social forms it may take) and culture as a form of stupefaction – are now more than ever at stake" (Scott 2000: 215). What is termed this "capitalization of the meaning of life" (Gordon 1991: 44) becomes, at the city level, the monitoring of external environments in terms of the appropriateness of internal responses (Sassen's 'endogenizing' process) whereby urban information units and knowledge sources feed the promise of possibility. Apparent complacency in the fulfilment of wishes becomes the enemy of innovation, whilst the paradox of the desire to be a resurgent city is: "the escalating contrasts between its surface glitter and its underlying squalor" (Scott 2008: 18).

Public admission of the absence of commitment to the promise can comfortably be read as not being a 'player' in the possibility to obtain higher stakes. The past becomes an impediment, or is selectively harnessed, for the future, and learning from the past evaporates in favour of representing 'best practice' when constantly 'moving forward'. We then find that: "the art of forgetting is an asset no less, if no more, important that the art of memorizing, in which forgetting rather than learning is the condition of continuous fitness" (Bauman 1997: 25). Learning is also hampered by institutional changes to the public sector in the name of the efficiencies assumed to be connected to neoliberal imaginaries. Therefore, they have found themselves subject to changes that seek to replicate the taken-for-granted efficiencies of the private sector in processes of constant change characterised by crisis. Whilst this creates anomalies, tensions and contradictions, it also contributes to depoliticised views of processes and practices. Fewer public servants able to exercise memory easily leads to an advantage for contracted-out services to the private sector. This works to bracket a history rooted in the provision of political checks upon the vagaries of the market system. Political-allocative values become displaced by administrative-technical issues informed by ever-increasing volumes of information. The overall consequence is the triumph of method over purpose and a movement away from a problem-solving orientation to a performance mode of operation (Mintzberg 1983).

These transformations mask their power effects by subverting and remoulding the idea of 'purpose'. Insofar as they are successful, they loosen the anchors that fix meaning, permitting power to flow in a manner which appears to have no nodal points. Power and responsibility collapse with the presupposition that all are responsible and exercise equal power. To this extent, celebrations of global flows are a reference to the new 'realities' in which cities have to participate. That leads to a focus on particular forms of knowledge to the exclusion of the value of others that are not part of the capitalisation of knowledge. A resulting practice becomes administration as depoliticisation, in which administrative-technical processes seek to mask and usurp their political-allocative values as if conducted in the name of reason, then emerges. Apparently outdated public service organisations become targets of neoliberal transformation fuelled by a change in climate informed by the enormous, but mundane work that goes into the naturalisation of competition. At a mezzo, or organisational level, we then find tactics, within overarching strategies, informed by a series of dominant assumptions concerning the differences between the state and the market with one being seen as constraining, closed and rigid and the other embodying freedom, flexibility and openness (see Bourdieu and Wacquant 2001).

A busy empiricism is then alive and well in the production of knowledge about knowledge against a background of these value oppositions that have emerged to complement and reinforce each other, thereby producing characterisations of urban performance. These pairings inform new practices and procedures designed to control and remould perceptions of success. In this process, it is the apparent indeterminacy of practice that becomes the target of new modes of control that are frequently justified by the supposed efficiencies of the private sector. The introduction of these forms of working practices, along with budgetary constraints, increasing use of private sector organisations in spaces where the public sector used to operate, give rise to a whole new language of continual transformation and benefit.

What the knowledge economy has done, in terms of its changes in practice at an urban level, is take the technological and knowledge-based infrastructures that came with modernity and turned those into overt, new forms of representation linked to their potential for urban transformation. Knowledge thereby becomes a 'tool' for managing the resolution of economic crisis in which denial, imposition of state-sponsored markets and the harnessing of expertise to militate against the effects of accumulation on the environment, all play their role (Mirowski 2014). Ideas of 'relevance' and 'usefulness', which have always been with us, assume an increasing importance in defining *what* knowledge should be produced and *how* it should be judged. Seen against the backdrop of the role of the state to predominately protect curiosity-driven research to one in which greater emphasis is placed on the application of knowledge for economic gain, we find the pervasive nature of 'relevance' as an allocation and evaluation 'tool' mixing with the promise of the knowledge economy. Politics, conducted in the imaginary of globalisation forms a wide gap between actuality and potentiality where knowledge and experimentation mix with the 'art of the global' (Roy and Ong 2011). Existing reality may be framed as the wicked problem of the present, whilst there is no apprehension when we look towards the future, but instead varying forms of comprehension informed by the steady reason of numerous studies by consultants and academics constituting the promise of the transcendence of the present. Blind-sided by this deluge leads us to being blinded to alternatives.

At the city-scale we see success not judged on contextual factors, which might include community-based alternatives, but according to aspirations fed by those 'experts' who are the intellectual jugglers of the permanent possibilities that feed an insatiable appetite to refashion context. These are the actions of those who tinker: "with machines and models to demonstrate the mechanics of economic interaction" (Gibson-Graham, Cameron and Healy 2013: 1). Markets become a 'belief in belief' (Žižek 2009a). To this extent, talk not only replaces action, but activity constituted in the name of promise becomes a denial of actually existing conditions or, when recognised, are explained away as the peculiarities of intransigent groups. Agnotology and rectification at the level of implementation become the focus points (Mirowski 2014). Some might even go as far as to say that things get done in cities to avoid thinking about them and nowhere was this more evident at national levels than by throwing $700 billion at the financial crisis (Žižek 2009a).

For Marx, contradictions in capitalist development were themselves the basis for its transcendence into a new social order. The knowledge economy turns that around through a set of circular justifications: that is, the condition of the impossibility of the continual reproduction of capitalism due to its being built in antagonisms, becomes the very condition of the possibility of the knowledge economy! As Slavoj Žižek puts it: "this notion of a society outside the frame of Capital, was a fantasy inherent to capitalism itself, the capitalist inherent transgression at its purest, a strictly ideological fantasy of maintaining the thrust of productivity generated by capitalism, by getting rid of the 'obstacles' and antagonisms that were – as the sad experience of 'really existing capitalism' demonstrates – the only possible framework for the effective material existence of a society of permanently self-enhancing productivity" (2014: 146–147).

The processes of globalisation that have constituted and enhanced the power of these processes are mediated in a way that curtails their complete domination of contexts. The effect of their increased power, however, is accompanied by a 'hollowing out' of control (Lash and Urry 1994). Different contexts require responses to conditions which mean that centralised command and control forms of organisation are not efficient for adaptation, leaving degrees of relative autonomy for responses to regional and local contexts. Such considerations are important in terms of the type of activity of the firm itself: "the creation of many of the most disintegrated cutting edge sectors, business services, finance services, and even high tech and telecommunications which themselves have become largely advanced producer services, is conditioned by the very centralised power of the transnationals themselves" (Lash and Urry 1994: 24). Here we see the dialectic in play in which, despite what are variable conditions, the firm will seek control even if such efforts become counter-productive for effective adaptation to different contexts. There are clear parallels between these changes and those of the formal administrative apparatuses of cities.

Winners and losers in the game of scales

These trajectories serve to sustain and deepen capitalist relations of uneven geographical development (Harvey 1989). The removal of national protective barriers in trade and services and the opening up of markets to global competition creates an environment in which inequalities and regional disparities worsen, and the gap between rich and poor is enlarged, in a world characterised by a 'survival of the fittest' mentality. The World Bank's own indicators illustrate that the gap between low and high-income countries is becoming wider and for the former: "the notion of entering the knowledge economy may appear to be beyond reach" (Madanipour 2011: 12).

Understanding differences in orientation to the issues surrounding knowledge and place is important for understanding the process of reproduction. All too often policies proceed in the absence of articulating underlying assumptions and presumptions – and how those relate to, or are disjointed from, expectations and desired outcomes. Drivers are assumed to be common between partners in the search for urban knowledge-based development. Despite this, global dynamics are manifest in different ways as they are mediated through governance, institutional, political and socio-cultural contexts. To develop more "progressive, socially just, emancipatory and sustainable formations of urban life" (Brenner, Marcuse and Mayer 2012: 5) requires greater sensitivity to the values and knowledges that produce and reproduce knowledge-based futures. Central to this endeavour are questions of social inclusion, participation and the forging of discourses and approaches that transcend, rather than replicate, narrow technological or economic viewpoints (Perry et al. 2013).

Cities become locked in a game of scales in which differences are generated as a result of the pursuit of knowledge which itself cannot be ultimately 'managed'. Therefore, they often enter a 'crisis management' role in which they are 'site and solution', with responses directly framed by the weight of prior state-led interventions. We thus see an increase in the intensity of oscillations between continuity and discontinuity. Whilst Park (1972) saw the city as a site of cooperation and competition, with the former providing the basis of solidarity among social groups, we now find an emphasis in the idea of some 'natural economy' that requires continual urban attraction efforts as a basis of survival. Thus, as the arena of competition becomes wider and expands at a faster rate, a political lag arises in which social problems become increasingly evident. In so doing, these forces clash and reflect the two hegemonic 'G-spots' of neoliberalism: governance and globalisation (Dean 2007). Irreconcilable pressures and tensions, which have not been mediated or resolved by international or national governments, are passed to cities to manage in conditions of crisis (May 2017).

Cities are differentially positioned in the game of scales through ambivalence between celebrating what exists (indigenous, context-based assets) and what can be (mediation of exogenous flows as part of the new realities of global positioning). Whilst that is structured by the resources and history upon which they draw, to dwell upon such matters may readily be dismissed as excuses in the face of an inability to rise to challenges. We thus seem to: "live in an era where the neoliberals demonstrably understand the politics of knowledge far better than do their opponents" (Mirowski 2014: 365). The desire for positional advantage mixes with a hierarchical evaluation of global success, so we get the idea of those who are 'lagging behind' and those who are the 'global leaders'. The former are characterised by 'second-rate thinking' and practice, and the latter become the exemplars of the promise of possibility. What we find is: "a breathtaking competition between similar regions in the hope of standing out in the increasingly homogenous global space, in which capital and information – and to a lesser degree high-skilled workers – can flow with some ease" (Madanipour 2011: 140).

The financial crisis did not deter this process. After 2008, enthusiasm for the city as a site of speculative accumulation increased (Harvey 2012; Norfield 2016). Conspicuous consumption, the power of multinational corporations and ever-increasing inequality, all play their role in a system that was on the brink of collapse until states and their citizens provided the welfare payments for the consequences of the actions of those in the financial sector (Crouch 2011; Dorling 2014; Gamble 2009). The push for ever-greater centres of excellence, networked across the globe, then accelerated, along with a preference for forms of knowledge and their representation (Chapain et al. 2009; May and Perry 2011b). What is illuminated is the regressive nature of policy with its narrow economic focus provided through the exclusion of cultural factors (Scott 2014). Opportunities are 'colonized' (Wyly 2013) within a process of capital accumulation, whose effects relate directly to how knowledge is seen, deployed and interpreted (Lave 2012).

Place, inequality and experimentation

Typically, cities are differentially positioned, with some being international 'exemplars' and others 'lagging behind'. In this climate, it is of no surprise that urban politicians, corporate managers and officials may not feel able to publicly admit of difficulties or that their activities run up against the harsh realities of the present.

This produces a falsity: localism is assumed to be able to harness the potentiality in global neoliberalism, despite it relying upon the inequalities that are evident in the constitution of its realities (Harvey 2014). In this climate, government can frame its role as creating 'opportunities' whilst actively creating the conditions for this state of affairs to flourish. Places judge themselves according to how imaginatively they have responded to opportunities. Anything less than full embrace is seen as a challenge and/or the reactivation of an apparently outdated politics of need. A symptomatic politics is allowed a free rein and holds up privileged places as 'leading the game' in the name of improving other cities.

Curiosity can inform experimentation. It offers the advantage of what is not yet known, but may be realised if possibility is permitted its free rein. It has been part of utopian thought which sees in distance from the present a future of hope (Levitas 2011). Yet experimentation under conditions of neoliberal practices does not positively benefit the populations of a city, but affirms an acceleration of a system producing staggering inequalities (Dorling 2014). Experimentalism can be seen as a way of testing responses to urban challenges without needing to attend to the structural inequalities or crises that may have given rise to those challenges in the first place. If experimentalism is a strategy for urban transformation, it is an 'affirmative' one (Fraser 2003) that runs the risk of bolstering business-as-usual outside the experimental bubble, tinkering at the edges of a broken system. What is called a problem of poverty from particular points of view is, from another, an issue of the riches of others (Sayer 2015).

Invoking experimentation may seem to challenge existing states of affairs, but may equally provide relief from ambivalence through a selectivity that omits so much (and so many) from its process. Whilst localised experiments claim to be opening up technological change to plural interests, the symbolism of experimentalism at a city scale represents the ceaseless, careful empiricism of the scientific attitude whose practices constitute rules and procedures for practitioners across continents and time. It is 'ignorant' to be against that which has not yet found its results, for to do so is to stand in the way of progress. Criticism of the validity of its adoption questions the very presuppositions upon which the decision-making process is based. Questions of 'why' and 'for whom' become luxuries in face of those who see experimentation as part of an insatiable desire for growth. In comparing experimentation in the eco-cities of Shanghai and Tianjin, Miao and Lang (2014: 254) stress the strong logic of economic growth and argue that: "the chances for success become slimmer if experimental initiatives pursue more comprehensive goals, like providing social goods". Experiments work, as they have done in history, not in terms of testing hypotheses, but as demonstrators (see Pickstone 2000; Poovey 1998). They work on context-revision, not sensitivity. They demonstrate adaptability and flexibility in the face of aspiration under conditions of uncertainty.

Within cities themselves, there are different manifestations of these dynamics. However, whilst uncertainty continues, we find evidence of continuity. The result of moves from Keynesian to supply-side post-Fordist economic strategies witnessed a shift to a thirst for real estate and property development in cities (Lash and

Urry 1994). In the UK, average house prices have increased by 300 per cent over the last twenty years, but in twenty boroughs in London, that figure exceeds 660 per cent (*The Guardian* 2016; available at: http://www.theguardian.com/money/2016/jan/15/house-prices-rocket-300-england-wales). As Doreen Massey wrote of London's global finance industries: "the fact that London's 'success' is one of the dynamics producing poverty and exclusion implied at least a query as to the meaning of this word 'successful' " (2005: 157). All this not only increases land values, but sidelines the potential for context-sensitive learning in favour of the perpetuation of an ideology that does not see place, but constitutes an absolute space of attraction with a whole set of consequences for the communities of a city as they become an income stream for those owning essential services (Meek 2015). Intellectual property rights increase to ensure knowledge exploitation, which restricts the rights of individuals and the poor to information (Drahos with Braithwaite 2002) through an artificial separation between democracy and expertise (Noveck 2015). Overall, these issues highlight the uneven impact of globalising processes on subnational economies and societies.

The city exhibits a visible and invisible morphology (Lefebvre 1996). One is manifested in the social realm – how people communicate, move between places and engage in various activities, for what reasons and with what consequences? The other is manifested materially in terms of buildings and spaces and is not assumed to be a fixed canvas upon which we can construct its flux (Massey 2005). There are interactions between the social and material which, in the above example, demonstrate a dependency between wealth, income and the ability to enjoy the social aspects of a city only if being able to do so through material acquisition. Underpinning the production of techno-economic views of urban futures lie dominant views perpetuated by a rich minority. A restriction to particular sets of actors who presume to speak on behalf of the city in the construction of urban strategies includes politicians and commercial organisations whose interests revolve around the production of replicable solutions to environmental issues. The effect is to frame the challenges of sustainable knowledge-based urbanism in very particular ways in which an ambivalence concerning the importance of contextual factors is apparent. A focus, for example, on slums and the urban poor as a problem, rather than a more nuanced reading that exposes the limitations of the epistemological lenses deployed for such purposes, leads to the depoliticising of issues within cities (Pieterse 2008).

These critiques may hit the hearts of those who find the consequences of our current trajectories to be nothing more than an apology for the accumulation of private wealth on the back of public poverty (Piketty 2014). However, if we take the reasons for its reproduction seriously, we should start with its discourse of social change which: "must make its appeal as wish-fulfilling dreams of omnipotent intentions or destined futures. From this perspective, every political programme is not only inherently fatalistic, but also mired in fantasy and narcissism from its inception. The discourse of social change takes place on the terrain of the Imaginary" (Rothenberg 2010: 153). If history is drawn upon, it is highly selective, for it also carries with it the denunciation of "a tacit contract of adherence to the established order which defines the original doxa" (Bourdieu 1992a: 127).

Explanations for this state of affairs of perpetual change enable a link to be made between elite reproduction and the circulation of global capital. When it meets barriers and limits, enormous efforts are made to overcome and circumvent those. In the process, we find a project that is: "Masked by a lot of rhetoric about individual freedom, liberty, personal responsibility and the virtues of privatisation, the free market and free trade" (Harvey 2010: 10). Traditional attachments may be maintained in the face of these pressures, but also re-contextualised and re-embedded with the influence of transnational communities, corporations and international governmental organisations producing new agendas and challenges for how we understand societal challenges (Turner 2006). 'Citizenship' and 'rights' are contested under the lead of complex and commanding influences of powerful organisations such as the World Bank, International Monetary Fund (IMF) and World Trade Organization (WTO), as well as private multinational corporations. Deliberative, democratic urban spaces focussing on present problems and possible futures may be easily filled by a frenetic search for competitive advantage or through the construction of particular problem populations to the exclusion of those who actually benefit from an unjust state of affairs (Dorling 2014). In the face of these circumstances and pressures, it is to the consumption patterns and inequalities in the developed world and their effects on other cities, that those seeking just sustainable futures turn (Agyeman 2013).

How does this then fit with place-based dynamics? History evaporates at one level, as the textures of communities are lost in the search for particular futures. The social dimension of a city is manifest in how people communicate, move between places and engage in various activities, and for what reasons and with what consequences. We find boundaries that provide physical and perceptual ordering, a diversity, but also evidence of the control of the urban poor in which the intersections of the historical and contemporary then reinforce: "the boundaries that confine and relegate people to place" (Hall 2012: 46). Lefebvre deployed the idea of implosion-explosion to capture how cities were both being destroyed, but also growing (Brenner 2014). It was with this twofold characterisation in mind that we wrote about a recent walk from a local community to the bright, shiny world of what was heralded as a new opportunity for Greater Manchester.

The community through which we started our walk was steeped in history. As we continued, we crossed a road and found ourselves in a place that seemed neither in, nor of, that community, yet so proximate. Here was a place whose sense of community appeared to be represented by social withdrawal and isolation. Indeed, those who live in these places have been characterised as buying: "their way out of their own activity, living in gated communities, eating organic food, taking holidays in wildlife preserves" (Žižek 2009b: 23). Office blocks have been built around docks that once provided the impetus for industrial growth and whose waters were now reflected in the glass façades of the shiny buildings of this post-industrial imaginary now rendered material. The docks themselves were devoid of boats, except for the occasional tourist boat travelling down the Liverpool-Manchester ship canal and those used for water sports.

History had been built upon in this area. At the same time, it has been eradicated and interpreted in particular ways in the name of a way of life that we are so often told provides 'trickle-down' opportunities for the community we had just left: one geographically close, but socially far removed. If the symptom of which a progressive, transformative politics speaks is the need to change lines of domination to bring voices and recognition to those who are not in the economic mainstream, it hits a serious impediment: the need not only to listen, but change the practices of those who benefit from this state of affairs. Instead, embodied in media mayhem is the myth of the individualistic entrepreneur, to whom all should aspire, despite the reality of varying starting points. Here we find massive investments in sealing the realm between the imaginary and the real in the offices of the chosen, and those who are not part of this are the inevitable casualties of this frenetic system. These casualties, however, are told they only have themselves to blame for their lack of aspiration.

The walk from one community to another represented a significant shift in architecture and feel for a place. It served as a reminder that such is the haste to deny the relevance of history and context to some imaginary future. It becomes easy to attribute potential to innovations whose existence often embodies a preference to forget. Learning takes place through experience of past actions and engagement with consideration to the issues that inform our lives. We are, quite simply, immersed in the actuality of everyday life with all its delights, desires and disappointments. A condition of understanding is to enter into varying degrees of oscillation between comprehension and apprehension. A resulting ambivalence in the former never quite catching the latter: "Consequently, temporality itself, 'as such', involves a gap between the apprehension of the dispersed multitude and the synthetic act of the comprehension of the unity of this multitude" (Žižek 2008: 46).

The walk led us to recall the words of Gøsta Esping-Anderson: "unless we succeed in broadly strengthening the cognitive capacities and resource base of citizens, the long term scenario might very well be a smattering of 'knowledge islands' in a great sea of marginalised outsiders" (2001: 134). When it comes to understanding these dynamics, we cannot simply separate the social from the environmental, nor allude to these changes as if a reflection of some economic natural order. They are the product of power relations operating at an international level whose intellectual underpinnings, on the occasions they are publicly contested and called upon to justify themselves, represent a new doxa: "Like the Catholic *doxa* of the Middle Ages, the new neoliberal *pensée unique* seemed to provide solutions for all kinds of social and ecological issues. Often neutralised in academic terms and amplified by associated intellectuals within and outside the mainstream media, these solutions are relentlessly preached – not least to students who will constitute the elites of the future" (Koch 2012: 190).

Summary: A knowledge economy for the few

In the struggle for distinction, innovation and creativity work to produce the exceptionality of place that is often divorced from its actual reality in terms of the lived experiences of diverse urban communities. There is a tension in scales between the desire for global positioning in order to attract inward investment, against local issues associated with distribution and fairness. In the competitive politics of global-urban hierarchies, cities seek to embrace experimentalism to promote to other cities, selected entrepreneurs, innovators and universities that they mean 'business'. In the process, particular cities are heralded as emblematic of how things can be achieved and thus serve as models for others to emulate. It is as if governmental support is not important, as they become nothing more than locations for aspirations – leaving intact the myth of global capital as inherently mobile, indiscriminate and innovative. References to growth and opportunity are accompanied by a seeking of emblematic status that others should emulate, without sensitivity to context. The result is that the city is a site of tension and opposition that produces a 'grudging tolerance' within the 'fragmentation of territories' (Banerjee-Guha 2010).

The knowledge economy acts as an animator of already existing practices and provides a means of mobilisation for different groups around apparently similar themes – to this extent, it adds 'value'. In another way, it represents a set of practices that breaks down and also reconstitutes boundaries around what can and cannot be said and by whom; it provides reasons for actions through the framing of world views as a basis for intervention. It is an organising idea that animates, constitutes and excludes. Therefore, it is about closure, but it is a slippery idea whose very plasticity provides it with power. It enables the population of aspirations from different groupings, but its pluralism is a disguise for the exclusion of knowledges that are not seen to contribute to, or reproduce, its basic assumptions: that knowledge relates to economic growth and science can be enabled to the extent that it will have technological applications. Here, the game of scales plays between application, representation and pursuit up the rungs of the global ladder of distinction and recognition.

The relations between belief and knowledge are the grit in this machine. If the knowledge economy concerns a belief in the application of knowledge for economic gain and markets have become a belief in belief, whilst knowledge is not manageable, how do all these relate? Whilst this becomes the wicked problem of the present, it is avoided in the name of permanent potential. Here, performance measurers, audit and the roles of knowledge about knowledge, play their role in the reduction of political ambivalence concerning development and positioning of cities. The overall effect is a "depoliticized simulation of truth" (Poster 1990: 62) which fails to recognise that: "The chances of translating knowledge for action into knowledge in action are immeasurably improved once it is recognized that the probability to realize knowledge is dependent on context-specific social, political and economic conditions" (Stehr 1992: 121). The population of the political imaginary may easily become saturated through the partiality of vision. So in steps the broad range of meanings to populate that in which everyone has an interest, but where a discussion of outcomes is silenced in terms of the marginality of forms of knowledge and populations. All this takes place in the movement from the factual basis of knowledge about a world of objects to the formulation of languages that attribute particular ideas of usefulness to its function – it is relevant and applicable when applied and everyone, of course, knows what that means.

How can knowledge be impervious to this weight of expectation? As Philip Mirowski (2014) noted, the neoliberals understand this politics of knowledge very well and there are many only too happy to peddle their wares to reproduce the frenetic search for competitive advantage. Yet the translation to context is missing in the view that knowledge is not context-dependent. So we search for evidence 'for' the knowledge economy, not evidence 'of' its values and purpose through participation and deliberation and its effects of marginalisation and contribution to inequality. It is an elite activity constituted through the idea of necessity over choice. Therein lies the paradox of the apparent freedom to choose: it is only if one chooses correctly and one has the capital to participate in the game.

These processes produce a democratic deficit. In steps justifications for interventions through the provision of particular economic models that rarely need scrutiny, let alone articulation of their basic premises and assumptions; all of which is exacerbated in the busy administration of city information units and the consultancies and academics who feed its appetite. The scales tilt in the work of translation and sense-making from the urban everyday to an abstract, organising principle whose rationale and effects are not part of public concern. After all, with so many highly skilled mobile people to not only attract, but also to retain, what are most of the public for? If capitalism cannot outsource the entire working class, they can at least find employment on minimum wages to provide the cappuccinos to lubricate the thoughts, flows and networks of the knowledge workers. So let us now turn to an institution where many of them are seen to work.

References

Agyeman, J. (2013), *Introducing Just Sustainabilities: Policy, Planning, and Practice*, London: Zed Books.

Alvesson, M. (2004), *Knowledge Work and Knowledge-Intensive Firms*, Oxford: Oxford University Press.

Andersen, H.T. and Atkinson, R. (eds.) (2013), *The Production and Use of Urban Knowledge: European Experiences*, Dordrecht: Springer.

Banerjee-Guha, S. (2010), 'Revisiting Accumulation by Dispossession: Neoliberalising Mumbai', in Banerjee-Guha, S. (ed.) *Accumulation by Dispossession: Transformative Cities in the New Global Order*, London: Sage.

Bauman, Z. (1997), *Postmodernity and its Discontents*, Cambridge: Polity.

Bernstein, R. (1983), *Beyond Objectivism and Relativism: Science, Hermeneutics and Praxis*, Oxford: Basil Blackwell.

Bourdieu, P. (1992), *Language and Symbolic Power*, edited and introduced by Thompson, J., translated by Raymond, G. and Adamson, M., Cambridge: Polity.

Bourdieu, P. (2000), *Pascalian Meditations,* translated by Nice, R., Cambridge: Polity.

Bourdieu, P. and Wacquant, L.J. (2001), 'NewLiberalSpeak: Notes on the New Planetary Vulgate', *Radical Philosophy*, 105: 2–5.

Brenner, N. (2004), *New State Spaces: Urban Governance and the Rescaling of Statehood*, Oxford: Oxford University Press.

Brenner, N., Marcuse, P. and Mayer, M. (2012), 'Cities for people, not for profit: an introduction', in Brenner, N., Marcuse, P. and Mayer, M. (eds.) (2012), *Cities for People, Not for Profit: Critical Urban Theory and the Right to the City*, London: Routledge.

Brenner, N. (ed.) (2014), *Implosions/Explosions: Towards a Study of Planetary Urbanization*, Berlin: Jovis Verlag.

Burchell, G., Gordon, C. and Miller, P. (eds.) (1991), *The Foucault Effect: Studies in Governmentality*, London: Harvester Wheatsheaf.

Burke, P. (2000), *A Social History of Knowledge*, Cambridge: Polity.

Chapain, C., Collinge, C., Lee, P. and Musterd, S. (eds.) (2009), 'Can we plan the creative knowledge city?', *Special Edition, Built Environment*, 32 (2).

Crouch, C. (2011), *The Strange Non-Death of Neoliberalism*, Cambridge: Polity.

Dardot, P. and Laval, C. (2013), *The New Way of the World: On Neo-Liberal Society*, translated by Elliott, G., London: Verso.

Dean, M. (2007), *Governing Societies: Political Perspectives on Domestic and International Rule*, Maidenhead: Open University Press/McGraw-Hill.

Doel, M. and Hubbard, P. (2002), 'Taking world cities literally: Marketing the city in a global space of flows', *City*, 6 (3): 351–368.

Dorling, D. (2014), *Inequality and the 1%*, London: Verso.

Drahos, P. and Braithwaite, J. (2002), *Information Feudalism: Who Owns the Knowledge Economy?*, London: Earthscan.

Esping-Anderson, G. (2001), 'A welfare state for the 21st century', in Giddens, A. (ed.) *The Global Third Way Debate*, Oxford: Blackwell.

Fraser, N. (2003), 'Social justice in the age of identity politics: redistribution, recognition and participation', in Fraser, N. and Honneth, A., *Redistribution or Recognition: A Political-Philosophical Exchange*, London: Verso.

Fraser, N. and Honneth, A. (2003), *Redistribution or Recognition: A Political-Philosophical Exchange*, translated by Golb, J., Ingram, J. and Wilke, C., New York: Verso.

Fuller, S. (2005), 'Knowledge as product and property', in Stehr, N. and Meja, V. (eds.) *Society and Knowledge: Contemporary Perspectives in the Sociology and Knowledge and Science*, New Jersey: Transaction.

Gamble, A. (2009), *The Spectre at the Feast: Capitalist Crisis and the Politics of Recession*, London: Palgrave Macmillan.

Gibson-Graham, J.K., Cameron, J. and Healy, S. (2013), *Take Back the Economy: An Ethical Guide for Transforming our Communities*, Minneapolis: University of Minnesota Press.

Giddens, A. (ed.) (2009), *The Global Third Way Debate*, London: Wiley.

Gordon, C. (1991), 'Governmental rationality: an introduction', in Burchell, G., Gordon, C. and Miller, P. (eds.) *The Foucault Effect: Studies in Governmentality*, London: Harvester Wheatsheaf.

Hall, P. (1998), *Cities in Civilization: Culture, Innovation, and Urban Order*, London: Phoenix.

Hall, S. (2012), *City, Street and Citizen: The Measure of the Ordinary*, Abingdon, Oxford: Routledge.

Harvey, D. (1989), 'From managerialism to entrepreneurialism: the transformation in urban governance in late capitalism', *Geografiska Annaler*, 71(B): 3–17.

Harvey, D. (2010), *The Enigma of Capital and the Crisis of Capitalism*, London: Profile Books.

Harvey, D. (2012), *Rebel Cities: From the Right to the City to the Urban Revolution*, London: Verso.

Harvey, D. (2014), *Seventeen Contradictions and the End of Capitalism*, London: Profile.

Koch, M. (2012), *Capitalism and Climate Change: Theoretical Discussion, Historical Development and Policy Responses*, Basingstoke, Hampshire: Palgrave Macmillan.

Krätke, S. (2011), *The Creative Capital of Cities*, Oxford: Wiley Blackwell.

Lash, S. and Urry, J. (1994), *Economies of Signs and Space*, London: Sage.

Lave, R. (2012), 'Neoliberalism and the production of environmental knowledge', *Environment and Society: Advances in Research*, 3: 19–38.

Lefebvre, H. (1996), *Writings on Cities*, selected, translated and introduced by Kofman, E. and Lebas, E., Oxford: Blackwell.

Levitas, R. (2011 [1990]), *The Concept of Utopia*, Witney: Peter Lang.

Lipsky, M. (1980), *Street Level Bureaucracy*, New York: Russell Sage Foundation.

Madanipour, A. (2011), *Knowledge Economy and the City: Spaces of Knowledge*, London: Routledge.

Marx, K. (1980), 'The Eighteenth Brumaire of Louis Bonaparte', in Marx, K. and Engels, F. (1980). *Selected Works In One Volume*. London: Lawrence and Wishart.

Massey, D. (2005), *For Space*, London: Sage.

May, T. (1991), *Probation: Politics, Policy and Practice*, Buckingham: Open University Press.

May, T. (2017), 'Urban crisis: bonfire of vanities to find opportunity in the ashes', *Urban Studies*, http://journals.sagepub.com/eprint/sgcNiC9nzUTeAJrGGxch/full (accessed May 2017).

May, T. and Perry, B. (2006), 'Cities, knowledge and universities: transformations in the image of the intangible', *Social Epistemology*, 20 (3–4): 259–282.

May, T. and Perry, B. (2011), 'Urban research in the knowledge economy: content, context and outlook', *Built Environment*, 37 (3): 352–368.

May, T. and Perry, B. (2016), 'Cities, experiments and the logics of the knowledge economy', in Evans, J., Karvonen, A. and Raven, R. (eds.) *The Experimental City*, Oxford: Routledge.

May, T. and Perry, B. (2017), *Reflexivity: The Essential Guide*, London: Sage.

May, T. with Perry, B. (2011), *Social Research and Reflexivity: Content, Consequences and Context*, London: Sage.

May, T. and Williams, M. (1998), 'Knowing the social world', in May, T. and Williams, M. (eds.) *Knowing the Social World*, Buckingham: Open University Press.

May, T. and Williams, M. (eds.) (1998), *Knowing the Social World*, Buckingham: Open University Press.

Meek, J. (2015), *Private Island: Why Britain Now Belongs to Someone Else*, revised edition, London: Verso.

Miao, B. and Lang, G. (2014), 'A tale of two eco-cities: experimentation under hierarchy in Shanghai and Tianjin', *Urban Policy and Research*, 33 (2): 247–263.

Mintzberg, H. (1983), *Structure in Fives: Designing Effective Organisations*, New Jersey, Englewood Cliffs: Prentice-Hall.

Mirowski, P. (2014), *Never Let a Serious Crisis Go to Waste: How Neoliberalism Survived the Financial Meltdown*, London: Verso.

Mokyr, J. (2002), *The Gifts of Athena: Historical Origins of the Knowledge Economy*, Princeton: Princeton University Press.

Norfield, T. (2016), *The City: London and the Global Power of Finance*, London: Verso.

Noveck, B.S. (2015), *Smart Citizens, Smarter State: The Technologies of Expertise and the Future of Governing*, Cambridge, Mass: Harvard University Press.

O'Mara, M.P. (2005), *Cities of Knowledge: Cold War Science and the Search for the Next Silicon Valley*, Princeton: Princeton University Press.

Only Lyon (2014), *Smart City: Experimenting Today for Better City Living Tomorrow*, Lyon: Greater Lyon Economic and International Development Delegation.

Park, R.E. (1972), *The Crowd and the Public and Other Essays*, edited by Elsner, H., translated by Elsner, C., Chicago: University of Chicago Press.

Perry, B. and May, T. (eds.) (2007), 'Governance, science policy and regions', *Special Edition, Regional Studies*, 41 (8).

Perry, B., May, T., Marvin, S. and Hodson, M. (2013), 'Rethinking sustainable knowledge-based urbanism through active intermediation: what knowledge and how?', in Andersen, H.T. and Atkinson, R. (eds.) *The Production and Use of Urban Knowledge: European Experiences*, Dordrecht: Springer, pp. 151–167.

Pickstone, J.V. (2000), *Ways of Knowing: A New History of Science, Technology and Medicine*, Manchester: Manchester University Press.

Pieterse, E. (2008), *City Futures: Confronting the Crisis of Urban Development*, London: Zed Books.

Piketty, T. (2014), *Capital in the Twenty-First Century*, translated by Goldhammer, A., Cambridge, Mass: Harvard University Press.

Poovey, M. (1998), *A History of the Modern Fact: Problems of Knowledge in the Sciences of Wealth and Society*, Chicago: University of Chicago Press.

Poster, M. (1990), *The Mode of Information: Poststructuralism and Social Context*, Cambridge: Polity.

Rothenburg, M.A. (2010), *The Excessive Subject: A New Theory of Social Change*, Cambridge: Polity.

Roy, A. and Ong, A. (eds.) (2011), *Worlding Cities: Asian Cities and the Art of Being Global*, Oxford: Blackwell.

Sassen, S. (2001), *The Global City: New York, London, Tokyo*, 2nd edition, Princeton: Princeton University Press.

Sayer, A. (2015), *Why We Can't Afford the Rich*, Bristol: Policy Press.

Scott, A.J. (2008), *Social Economy of the Metropolis: Cognitive-Cultural Capitalism and the Global Resurgence of Cities*, Oxford: Oxford University Press.

Scott, A.J. (2014), 'Beyond the creative city: cognitive-cultural capitalism and the new urbanism', *Regional Studies*, 48 (4): 565–578.

Scott, J. (1998), 'Relationism, cubism, and reality: beyond relativism', in May, T. and Williams, M. (eds.) *Knowing the Social World*, Buckingham: Open University Press.

Scott, J. (2000), *Social Network Analysis: A Handbook*, 2nd edition, London: Sage.

Stehr, N. (1992), *Practical Knowledge: Applying the Social Sciences*, London: Sage.

Stehr, N. and Meja, V. (eds.) *Society and Knowledge: Contemporary Perspectives in the Sociology and Knowledge and Science*, New Jersey: Transaction.

The Guardian (2016), 'House prices have rocketed 300% in England and Wales since 1995 – analysis', http://www.theguardian.com/money/2016/jan/15/house-prices-rocket-300-england-wales (accessed May 2017).

Thrift, N. (2005), *Knowing Capitalism*, London: Sage.

Turner, B.S. (2006), *Vulnerability and Human Rights*, Pennsylvania, PA: Pennsylvania State University Press.

Weick, K.E. (2009), *Making Sense of the Organization, Volume 2: The Impermanent Organization*, Chichester: John Wiley.

Wyly, E. (2013), 'The city of cognitive cultural capitalism', *City*, 17 (3): 387–394.

Žižek, S. (2008 [1999]), *The Ticklish Subject: The Absent Centre of Political Ontology*, London: Verso.
Žižek, S. (2009a), *First as Tragedy, Then as Farce*, London: Verso.
Žižek, S. (2009b), *Violence: Six Sideways Reflections*, London: Verso.
Žižek, S. (2014), *Trouble in Paradise: From the End of History to the End of Capitalism*, London: Allen Lane.

4

UNIVERSITIES AS ENGINES
OF GROWTH

Introduction

Global cities want global universities. An increased relevance attached to knowledge has led to a plethora of actors focussing upon and positioning themselves within a sphere of activity characterised by what seems to be limitless potential. Pressures for universities to engage with their cities are mediated through global forces. Approaches across national contexts to common pressures of globalisation, the knowledge economy and the desire for new technological fixes to particular problems can be detected. As we have seen, these pressures are mediated through contexts. So, as with cities, whilst we see global trends, there are contextual factors that are of importance in understanding the relations between the knowledge economy and universities. These factors can be seen to accelerate, mitigate and challenge the power of global flows (Marginson and Rhoades 2002).

In this chapter, we examine the implications of the knowledge economy for the position and purpose of the university in society and how this is manifest in practices within these institutions. The same dynamics that work to define and shape knowledge-city politics are also manifest in centres of knowledge production, especially the university. These institutions are not immune to the pressures we have charted in previous chapters: "In the last analysis, higher education cannot be understood except in the context of the wider social and political environment in which it is located. As in all social activities, there is an inherent tension between the collective public and individual private benefits and responsibilities. In the long term, the ideological climate tends to swing from one to the other. At present, individual costs and benefits of both suppliers and users of services are in the ascendant" (Williams 2016: 140). Therefore, we examine the changes in terms of pressures of convergence and divergence, but also the forms of knowledge-based development which are manifest in the process. We then turn to a critical assessment of these before moving on, in the next chapter, to the issues that inform the reproduction of current practices that need to be addressed when it comes to the possibilities for change.

The place and space of universities

Whilst universities have traditionally been seen to occupy a space apart from society, they were never as independent or autonomous as such accounts tend to portray. The idea of the 'ivory tower' was a phase in its development (Barnett 2000: 41). In Germany, there has always been a close association between engineering departments and laboratories, and the US land-grant universities were set up to meet local needs in agriculture and only subsequently became excellent in research. Similarly, the Ivy League universities always had close associations with industry (Newfield 2003). Nevertheless, whilst engaged, universities had a distance from mainstream society and this has been seen to afford them a limited buffer zone from external demands, maintained through the trust of government funds to scientists to manage their own affairs (Guston 2000). Indeed, it could be argued that this distance constitutes the distinctiveness of the university as a site of knowledge production.

Knowledge has always played an important role in relation to social, cultural and political understandings and been attributed with varying powers and value. Any history of ideas shows periods of greater or lesser circulation of influence between the direction of research and broader developments (Burke 2000). Universities have never been simply protected or insulated from social, economic or political forces. Whilst the ivy and industry connection should not be downplayed in nostalgic yearnings for a bygone era of supposed autonomy, the interaction is two-way in which ideas and practices shape each other. As those who have studied American universities note: "The research university has always had enormous experience with business. It has had nearly a century and a half of practice pursuing truth and personal development, in the context of economic development. Even in instrumentalist terms, the university was the place where knowledge would determine the shape of economics, and not the other way round" (Newfield 2003: 223).

In many countries, links between universities, the state and industry became stronger after 1945, especially in the context of the Cold War and the role of science. Much applied scientific research was carried out in specialist state research institutions (Gummett 1991; Piganiol 1991). However, the university's main focus remained the pursuit of basic, 'blue skies' research in science, the social sciences and the humanities. Ruivo (1994) considers this first 'paradigm of science' in the postwar years as the era of 'science as the motor of progress'. Here we find an almost unquestioning belief in the inherent value of pure science and proportionately high levels of basic research funding. Nevertheless, by the 1970s the ability of science to deliver social and economic benefit was being questioned. The focus shifted to the ways in which science could be directly applied to 'solve' national problems and to how scientific knowledge in general could have increased relevance. From the 1980s, this conception of science gave way to a third paradigm – 'science as a strategic opportunity' with a focus upon growth, the development of foresight, university-industry links and developing relations between science and innovation (Ruivo 1994). Inherent in this is a different conception of the function of the university in relationship to the state and the market, which can be explained primarily in the context of the development of the knowledge economy.

Whilst the notion of an ivory tower does not bear close scrutiny, we do find a degree of acceptance around a view of relative academic autonomy and the unique position of knowledge as pertaining to a tolerated, yet elite, set of cultural practices. That view persists until the late 20th century. Despite political, economic and social upheaval and change, the university remained a relatively stable, though evolving institution from its medieval roots until the second half of the 20th century (Barnett 1990). The two primary functions of the institution, the pursuit of knowledge – or 'science' for short – in a range of academic disciplines (Fuller 2000) and the provision of a liberal education to an elite, were part of a more general aim to create a more knowledgeable and enlightened population (Scott 2000).

Changes have seen the university as more central to economic and social development, with a pivotal role in the production and reproduction of societies and the achievement of visions of the 'learning region' (Archibugi and Lundvall 2001), 'ideopolis' (Work Foundation 2006) or 'knowledge society' (Stehr 1994). As spaces of expectation, universities are informed by their environments and this drives the idea of being a 'service' to the economy. The trends of globalisation and knowledge-based development have reshaped expectations of universities and with that the roles of research in society (Odin and Manicas 2004). As in the case of the urban, resulting forms of commodification produce tensions that are played out in contexts with different consequences for the content of the knowledge produced (Allen and Imrie 2010; Radder 2010). Universities in Europe have been told that they cannot continue with some medieval conception of their role in present times and that they should be more like businesses by accessing 'third stream funding' outside of research and teaching. Such a move is indicative of the discourses on 'enterprise' that we charted in earlier chapters (Marginson and Considine 2000). As with many urban dwellers, conflicting pressure can leave researchers bewildered about the form of university development, and reactions can be manifest in denial and retreat and allusions to particular ideas of professionalism (May and Perry 2013), along with calls to slow down these cultures to reclaim the university (Berg and Seeber 2016).

So the narrative of convergence, divergence and conflict remains. We do not find a simple alignment between the mission of universities and the immediate economic and social development needs of states, markets and localities, with research being driven by the advancement of knowledge, rather than the world of application and teaching based on a broad educational, rather than selective training function. As we have argued in relation to the knowledge economy, what we find is an intensification of particular issues manifest in pressures for convergence. By 2010 it was estimated that 60 per cent of the world's research and development spending came from industry with the result that contemporary science is 'big business' (Resnik 2010). Eurostat, the statistical office of the European Union, estimated this amount to be 64 per cent in 2014, with the higher education sector accounting for 2 per cent, the government sector at 12 per cent and the private, nonprofit sector being 1 per cent: "With respect to other major economies, R&D intensity in the EU was much lower than in South Korea (4.15% in 2013) and Japan (3.47% in 2013) and lower than in the United States (2.81% in 2012), while it was about the same level as in China (2.08% in 2013) and higher than in Russia (1.15%). In order to provide a stimulus to the EU's competitiveness, an increase by 2020 of the R&D intensity to 3% in the EU is one of the five headline targets of the Europe 2020 strategy" (Eurostat 2015: 1).

With 238 billion euros spent on research and development in 2014, expectations of knowledge in the European Union are high. The boundaries between universities and these expectations inevitably become more porous in these circumstances. In terms of funding, public universities have less immunity to the pressures for change, reform and accountability, whilst universities as a whole exist in increasing climates of competition between sectors to secure resources. They are now expected to deliver a range of benefits, outputs and deliverables in teaching, outreach and exploitation; all to the same high standards as before, yet within quicker time frames and conditions of reduced resources. While attention is focussed on the need to increase business expenditure on R&D and exploit private, scientific research, policy mechanisms for such activities are more limited in the context of state-aid rules, rendering the university a tool and target for public policy and a transformative agent to accelerate the promise of the knowledge economy for city benefit. As the UK Russell Group of universities put it from their studies of impact, they can: "show that research underpinning the case studies has resulted in at least £21 billion of wider economic benefits – 100 times the initial investment" (2015: 4).

While reforms can be instigated from the 'bottom-up', that is by universities themselves, they are more widely driven by governments and the pressures of globalisation. Increasingly science is not trusted to reform itself in the ways that are deemed necessary. The successful extraction of scientific value is predicated on greater intervention into university life which poses key challenges for institutional design. For many, the realisation of value from the university is contingent upon its adoption of different institutional forms and accompanying this are demands for increased relevance manifest in indicators of excellence that include international league tables. The Times Higher Education and the company Quacquarelli Symonds (QS) are two such examples. Universities are judged in terms of their business performance through extended regulatory systems, performance indicators and so forth, not by the traditional reference to a public service ethic or a set of professional values. A shift from a public service to entrepreneurial ethos is one from accountability based on trust and mutuality to audit based on an ever-increasing array of indicators.

Boundaries under pressure

The knowledge economy is based upon a different university. It is one assumed to be more reflexive, innovative and streamlined (Clark 1998; Van der Sijde and Schutte 2000; Jongbloed and Goedegebuure 2001). Given neoliberal pressures on convergence, issues emerge between for-profit and nonprofit institutions that lead to particular consequences. Thus, writing about the forms of governance of such institutions in the US and pressures on convergence, the following observation remains relevant today: "Little is currently known about how convergence will shape under provision to particular educational markets, the tension between long-term strategic planning, and ad hoc decision-making, or the role of research and teaching in faculty responsibilities" (Pusser and Turner 2004: 256–257). Trends, however, are apparent.

We can say that aspirations are embodied in the 'entrepreneurial' or 'enterprise' university, actively engaging with stakeholders and societal actors. Through examination of the Universities of Warwick, Strathclyde (both UK), Twente (Netherlands), Joensuu (Finland) and Chalmers University of Technology (Sweden), Clark (1998) identified five core elements to the entrepreneurial university: a strengthened steering core; expanded developmental periphery; diversified funding base; stimulated academic heartland and an integrated entrepreneurial culture. Whilst the subject of debate on the extent to which this can be seen in practice, case studies from universities across the globe formed the basis of an International Management in Higher Education (IMHE) conference in 2000. The contributions revealed varying degrees of convergence and divergence in response to external engagements. There was, however, a general sense that the 'entrepreneurial/innovative university' is likely to be inevitable as a result of external pressures (Davies 2000).

At the turn of the 21st century, neoliberal market-oriented practices came into universities in these changing circumstances (Baker and May 2002). It was linked in those countries with publicly funded institutions to a wider shift from a public service to a performance and audit-based ethos, with a focus on user relevance, managerial efficiency, cost effectiveness, employability, benchmarking, league-tabling and audit accountability (Pels 2003). Reference to the 'new managerialism', the rise of the audit society and a 'new policy language' were deployed to characterise these shifts (Delanty 2001). Now, as Western countries adopt increasing economies within an austerity politics: "most parts of the public sector experience austerity not as something optional or avoidable, but as something imposed" (Pollitt 2016: 135). A mix of audit and austerity was driven home to us during one of our times when we worked for universities advising them on socio-economic engagement. A former vice chancellor introduced a strategy group meeting with the following: "you are only as good as your current metrics … we are not where we should be … we are aligned with government direction, the only true measure of our success is operational surplus". This is all part of a culture where: "concerns about money, audits and budgets come to the fore, with incumbents wrestling to combine informal and relatively non-hierarchical ways of organizing academic work through collegiality with new ways of doing things under a harsher policy and funding regime" (Deem 2003: 59).

For-profit universities, such as the University of Phoenix (US), or private, non-profit universities such as Harvard and Stanford, are in a different position and are not subject to the same pressures as publicly funded institutions. Then we have 'corporate' universities. One estimate is that there are over 4,000 worldwide, with their numbers doubling to 2,000 in the US in the ten years up to 2007 (Boston Consulting Group 2014). These new institutional forms, as well as mechanisms for service delivery through online provision, represent challenges to traditional university systems and their capacities to deliver all that is expected of them. What is evident is a pressure to meet corporate needs and a focus on 'doing' leading to a hybrid between further and higher education (Jarvis 2001). To these changing factors we can add national state policies and the effects of globalisation and region-alisation that influence and shape the direction of *all* universities and the demands upon them with UK higher education policy, for example, being opened up to private equity interests (McGettigan 2013). Indeed, as we write, the latest Higher Education and Research Bill (2017) in the UK seeks to introduce private inter-ests in the provision of degrees as if that were some guarantee of student choice and higher quality through greater competition to meet the needs of the future economy.

International student markets are expected to grow throughout the world and the search for the promise of success is leading to the emergence of new configura-tions of institutions, both public and private, to create economies of scale, such as international consortia and collaborations leading to transnational higher education (Caruana 2016). Institutional reform is thereby embedded in wider processes aimed at producing world-class competitive higher education systems able to succeed in a global knowledge market, characterised by diversification, stratification and hierarchies. Indeed, in the United Arab Emirates (UAE) the number of licensed colleges and universities grew from five to fifty-eight between 1997 and 2008. Of these, only three are government funded. As a study on the movement from an oil to knowledge economy in the UAE notes: "The expansion in higher education opportunities was mainly driven by high economic growth in the UAE economy and the increase in investment made by the private sector in higher education insti-tutions in the Gulf region in general" (Ahmed and Alfaki 2016: 53).

Searching for markets, focussing on the privatisation of services and facilities in universities, along with doing more with less resources and transferring the costs of university provision from state-acquired taxation to students, all promote the idea of higher education as a private, rather than public good. Aside from the UK, Europe, New Zealand and Hong Kong are just some of the places where these trends are apparent and the introduction of performance management and audits to measure the quality of teaching and research became more mainstream (Deem, Hillyard and Reed 2007). An increasing move towards transnational higher educa-tion can be seen in terms of diminishing national resources measured against global ones in terms of pressures for competition. As with cities in general, networks of forces play out at the local level in higher education. Whilst seeking to avoid the determinism of the structure of global forces on local autonomy, a study reviewing published research on these processes between 2006 and 2016 concludes that it still remains important to: "acknowledge the force of network power assumed by the global standard that constrains individual and collective agency, progressively eliminating all possible perspectives save that of the knowledge-based economy underpinned by global neoliberalism. In an environment where the alternative to convergence – which assures membership of 'the club' – is isolation, the local works in symbiosis with the global and local adaptation and divergence become functional for convergence on the main global principles" (Caruana 2016: 66).

As the need to be competitive, cost-effective and to respond to market pressures is impressed upon universities, this has the effect of commercialising activities in research and teaching. In the context of constraints on public funding, universities have turned to alternative support from the private sector. In teaching, a wider range of groups and interests now claim a concern in shaping university education. Two constellations stand out: government and industry and the new mass of potential consumers of higher education. Increasingly, what universities teach and how they do it is changing in response to pressure from both these sources. Government and industry stress the need for graduates with better 'key' or 'generic' skills and the need for the universities to focus on the new skills required by the knowledge economy. Students become market-oriented and are attracted to courses that offer a passport to employment in what are seen as the dynamic sectors of the economy. Many disciplines, in order to survive, have to reinvent themselves by extolling market friendly forms. Equally, an increasing recognition of science's capacity for economically productive innovation involves a movement from support for 'basic' or 'pure' scientific research whose evolution is determined by the 'advancement of knowledge' and whose direction is controlled by (mainly academic) scientists, to support for research that is closely linked to other priorities. Funding is increasingly tied to the production of 'socially robust' research involving new partnerships with business and industry, the public sector and the community. Quality control then involves forms of social accountability and acceptability that go beyond those set by the purely cognitive context of the epistemically less permeable 'Mode 1 science'.

It is for such reason that scholars are concerned with the 'university in ruins' and its infantilisation (Maskell and Robinson 2001; Furedi 2017). Intensification of the issues we have charted becomes apparent (Radder 2010) within the emergence of an 'academic capitalism' (Slaughter and Rhoades 2004) and this runs alongside calls to resist the applicability of the market model on the grounds of universities being part of 'cultural infrastructures' (Wagner 2004). These calls are a reaction to a steady process of re-engineering by stealth manifest in: "a directed process of market construction, each move designed to protect the elite and expose the majority. At the same time, the gamble involves running the risk of subprime degrees. Existing quality assurance, which has its faults, is supplanted by 'value for money', a 'risk-based' system, and a regulator tasked with promoting competition.

Caveat emptor!" (McGettigan 2013: 185). Roland Barnett, while accepting much of the validity of the 'end of knowledge' thesis, suggested there was a new epistemology awaiting the university that is: "open, bold, engaging, accessible and conscious of its own insecurity" (Barnett 2000: 409). It is one based on the ability of the university to become entrepreneurial and market its wares through the adoption of academic capitalism.

The rise of the 'market-university' has been characterised as a loss in academic quality, academic autonomy and uniqueness of the university as an institution. Subject to a process of McDonaldisation, it is seen to be an irrational and dehumanising place (Ritzer 2015). Research groups are prioritising commercial return over academic standards, with 'quick hits', the 'bottom line' and meeting 'market needs' becoming the underlying rationale for research to the detriment of the 'pursuit of knowledge' that formed the university's traditional raison d'être (Coombs and Metcalfe 2000). There is concern that the market-needs focus of research and teaching precludes innovations that are not assumed to be linked to them. The search for innovation implies freedom and risk and this is incompatible with too great a focus on efficiency, public sector auditing requirements, user engagement and identifiable outputs (Fuller 2000) whilst it accords the private sector with attributes that do not stand up to examination (Meek 2015). A further set of policy and academic tensions and contradictions thereby emerge that universities must manage. Issues include the pressures on traditional methods of management and governance, systems of remuneration and reward, the culture of collegiality and on evaluations of worth and status based on respect for knowledge production for its own sake. As Davydd Greenwood puts it: "if universities do not invest in deep, specialized knowledge creation, then they soon will have nothing at all to offer to the world beyond their walls and they will simply be private and public sector research shops and vocational schools" (2009: 15).

Univer-cities

In the face of these factors it would be easy to forget the historical roots of universities and long associations with locality (Newfield 2003; Pickstone 2000). The relationship between universities and cities may be characterised as one of occasional conflict, negotiated tolerance, ambivalence and mutual benefit. Whether through disagreements between 'town' (the city) and 'gown' (the University) in medieval Cambridge or Oxford, the establishment of civic universities and those emerging from the industrial, science or technological institutes of the 19th century (for example, Manchester), or the land-grant universities of the US (for example, Cornell), universities have cohabited in the same spaces as multiple actors, communities and authorities that have comprised the 'city'. Proximity and distance, engagement and relative autonomy, go together. On the whole, however: "the university has always claimed the world, not its host city, as its domain. Whatever its local roots, the university historically has striven for learning that at least reaches towards universal significance" (Bender 1988: 294). For scholars of the Chicago

School, the city was a laboratory providing: "a miniature replica of problems frequently encountered within the society" (Hamel et al. 1993: 15). Studies were
based on the assumption that societies could be delimited and had sufficient homo-
geneity that the city was a mirror for a broader social system, seen through the lenses
of various research techniques. The city provides access to human resources and an
environment that supports the core missions of teaching and research. Universities
have generally been part of the urban landscape and institutional architecture, contributing to economic and cultural life via spending and employment or broader
practices of civic engagements (Hall 1997).

Whilst accounts can emphasise a passive relationship between universities and
cities, the changes we have charted point to a more dynamic relationship. What
we see are universities rebranding themselves as distinctive given their histories in
particular places. Increasingly, they seek to meet the demands of external parties
and the expectations of their roles in the knowledge society through mediated
forms of governance (Friedrichsmeier and Marcinkowski 2016). The parallel processes of globalisation and localism are leading both universities and cities to seek
closer relations in building knowledge cities through intensification of activities
under new sets of pressures. The appropriateness of different levels of scale for
economic development and social cohesion led to increased interest in the roles of
cities in knowledge-based growth, in the context of wider shifts to multi-actor and
multi-scalar governance regimes (Brenner 2004; Neuman and Hull 2009). As cities
seek to build their image around knowledge, science and technology, they cannot
ignore one view of universities as being to the: "information economy what coal
mines were to the industrial economy" (Castells and Hall 1994: 231).

The dynamics of the knowledge-based era combine with those of a
multi-scalar international political economy to produce a 'glocalization' of science
(Swyndegouw 1992; Perry 2006). As we noted, public policies at supra-national
and subnational scales have been repopulated through ideas of clusters, knowledge
spillovers, innovation and knowledge transfer, as science and technology are seen to
be revolutionising approaches to urban and regional development. A clear emphasis emerges whereby economies are reoriented to build knowledge regions and
cities and enhance urban growth through alliances with universities, industries and
policymakers (Wong et al. 2006; Clua and Albet 2008; Fernandez-Maldono and
Romein 2010). Within this context, universities are required to operate at a
number of spatial scales, interweaving international, national and subnational roles
(Benneworth, Charles and Madanipou 2010). A multi-level governance of science
policy implies both the complex and often subtle rescaling of activity vertically
between levels of government and horizontally across different public/private
actors (Perry 2007). In the process attention is directed towards the research base
in 'supply-oriented' approaches and the emerging relationships between universities and subnational actors (Crespy, Heraud and Perry 2007; Koschatsky and Kroll
2007). Subnational actors have sought to build 'knowledge cities' through linking
science with industry and harnessing the power of science as a driver for wealth
creation and economic growth.

With parallels apparent in the aspirations of cities in the context of the knowledge-economy, universities have become part of urban growth coalitions that assist in delivering urban renaissance in countries such as Mexico, Japan, Indonesia, South Korea, Israel, Finland and Germany (Wiewel and Perry 2008). Once we move into attributing value to knowledge in terms of the contexts of its application we enter the terrain of knowledge-based urban development where we find cities: "characterized by a focus on entrepreneurial activities concerned with economic development and issues of production, rather than a concern with the more managerial issues of social welfare and collective consumption" (Wilks-Heeg et al. 2003: 30). Cities and universities then move into a focus on marketing, branding and global success and position. Their positions align: "London accounted for over 23% of the UK's economic output in 2014, having grown by 18% since 2009, compared to 8% for the country as a whole (Experian). London has a highly qualified workforce, with 53% of employees having a degree. Imperial College London is ranked as the 7th best university in the world, with a further three London universities in the Top 40. Importantly, 22% of all overseas students based in the UK are in London" (Bilfinger GVA 2015; available at: https://www. gva.co.uk/research/london-and-the-knowledge-economy). Cities that aspire to be global want global universities to climb up the ladder of international league tables. If cities have been passive sites, lenses or objects for academic study, the knowledge economy signals a changing set of expectations of these institutions.

Those expectations meet changing funding and policy regimes, and branding at the institutional level occurs in universities. As we noted in the last chapter, it is the reconfiguring of institutions in the name of particular economic views that adds to the characteristics of current times. In universities there are patterns of specialisation in niche areas or around clusters and centres of excellence as they pursue and market their positions in global league tables. As with cities, the knowledge economy is not just a description for a set of external changes, but a persuasive exercise in the reformulation of the economy and those institutions and organisations involved in knowledge production, transmission and circulation. It is no wonder that universities as a principle site of these activities find themselves adopting similar strategies to the cities in which they are located.

In the formulation of urban strategic direction, universities are seen as significant actors which, by virtue of the physical nature of their estates or engagement through cultural activities, are bound up with their cities. A dominant consensus emerges around the need to increase the interrelationships between universities and their localities for the mutual benefit of all involved. However, in practice there are a complex set of interrelationships, dynamics and motivations underpinning engagement at the urban scale, from the altruistic to the instrumental and strategic. A particular set of issues surrounds the balance between public and private interests and the way private interests may be reframed as public (Perry 2006). Universities can be driving forces for urban development, provided cities are successful in embedding knowledge in local, social and economic networks which, in turn, depends on the balance in the process of exchange between the various stakeholders in higher education (Russo, van den Berg and Lavanga 2007).

Universities have become more adept at playing the game of scales, seeing local relevance and global excellence as equal partners depending on their location and position in league tables. The UK's Russell Group of universities is typical: "Our research-intensive, world-class universities play an important part in the intellectual life of the UK and have huge social, economic and cultural impacts locally, across the UK and around the globe" (http://russellgroup.ac.uk/about/). For the Alliance universities: "we are leaders in our cities and regions ... we are locally-rooted and globally-connected" (http://www.unialliance.ac.uk). Subnational expectations are not, however, equal upon all universities. Elite universities are valued for their assumed benefits, leaving other institutions to deliver on agendas relating to the third mission or attracting local students. Organisational culture comes into play here along with the regulatory regime: the autonomy of the professor and their right to determine their own affairs is constitutionally enshrined in Germany, whilst the widespread striking of French scientists in reaction to proposed reforms to the research system in 2004 led to a reversal in French policy. Even in more neoliberal systems, regional demands on universities are largely restricted to being physical agents, attractors and political partners. What we see then is a certain power of science to protect itself in the face of an encroaching relevance, but this power relates to a position in regional, national and global hierarchies with varying consequences for what can be embraced, denied and ignored.

A missing middle

Whilst universities and the workers within them may be differentially positioned, in the main they may be singularly inappropriate organisations for delivering the kinds of promises that the knowledge economy expects of them. There remains a considerable gap – a 'missing middle' – between societal expectations and the institutional capacity of universities to deliver. Universities are not single purpose institutions commonly united around clearly defined missions, but bring together different communities and networks of academics with divergent motivations: from curiosity to social relevance, linked closely to incentive structures that inform research behaviour. External expectations consequently highlight the need for reform from within universities at the levels of management, governance and steering (Harloe and Perry 2005). Management issues cannot be divorced from the cultures of universities and the activities of academics themselves and there is an often uncomfortable affinity between the clamour for academic recognition in a competitive environment and the forms of managerialism they exhibit (May and Perry 2013).

Universities have varying capacities to position themselves in relation to these pressures and thus to mediate their effects on academics and researchers. Universities would reject the idea of being purely contemplative institutions, claiming instead to pursue the importance of the relevance of their activities at varying scales of activity: from the local, to city-regional, national and international. They would point to numerous examples of successful partnership between academics and stakeholders at local, national and international scales, from business, government and community groups. Whilst clear intra-institutional differences exist between disciplines and where they are positioned within faculties, particularly when it comes to resource allocation, inter-institutional differences also play a significant role. University managers acting at the boundaries of their institutions perform roles from capture and insulation, to amplification and an increase in uncertainty. Marketing their localities and places means an ever-increasing link to their contexts at the same time as cities have become more concerned with marketing, branding and global success and positioning in city-hierarchies. Here, we find a mix of the futurity of the promise with nostalgia in developmental configurations whereby it holds up a mirror to centre the university. This is ably assisted by the introduction of whole new tiers of personnel in university concerned with an image that so easily appears at a disjuncture with the everyday practices of academics. This is hardly a mix in which critique is enabled to flourish (Brenner 2009; May with Perry 2011; Morris 2010).

As a result of these pressures, institutions tend to compete, rather than collaborate, aiming for the elusive label of being 'world-class'; except where collaboration is itself a stepping stone to global visibility. New managers enter institutions in the promise of delivering them to new heights in a struggle that is rarely questioned through an alignment of interests. For these reasons, we continue to find many universities that are 'in', but not 'of' their localities as the intangible goes in pursuit of the unattainable and academics exhibit ambivalent attitudes towards the places in which their institutions are housed. Those elements of 'third mission' activities that support this 'world-class' role, such as collaborations with industry or the receipt of regional monies, are embraced as a means to further international profile which is ably assisted if situated within a 'global' city; the result being that the less visible, yet arguably more socially relevant work which is not seen as excellent, can easily be relegated to the domain of less prestigious activities.

Inherent in these diverse roles are sets of expectations that embody different values. Their overall balance is mediated via frameworks for action at multiple levels of scale with incentives via alternative funding streams. It is here that the international political economy described earlier comes into play. Mixed messages are apparent in the drives for international excellence and collaborations for more proximate benefit. It is held that research needs to be conducted at an international level in order to meet criteria of world-class excellence. Yet it also needs to be embedded in local and regional contexts if the kinds of benefits expected from knowledge for the economy are to be realised. The decontextualised nature of the neoliberal paradigm leads to sets of assumptions that research excellence will lead, in some way, to relevance in a given locality, as if there were some automatic connection between the place in which a university is located and its benefits to that area.

In these circumstances, different academics play particular roles, bolstered by the contexts of their knowledge production about which they are often indifferent when it comes to its relationship to the content of their work. The idea that individual characteristics are solely responsible for excellence and/or innovation is promoted through, for instance, the teaching of entrepreneurialism and enterprise as specific fields of study, thereby replicating an abstract individualism. Character is, of course, an important component in understanding social identity and action, but focussing on this alone gives rise to an indifference to institutional conditions of knowledge production that allow claims to expertise to be made free from context. These contexts are political as well as social, economic or cultural (Bauman and May 2018). For instance, Dresner notes how the scientific community in Germany exploited the difficulties in reaching political agreement between the Federal and *Länder* governments to obtain an unusually high degree of autonomy (Dresner 2001: 110). Individualistic cultures are perpetuated whereby claims to professional autonomy on the part of the academic are prioritised over the necessary condition for its attainment: that is, institutional autonomy (May 2005; 2007). What is then created is a vulnerability to the effects of changes upon academic cultures which seek alterations in 'how' practices occur by measuring 'what' they produce.

The results are twofold. First, a confusion of expectations and incentive structures leads to demands from policymakers, politicians and university managers for programmes in the short term to demonstrate relevance. The idea of 'quick hits' drive criteria of relevance in ever-greater demands to service the economy through an assumed relationship between supply and demand when applied to knowledge. That process is ably assisted by knowledge exchange and transfer units applying these limited models and reproducing the assumption that policy and practice 'demand' knowledge in even tighter time frames. The absence of time on the part of these recipients to actually learn is left to one side through this invoking of a deficit model of academic practice. Equally, the search for excellence produces hierarchies according to abstract league tables whose flaws may be noted, but this does not stop the frenetic drive to attain a higher place in the rankings. Diversification then accompanies stratification in university systems with the 'third mission' becoming a resort for new streams of revenue as well as those universities outside the upper echelons of the global hierarchy. We then see a mix of scalar discourses and a tension between a modernist, universalising and international discourse and other more local historical layers, apparent not merely at the level of the organisation or the national HE sector, but also within regions (Burtscher, Pasqualoni and Scott 2006).

As with city administrations, these pressures have led to a series of organisational transformations within universities that have varying institutional consequences. First, the balance between steering and autonomy of universities is changing (Wagner 2004). In Germany and France, increased efforts to direct universities and programmes of research have been paradoxically accompanied by increased autonomy for universities. Autonomy is seen as a prerequisite for both scientific excellence and economic relevance, with incentives and project-based funding used as policy levers to influence academic behaviour. The aim is to replicate a UK competitive model of higher education and research, through reducing direct state influence, increasing indirect mechanisms of incentivisation and introducing greater instability and flexibility into the system through, for instance, a reduction in recurrent funding. Second, internal coordination within the university needs to be appropriate to meet external expectations. The traditional centralised and bureaucratic mode of organisation of the university is challenged by the need to respond flexibly to increasingly unpredictable environmental changes and engage with the varying needs of different localities and social groups.

New organisational forms are said to be required that enable interpretations of environmental changes to be rapidly implemented into organisational responses. A balance between centralised bureaucracy and flexible forms for the university demands not only imaginative management and appropriate design, but also the right mix of skills, values and knowledge among personnel across organisational units. Yet this raises a complex set of issues for those working in universities in respect to their purpose, as well as questions over what can be reasonably expected of higher education in relation to its positive impact upon social and economic development. Translating opportunities into tangible realities poses a number of significant challenges. These need to be managed in ways that are not indifferent to current practices and sustainable futures in particular contexts.

Meeting such challenges raises issues of leadership and management. Universities may have ambitions to be international in order to attract inward investment, but they need to be subregional and regional to be of benefit, to attract additional types of funding and to mobilise the type of political support they require to survive. This means examining the relationship between intended and actual results, as well as political leadership, which affects closure on otherwise open-ended terrains and which is willing to learn and to admit of mistakes. The presence of such leadership is not a sufficient condition to prevent the free play of different interests. It is, however, a necessary condition to ensure benefit beyond the narrow interests of associated institutions, organisations and professions. Difficult questions are then raised in terms of the management of conflicting aims which can easily become internalised within the organisation and heighten degrees of politicisation of its purpose and processes. These issues are often ignored and instead manifest in the need to engage in organisational restructuring that focusses on process without due regard to purpose, or the constitution of visions that have no meaningful content in terms of any specific activities that will make a difference to its future.

What is apparent in cities can also be seen in the idea of success in universities measured by such criteria as: external income generation, citation indexes, staff-student ratios, league tables and what has been termed 'journal list fetishism' (Willmott 2011). In addition, the effects of globalisation are argued to be manifest in campuses through less tolerance and freedom of expression (Furedi 2017). University transformation rhetoric also rapidly overtakes action, as well as the pursuit of product over consideration of purpose and value (May 2001). Such is the speed at which change is sought, little attention is given to a number of underlying issues that need to be clarified and addressed as a sound basis upon which the distinction of the university as a site of knowledge production may be sustained.

As a result, potential remains unrealised, but frenetic action abounds. Universities need to be far better at processes of communication internally and cross-institutionally, particularly given the difficulties created by an audit culture. People working in universities are unlikely to find yet more initiatives for third mission activities appealing when suffering from initiative fatigue. As we have said, innovation is no more than the triumph of forgetting over memory and this is paradoxically so in what is supposed to be a learning organisation. In the case of countries outside the Global North, the pursuit of globally induced objectives, without the level of investment that is enjoyed in the West for universities, will only exacerbate the problems. In context, it is the reasonable and attainable gap between the actual and potential according to particular values and goals that needs to be addressed in partnership with communities, the voluntary sector, local, regional and national government and business. That means open and honest conversations that do not invoke the falsehoods perpetuated by the forces we have charted.

Relatively little is known about the contexts which enable and constrain the relations that exist between policy expectations and the actual capacity of universities to deliver to different groups. Instead, we move from initiative to initiative without sufficient learning from experience, leaving expectations being either too impractical or unmet. Contexts matter, yet models are pedalled as one-size-fits-all solutions or as development fixes. Beware those who have ready-made solutions to problems, as they commit the fallacy of believing that the model of reality has become the reality of the model. Content-less policy initiatives are left to be populated by varying interests, without sufficient time for consultation or a general understanding of the conditions for success. As a result, a 'missing middle' exists (May, Perry and Wilmott 2016) between the aspirations for universities in relation to socio-economic development, the nature of policy frameworks, the governance of spatial relations and organisational forms and capacities. Policy initiatives are driven by a self-perpetuating hype in which the search for excellence becomes its own raison d'être. What we need is the intelligent regionalisation of universities (Levin and Greenwood 2016), given that universities are not driving local and regional economies, nor are they managed with this sole objective in mind.

Summary: Institutions and the knowledge economy

In this chapter, we have covered the issues that are raised by the promise of knowledge and the positioning of universities in terms of these pressures. Universities are strategic partners enrolled in the game of scales. These institutions mediate these relations, but those with the power to challenge the frenetic search of the promise to reconfigure our cities in a particular image, often reflect and accelerate those. This, in turn, raises contentious issues and informs practices of resistance at odds with the dominant rhetoric. Indeed, if those in universities are all producing new knowledge, as is so often required of their performance cultures and professional justifications, then why are there so many problems so routinely faced by the populations who live not far from their campuses? What exactly are the expectations that inform the relations between knowledge and action?

In the process of charting these changes, uneasy parallels are traced between the knowledge politics of the city and those of universities who search for global competitiveness and 'world class' excellence. These are apparent in international university rankings and the race for citations and scientific output indicators. Although the university is not a homogeneous entity, organisational structures and cultures prioritise particular forms of knowledge and methods of engagement, linked to incentive systems and peer recognition and review. Tensions are then raised in positioning the university in relation to urban development, and how that relates to forms of engagement, with whom and for what reasons?

When we get closer to home in our critique, it gets more uncomfortable. After all, many call the world into question, but fewer: "call the intellectual world into question" (Bourdieu 2007: 23). It is productive as we start to examine the very conditions and cultures that enable the perpetuation of those states of affairs that are advantageous to elites who have never been as evident as now in the outcomes of their acquisitive actions. Not only do relations between actions and knowledge need questioning, but also the role of power in all the rhetoric that surrounds the knowledge economy. However, as we have argued, it cannot be simply dismissed as empty, for it clearly informs actions and aspirations, as well as the attributions made to particular forms of knowledge. We need, therefore, to explore this politics of reproduction in more depth before moving on to the possibilities for cities to be more than spaces of extraction and reward for a few.

References

Ahmed, A. and Alfaki, I. (2016), *From Oil to Knowledge: Transforming the United Arab Emirates into a Knowledge-Based Economy towards UAE Vision 2021*, Sheffield: Greenleaf Publishing.

Allen, C. and Imrie, R. (eds.) (2010*), The Knowledge Business: The Commodification of Urban and Housing Research*, Farnham: Ashgate.

Archibugi, D. and Lundvall, B. (eds.) (2001), *The Globalising Learning Economy*, Oxford: Oxford University Press.

Baker, G. and May, T. (2002), 'Auditing the eternal present: organisational transformation in British higher education', *European Political Science*, 1 (3): 12–22.

Barnett, R. (1990), *The Idea of Higher Education*, Buckingham, Society for Research into Higher Education and Oxford University Press.

Barnett, R. (2000), *Realizing the University in an Age of Supercomplexity*, Buckingham: Open University Press.

Bauman, Z. and May, T. (2018), *Thinking Sociologically*, 3rd edition, Oxford: Blackwell-Wiley.

Bender, T. (ed.) (1988), *The University and the City: From Medieval Origins to the Present*, Oxford: Oxford University Press.

Benneworth, P., Charles, D. and Madanipour, A. (2010), 'Building localized interactions between universities and cities through university spatial development', *European Planning Studies*, 18 (10): 1611–1629.

Berg, M. and Seeber, B.K. (2016), *The Slow Professor: Challenging the Culture of Speed in the Academy*, Toronto: University of Toronto Press.

Bilfinger GVA (2015), *London and the Knowledge Economy Report*, https://www.gva.co.uk/research/london-and-the-knowledge-economy (accessed May 2017).

Boston Consulting Group (2014), *Corporate Universities: An Engine for Human Capital*, https://www.bcgperspectives.com (accessed May 2017).

Bourdieu, P. (2007), *Sketch for a Self Analysis*, translated by Nice, R., originally published in 2004 as *Esquisse pour une auto-analyse*, Cambridge: Polity.

Brenner, N. (2004), *New State Spaces: Urban Governance and the Rescaling of Statehood*, Oxford: Oxford University Press.

Brenner, N. (2009), 'What is critical urban theory?' *City*, 13 (2–3): 198–207.

Burke, P. (2000), *A Social History of Knowledge*, Cambridge: Polity.

Burtscher, C., Pasqualoni, P. and Scott, A. (2006), 'Universities and the regulatory framework: the austrian university system in transition', *Social Epistemology*, 20 (3–4): 241–258.

Carillo, F. (ed.) (2006), *Knowledge Cities. Approaches, Experiences and Perspectives*, Oxford: Butterworth-Heinemann.

Caruana, V. (2016), 'Researching the transnational higher education policy landscape: exploring network power and dissensus in a globalizing system', *London Review of Education*, 14 (1): 56–69.

Castells, M. and Hall, P. (1994), *Technopoles of the World*, London: Routledge.

Clark, B.R. (ed.) (1998), *Creating Entrepreneurial Universities: Organizational Pathways of Transformation*, Oxford: Pergamon.

Clua, A. and Albet, A. (2008), '22@bcn: bringing Barcelona forward in the information era', in Yigitcanlar, T., Velibeyoglu, K. and Baum, S. (eds.) *Knowledge-Based Urban Development: Planning and Applications in the Information Era*, London: IGI Global, pp. 132–148.

Coombs, R. and Metcalfe, J.S. (2000), *Universities, the Science Base and the Innovation Performance of the UK*, Centre for Research on Innovation and Competition, University of Manchester.

Crespy, C., Heraud, J-A. and Perry, B. (2007), 'Multi-level governance, regions and science in France: between competition and equality', *Regional Studies*, 41 (8): 1069–1084.

Davies, J.S. (2000), 'The hollowing out of local democracy and the fatal conceit of governing without government', *The British Journal of Politics and International Relations*, 2 (3): 414–428.

Deem, R. (2003), 'New managerialism in UK universities: manager-academic accounts of change', in Eggins, H. (ed.) *Globalization and Reform in Higher Education*, Maidenhead, Berks: Open University Press/McGraw-Hill.

Deem, R., Hillyard, S. and Reed, M. (2007), *Knowledge, Higher Education, and the New Managerialism*, Oxford: Oxford University Press.

Delanty, G. (2001), 'Ideologies of the knowledge society and the cultural contradictions of higher education', *Policy Futures in Education*, 1 (1): 71–82.

Dresner, S. (2001), 'A comparison of RTD structures in EU member states', in Dresner, S. and Gilbert, N. (eds.) *The Dynamics of European Science and Technology Policies*, Aldershot: Ashgate, pp. 109–135.

Dresner, S. and Gilbert, N. (eds.) (2001), *The Dynamics of European Science and Technology Policies*, Aldershot: Ashgate.

Dunford, M. and Kafkalas, G. (eds.) (1992), *Cities and Regions in the New Europe*, New York: Belhaven Press.

Eggins, H. (ed.) (2003), *Globalization and Reform in Higher Education*, Maidenhead, Berks: Open University Press/McGraw-Hill.

Ehrenberg, R.G. (ed.) (2004), *Governing Academia*, Ithaca, NY: Cornell University Press.

Eurostat (2015), 'First Estimates of Research and Development Expenditure', *Eurostat News Release No 209*, http://ec.europa.eu/eurostat/documents/2995521/7092226/9-301120 15-AP-EN.pdf/29eeaa3d-29c8-496d-9302-77056be6d586 (accessed May 2017).

Fernandez-Maldono, A. and Romein, A. (2010), 'The role of organisational capacity and knowledge-based development: the reinvention of Eindhoven', *International Journal of Knowledge-Based Development*, 1 (1–2): 79–97.

Friedrichsmeier, A. and Marcinkowski, F. (2016), 'The mediatisation of university governance: a theoretical and empirical exploration of some side-effects', *Policy and Politics*, 44 (1): 97–113.

Fuller, S. (2000), *The Governance of Science*, Open University Press, Buckingham.

Furedi, F. (2017), *What's Happened to the University? A Sociological Exploration of its Infantilization*, London: Routledge.

Greenwood, D. (2009), 'Are research universities knowledge-intensive learning organizations?', in Jemielniak, D. and Kociatkiewicz, J. (eds.) *Handbook of Research on Knowledge-Intensive Organizations*, London: Information Science Reference.

Gummett, P. (1991), 'The evolution of science and technology policy: a UK perspective', *Science and Public Policy*, 18 (1): 31–37.

Guston, D. (2000), *Between Politics and Science: Assuring the Integrity and Productivity of Research*, Cambridge: Cambridge University Press.

Hall, P. (1997), 'The university and the city', *Geojournal*, 41 (4): 301–309.

Hamel, J. with Dufour, S. and Fortin, D. (1993), *Case Study Methods*, English translation, London: Sage.

Harding, A., Scott, A., Laske, S. and Burtscher, C. (eds.) (2007), *Bright Satanic Mills: Universities, Regional Development and the Knowledge Economy*, Aldershot: Ashgate.

Harloe, M. and Perry, B. (2005), 'Rethinking or hollowing out the university? External engagement and internal transformation in the knowledge economy', *Higher Education Management and Policy*, 17 (2): 11–16.

Higher Education and Research Act – available at: http://www.legislation.gov.uk/ukpga/2017/29/contents/enacted/data.htm

Jarvis, P. (2001), *Universities and Corporate Universities*, London: Kogan Page.

Jemielniak, D. and Kociatkiewicz, J. (eds.) (2009), *Handbook of Research on Knowledge-Intensive Organizations*, London: Information Science Reference.

Jongbloed, B. and Goedegebuure, L. (2001), 'From the entrepreneurial university to the stakeholder university', in *Paper for the International Congress 'Universities and Regional Development in the Knowledge Society'*, pp. 12–14.

Koschatzky, K. and Kroll, H. (2007), 'Which side of the coin? The regional governance of science and innovation', *Regional Studies*, 41 (8): 1115–1128.

Levin, M. and Greenwood, D. (2016), *Creating a New Public University and Reviving Democracy: Action Research in Higher Education*, Oxford: Berghahn.

Marginson, S. and Considine, M. (2000), *The Enterprise University: Power, Governance and Reinvention in Australia*, Cambridge: Cambridge University Press.

Marginson, S. and Rhoades, G. (2002), 'Beyond national states, markets, and systems of higher education: A glonacal agency heuristic', *Higher Education*, 43 (3): 281–309.

Maskell, D. and Robinson, I. (2001), *The New Idea of the University*, London: Imprint.

May, T. (2001), 'Power, knowledge and organizational transformation: administration as depoliticisation', Special Issue 'Social epistemology and knowledge management', *Social Epistemology*, 15 (3): 171–186.

May, T. (2005), 'Transformations in academic production: context, content and consequences', *European Journal of Social Theory*, 8 (2): 193–209.

May, T. (2007), 'Regulation, engagement and academic production', in Harding, A., Scott, A., Laske, S. and Burtscher, C. (eds.) *Bright Satanic Mills: Universities, Regional Development and the Knowledge Economy*, Ashgate: Aldershot, pp. 95–117.

May, T. and Perry, B. (2013), 'Universities, reflexivity and critique: uneasy parallels in practice', *Policy Futures in Education*, 11 (5): 505–514.

May, T. with Perry, B. (2011), *Social Research and Reflexivity: Content, Consequences and Context*, London: Sage.

May, T., Perry, B. and Willmott, H. (2016), 'Cities, universities and urban knowledge exchange: lessons from a regional experiment in the UK', in Mercurio, R. (ed.) *Organizational Networks for Innovation*, Milan: Egea.

McGettigan, A. (2013), *The Great University Gamble: Money, Markets and the Future of Higher Education*, London: Pluto Press.

Meek, J. (2015), *Private Island: Why Britain Now Belongs to Someone Else*, revised edition, London: Verso.

Mercurio, R. (ed.) (2016), *Organizational Networks for Innovation*, Milan: Egea.

Morris, R.C. (2010), 'Introduction', in Morris, R.C. (ed.) *Can the Subaltern Speak? Reflections on the History of an Idea*, New York: Columbia University Press.

Morris, R.C. (ed.) (2010), *Can the Subaltern Speak? Reflections on the History of an Idea*, New York: Columbia University Press.

Neuman, M. and Hull, A. (2009), 'The Futures of the City Region', *Regional Studies*, 43 (6): 777–787.

Newfield, C. (2003), *Ivy and Industry: Business and the Making of the American University: 1880—1980*, Durham and London: Duke University Press.

Odin, J.K. and Manicas, P.T. (eds.) (2004), *Globalization and Higher Education*, Honolulu: University of Hawaii Press.

Pels, D. (2003), *Unhastening Science: Autonomy and Reflexivity in the Social Theory of Knowledge*, Liverpool: Liverpool University Press.

Perry, B. (2006), 'Science, society and the university: a paradox of values?', *Social Epistemology*, 20 (3–4): 201–219.

Perry, B. (2007), 'The multi-level governance of science policy in England', *Regional Studies*, 41 (8): 1051–1067.

Pickstone, J.V. (2000), *Ways of Knowing: A New History of Science, Technology and Medicine*, Manchester: Manchester University Press.

Piganiol, P. (1991), 'Laying the foundations of French science policies', *Science and Public Policy*, 18 (1): 23–30.

Pollitt, C. (2016), *Advanced Introduction to Public Management and Administration*, Cheltenham; Edward Elgar.

Pusser, B. and Turner, S.E. (2004), 'Nonprofit and for-profit governance in higher education', in Ehrenberg, R.G. (ed.) *Governing Academia*, Ithaca, NY: Cornell University Press.

Radder, H. (ed.) (2010), *The Commodification of Academic Research*, Pittsburgh, PA: University of Pittsburgh Press.

Resnik, D.B. (2010), 'Financial Interests and the Norms of Academic Science', in Radder, H. (ed.) *The Commodification of Academic Research*, Pittsburgh, PA: University of Pittsburgh Press.

Ritzer, G. (2015), *The McDonaldization of Society*, 8th revised edition, Thousand Oaks, California: Sage.

Ruivo, B. (1994), 'Phases' or 'paradigms' of science policy?', *Science and Public Policy*, 21 (3): 157–164.

Russell Group (2015), 'Engines of growth: the impact of research at Russell Group universities'.

Russo, A.P., van den Berg, L. and Lavanga, M. (2007), 'Toward a sustainable relationship between city and university: a stakeholdership approach', *Journal of Planning Education and Research*, 27 (2): 199–216.

Salet, W., Kreukels, A. and Thornley, A. (eds.) (2003), *Metropolitan Governance and Spatial Planning: Comparative Case Studies of European City-regions*, Aldershot: E and FN Spon.

Schütte, F. and Van der Sijde, P. (2000), *The University and its Region: Examples of Regional Development from the European Consortium of Innovative Universities*, Twente University Press.

Scott, A.J. (2000), *The Cultural Economy of Cities*, London: Sage.

Slaughter, S. and Rhoades, G. (2004), *Academic Capitalism and the New Economy: Markets, States, and Higher Education*, Baltimore, Maryland: Johns Hopkins University Press.

Stehr, N. (1994), *Knowledge Societies*, London: Sage.

Swyndegouw, E. (1992), 'The mammon quest: "glocalisation", interspatial competition and the monetary order - the construction of new scales', in Dunford, M. and Kafkalas, G. (eds.) *Cities and Regions in the New Europe*, New York: Belhaven Press.

Van der Sijde, P.C. and Schutte, F. (2000), 'The university and its region – an introduction', in Schutte, F. and Van der Sijde, P. (2000), *The University and its Region: Examples of Regional Development from the European Consortium of Innovative Universities*, Enschede: Twente University Press.

Wagner, P. (2004), 'Higher education in an era of globalization: what is at stake?', in Odin, J.K. and Manicas, P.T. (eds.) *Globalization and Higher Education*, Honolulu: University of Hawaii Press.

Wiewel, W. and Perry, D.C. (eds.) (2008), *Global Universities and Urban Development: Case Studies and Analysis*, New York: M.E. Sharpe.

Wilks-Heeg, S., Perry, B. and Harding, A. (2003), 'Metropolitan regions in Europe: regimes, rescaling or repositioning?', in Salet, W., Kreukels, A. and Thornley, A. (eds.) *Metropolitan Governance and Spatial Planning: Comparative Case Studies of European City-regions*, Aldershot: E and FN Spon.

Williams, G. (2016), 'Higher education: public good or private commodity?', *London Review of Education*, 14 (1): 131–142.

Willmott, H. (2011), 'Journal list fetishism and the perversion of scholarship: reactivity and the ABS list', *Organization*, 18 (4): 429–442.

Wong, C., Choi, C-J. and Millar, C. (2006), 'The case of Singapore as a knowledge-based city', in Carillo, F. (ed.) *Knowledge Cities: Approaches, Experiences and Perspectives*, Oxford: Butterworth-Heinemann.

Work Foundation (2006), *Ideopolis: Knowledge City-Regions*, London: The Work Foundation.

Yigitcanlar, T., Velibeyoglu, K. and Baum, S. (eds.) (2008), *Knowledge-Based Urban Development: Planning and Applications in the Information Era*, London: IGI Global.

5

KNOWING THE CITY

Introduction

We have examined how cities and universities mediate global pressures in the knowledge economy. Whilst the city and university construct particular views of what counts as knowledge in these circumstances, what results is an under-examination of the relationship between expertise and the city, the expectations of knowledge and how dominant ways of knowing the city reinforce a particular approach to urban development. This chapter aims to address this deficit. Without such an understanding in place, the viability of alternatives is diminished.

To undertake this analysis we discuss what knowledge is valued in urban development and argue that the 21st century city has been predicated on particular forms of technocratic and economic knowledge. Expectations of knowledge within and outside universities are to address issues, but certain ones are prioritised over others. What we see is a tendency towards data, rather than intelligence, and quick fixes, rather than understanding and learning, being prioritised. We examine the ways in which a narrow understanding of expertise and knowledge is reproduced in elite, epistemic groups. We then turn to the spatial dimensions of expertise and present a typology for understanding the relationship between excellence, relevance and scale. Here we find narrow understanding of expertise and its relationship to scale and, as with the last chapter, this provides us with a basis upon which to consider alternative possibilities in university-city relations in the third part of the book.

Knowledge matters

The idea that the urban exists as a self-sufficient entity has become taken for granted through the practices of those politicians who have sought global status for their cities through a bounded conception of territory. Such a formulation assumes there is a coherent entity into which is poured the perpetuation of growth through a denial of 'causal responsibility' (Garvey 2008). A technological view of innovation that emphasises linearity, products, outputs and patents, or an economic view extracted from the social, cultural and political will not result in improvements in our cities, nor denial or indifference to the effects of global warming. Epistemic hierarchies exist through which this is perpetuated, in which knowledge for understanding outside narrowly defined agendas is valued less than the attributed value of commercially exploitable technological outputs and the perpetuation of highly limited models of human behaviour.

How can this be explained? A clear tendency in urban development has been to allude to particular forms of technocratic and economic knowledge with judgements of benefit to particular groups and organisations, accompanied by assumptions of 'radiated' or 'trickle-down' effects. That idea has been widely discounted: "If the top 1 per cent actually created more jobs as they became wealthier, then ordinary people would be surrounded by employment opportunities in both the US and the UK" (Dorling 2014: 23). Danny Dorling charts clear reductions in inequality when the state intervenes through taxation and a curtailment on bonus payments, to ensure greater equity. With stagnancy in aggregate demand increasing over time in rich countries – with what there was provided through credit – less could be made out of producing goods. Thus, we see a movement towards the increasing power of finance; in other words, those who make money out of money. With such a shift in national income going to the rich we would expect to see an increase in spending. However, this does not occur due to an overall lower proportion of their income being spent: "*This means that 'trickle-down' arguments are wrong.* Yes, the rich employ a few servants and provide demands for accountants, tax advisors and luxury services, but far fewer jobs result from this that would be the case if their income were redistributed back to ordinary people with a much higher propensity to consume" (Sayer 2015: 121. Original italics). The need to reduce inequality in order to increase the overall quality of life in society is clear (Latouche 2009; Wilkinson and Pickett 2010).

Against this backdrop, in the forms of urban development we have charted in this book, knowledge is poured and filtered according to frames that constitute what is admissible and useful. These frames bracket political-redistributive issues that are ignored or denied in favour of administrative-allocative functions. Necessity of action is attributed to aspects of the urban domain, in all of its various manifestations, through invoking particular values that work to saturate, displace and devalue alternatives. These dynamics reflect the relations between facts and values where, in the rise of positivism, facts were substituted for values as if the two could be separated. The promise saturates the value of alternatives as it becomes a factual necessity in the image of particular ideas of what the economy is and how it must operate. What we find is action orientated to 'success', rather than 'understanding' (Habermas 1981). Action orientated to success is measured by the supposed rules of rational choice, while action orientated to understanding takes place through the work of communication. That materialises by the mutual and cooperative effort of understanding amongst collective participants. It is this distinction which preserves what is necessary to constitute understanding and does not collapse the construction of human behaviour into narrow and destructive neoliberal frames. These models of human behaviour remove the realities from the world and it is this image that informs what is to count as 'legitimate' knowledge. As the financier George Soros puts it: "The assumption of independently given conditions of supply and demand eliminates the possibility of any reflexive interaction" (1998: 38).

We are dealing with the collapse of different forms of knowledge through the dominance of a belief that seeks to saturate all before it. Take political knowledge. It is concerned with the strategy of social action and the spontaneous and reflective knowledge that informs that and whose intention is to contribute to the denunciation of the established doxa (Bourdieu 1992; Gurvitch 1971). Such knowledge is: "a combination of value judgement and judgements of fact, this political knowledge nevertheless could not be reduced to a profession of faith, *since it is first and foremost knowledge*: a very precise and realistic knowledge concerning opposing forces and the settings in which such action occurs. Political knowledge implies, therefore, clear awareness of difficulties to be overcome, and an acute sense of the action to be taken in any social situation" (Gurvitch 1971: 31. Original italics). That is displaced in the processes we have described.

Political knowledge inspires action aimed at change and informs calculations concerning possibilities and perhaps even when to withdraw from the political field. It comprises knowledge of the group ('we') to which one belongs as well as the Other, along with elements of common sense, technical knowledge and aspects of social reality manifest in 'global conjunctures' (Gurvitch 1971: 32). Once turned into an ideology that fails to see its assumptions it works to blinker, denounce, ignore and deny. Enormous energies go into the avoidance of alternative ways of seeing as if there were some 'natural order' to existing states of affairs. Such ideology disguises itself in the name of the real. The promise of knowledge encapsulated in relation to the economy represents a powerful dream that parks the present in the name of a future. Through its restrictions, omissions and supposed openness, it ends up being relatively uncontested, leaving only debate about the technical means to achieve the dream. It is not the visible spectacle of particular acts and their consequences that are amplified to us in its operation, but a sustained vision manifest in the mundane routinisations that replaces ends with means and obliterates alternative values through: "bracketing the 'end' or drawing it back into the system of pure means in such a way that the end is merely the empty aim of realizing these particular means" (Jameson 2013: 239).

Combining feeling and knowledge serves as assurance against ambivalence enabling that which is not regarded as 'feasible' in terms of alternative ends, to be discounted. We can see this form of control in Stan Cohen's vision when he writes: "The atmosphere is calm. Everyone present knows that no amount of criticism of individual treatment methods, no empirical research, no dodo-bird verdicts can slow the work down. The reverse is true. The more negative the results, the more manic and baroque the enterprise of selection becomes" (1985: 185). Whilst he is referring to the professionalisation of the penal system, this is the vision for the knowledge economy. More is needed: more information; more consultancy reports about the potential of the promise; more marketing; more opportunities for science parks; more global measures of excellence; more cultural attractions for the knowledge workers and more connectivity to the global without which the abstract oxygen of the whole enterprise would leave us lagging and starved.

To achieve this means the deployment of technical knowledge. Here we find a form of knowledge that is: "*concerned with every kind of effective manipulation – artificial and subordinate, but tending to become independent and valued as such – precise, transmissible, and innovative, its acquisition is inspired by the desire to dominate the worlds of nature, humanity, and society, in order to produce, destroy, safeguard, organize, plan communicate and disseminate*" (Gurvitch 1971: 29. Original italics). With the power of the conjunction of image and the making of a reality in order to overcome the present we are left with a peculiar mixture of utopia and dystopia. For some, that means we need to take a different starting point for critique which: "should not begin with critiquing reality, but with the critique of our dreams" (Žižek 2014: 193).

The dream is apparent in target-driven mentalities that produce particular preferences for data over intelligence which concerns the use of knowledge in context. Yet it is that context which is problematic as it falls into a realm of understanding informed by the image. The emphasis on technical solutions, rather than the work of understanding and learning, adds to a sense of disempowerment among those urban populations who are excluded in voice and participation, but sometimes included in attributions of eventual gratitude over the 'medium term'. Through the narrow deployment of concepts of expertise and its relationship to place, this technocracy is transforming the nature of democracy from a politics of sovereign citizens to a politics of diffused experts in which electoral struggle is replaced by expert bodies and specialised technical discourse (Turner 2003). We are seeing a disjuncture between analysis and deliberation that is part of the dislike of democracy that informs neoliberalism and those who sell simplistic solutions through populist means.

Armed with a permanent possibility based on particular imaginary futures, politicians and officials can readily turn to the instrumental-technical mode of operation whereby ever-greater amounts of information are gathered about 'performance' in a sidelining of justification over application (May and Perry 2006). Recognition and analysis of crisis may be averted through processes of meticulous data gathering by armies of technicians who provide the grounds for growth as everyone is 'moving forward'. These ready-made pieces of scientism relieve their recipients of critical analysis through the provision of information that slips from political decision-making to constructed necessities in order to monitor the economy and attract the talent and companies for future urban vitality and viability. The tendency for public, democratic deliberations to take place diminishes and public sector organisational efforts aim to create private sector benefits as if they were a 'magic pill' for the diagnosis of economic ills. A frenetic set of activities may be constructed around servicing in the guise of a quiet and sustained production of information gathering. Accompanying this is a particular view of the formulation of policy. That is often translated into the less polemically stated problem of 'policy-based evidence' leading to the view that politics is: "so pathological that no decision is based on an appeal to scientific evidence if it gets in the way of politicians seeking election" (Cairney 2015: 3).

Differences in the relative autonomy that cities have with their states exist, but they are increasingly seeking to act on a global stage and that sets a hierarchy among them. Within them, centralised command and control models in which communication over the conception of policy is taken as a prerogative is common. A model of action is then posited that separates the information from which the policy draws from the social and economic conditions under and through it will be enacted in given localities (May and Marvin 2009). It then becomes the promotion of exceptionality, rather than collective capacity, that rules the day and acts as an impediment to the creation of such cultures and this is ably assisted by the forms of knowledge that go into justifying this process. What is lost is the opportunity to examine the value of different types of knowledge in terms of the speed, content and context of their production, transmission and reception. A triumph of process and product, over that of purpose, drives this forward with the overall result being that the relations between the 'why' and 'how' of knowledge are subsumed within the narrow confines of 'what' measures (May 2001).

We have a narrow, selective view for which we are paying a high price. The idea of focussing upon the optimal means of allocating scarce resources to ensure the production and distribution of commodities starts to look rather weak when it comes to the destruction of natural resources, huge inequalities and injustice. Economics has adapted to this by treating information as a commodity, along with new means of measuring knowledge, managing knowledge and seeking to secure or utilise tacit knowledge and so on. That is based upon an idea of the individual person with which we currently work and that forges so much contemporary thinking and practice. In one historical study of this relationship in the West we reach a 'disturbing moment' in contemporary times where several factors combine: a reduction of historical understanding, an endorsement of market economics and a retreat into private spheres at the expense of civic spirit and political participation (Siedentop 2015). The constructions of people as rationally calculating according to individual preferences has been exposed as highly limited (Etzioni 1990; Pratten 2014) with the failure of the form of economics that feeds this view being placed at the door of: "often quite irrelevant, typically formalistic, methods and techniques which economists naively and unthinkingly wield in a forlorn hope of thereby gaining illumination of a social world that they do not 'fit'" (Lawson 1998: 169).

Instead of confronting that issue, it is turned into mechanical means of filtration and framing and new laws of intellectual property are not uncommon answers. In turn, they constitute new boundaries in order that it is scarce again and so the reproduction of competitive advantage continues apace. Without the idea of an autonomous economic sphere, the edifice collapses. Its perpetuation produces anomalies that are so evident around us. What we are dealing with here is not so much a need for an economics of things, but one of attention: "Information purchases must assess the informational signal, the category of information the perceiver is prepared to perceive, the motivational structure that animates the communication, and the global assumptions about the human world within which human communication takes place. In an economics of attention, we must ask not only how people go about achieving their goals but where the goals come from. Economics in an information economy is about how choices of attention are made and thus, about human motive" (Lanham 2007: 180). It is to these motives in the context of academic practices in the university that we now turn.

Expertise and the university

Writing on reform and resistance in the American university, Louis Menand charts the changes in higher education and asks some uncomfortable questions of the professors within these institutions. Different training, changes in what is culturally important in terms of the production and audience for knowledge and the role of interdisciplinarity, are just some of the issues he considers. A balance also needs to be maintained between universities and those who see in them reward and potential which does not simply replicate a basis of exchange informed by supply and demand. One consequence, for example, is that knowledge becomes nothing more than a justification for preexisting preferences and we have seen where that takes us! With such issues in mind, his conclusions remain of considerable importance: "Academics need to look to the world to see what kind of teaching and research needs to be done, and how they might better train and organize themselves to do it. But they need to ignore the world's demand that they reproduce its self-image" (Menand 2010: 158).

Resistance to the image of the knowledge economy is understandable. There are a variety of opinions on the desirability for such changes. For some, the distinction of the university from other sites of knowledge production is the provision of more sustained periods of contemplation in an age in which there is a frenetic search for adaptation to new demands that are taken as self-evident, rather than subjected to sustained scrutiny. If universities are not able to provide legitimacy for the distinction of the knowledge they produce relative to other sites such as consultancies, think tanks and the research and development arms of multinational companies, then their absorption into the neoliberal mainstream seems guaranteed. As communities of communication which informs their distinction, universities reflect the pragmatic idea of cooperation as a basis for preventing them from succumbing to the pressures of increasing competition. In line with such a view, advances in understanding, of which knowledge is a part, is argued to be valuable for its own sake (Graham 2005), whilst 'useless' knowledge is seen as vital for the cultivation of a contemplative mind (Russell 2004).

The consequences of commercialisation have been raised for some time now and responding to the needs of governments, industry and 'customers' have been embodied in the idea of 'academic capitalism' (Slaughter and Leslie 1997). Pressures on established methods of management and governance and implications for the cultures of universities, in terms of revised systems of remuneration and reward, evaluations of worth and status and a heightened degree of individualisation, easily lead to the undermining of any sense of collegiality (Harloe and Perry 2005; May and Perry 2013). As Chris Shore and Susan Wright observed of the consequences of the introduction of an audit culture in universities: "University lecturers have always been flexible workers: adaptable, multi-skilled, self-managed and largely self-driven professionals who are willing to work far longer hours that they are contractually obliged to do. What is perverse and counter-productive about the new audit culture is that it militates precisely against that kind of professionalism" (2000: 79).

How are academics positioned in the processes and what are the conditions that inform their reproduction? On the one hand academics are at the frontier of the mania of the knowledge economy. Ideas generated in the academy have been instrumental in the formation of the knowledge economy (Kenway et al. 2006). As we noted in Part I, the management scholar Peter Drucker is credited with coining the terms 'knowledge worker' and 'knowledge work' in the 1950s. Fritz Machlup, an economist at Princeton, produced an analysis of the production and distribution of knowledge in the US economy which was subsequently popularised by Clark Kerr in 1963. In the 1980s, academics in the Science Policy Research Unit at Sussex University emphasised the role of innovation as a driver in economic growth drawing on Schumpetarian ideas. 'New Growth Theory' (Romer 1986), the 'Mode 1/Mode 2' thesis (Gibbons et al. 1994) and the 'Triple Helix' (Etzkowitz 2008) are all examples of how academic analysis is not only reflecting the knowledge economy but may also be actively constituting its promise.

In a special edition of *Ephemera* (2008: 273–274), discussions between Stephen Dunne, Stefano Harney, Martin Parker and Tony Tinker reveal the following: the right-wing nature of most American business schools and "implicit denigration of all state and 'social' interests that might stand opposed to the accumulation process"; how business schools position themselves as the voices of 'labour' or 'capital' and the interrelationships between universities and the reproduction of capital. Business schools are dubbed the 'Trojan Schools' of modern capitalism and there are limits to how critical management studies can productively engage and transform these wider forces. Little wonder that business schools and technological universities want states to invest in innovation and technology transfer to realise the promise of the knowledge-based economy. We do not know the motives and beliefs of these academics, nor can we easily distinguish between those that see their role as analysing the world and those that are peddling models to further their own careers. Some are uncomfortable with the way in which their works have been taken up: for example, Sheila Nowotny, Peter Scott and Michael Gibbons regard their thesis as having been misappropriated and manipulated, leading to a need: "to reach beyond the knowable context of application to the unknowable context of implication" (Nowotony et al. 2003: 192).

The practices of academics are frequently justified according to the exercise of academic autonomy which, itself, would mean insulation from the effects of the knowledge economy and thus the potential for the production of alternative forms of knowledge. If, however, we place this belief under scrutiny, the idealised picture starts to melt away. We have seen how these institutions have adapted in varying ways to the environment of which they are a part and this means that: "If the defenders of academic freedom only attend to its abrogations, they will not see the ways it is foreclosed" (Butler 2006: 16). To resist these pressures, we should be clear about several questions: what is being resisted, under what circumstances, utilising what resources and working with whom to produce the potential for alternatives? Yet here is a double-edged issue: on the one hand, universities provide a distance from necessity that enables alternative types of analysis to emerge from those that typify the urban policy practices we have charted and on the other, that very distance can anaesthetise researchers from what really matters to urban populations.

If the university provides an environment as a basis of knowledge about the world that is not available in other sites of activity, then those within the university must also work at the social conditions of their practice in order to obtain a distance from that world as an object of knowledge, whilst also being engaged in the issues of that world. As we have seen, universities are part of the knowledge economy and share the practices that are apparently 'external' to them. Once we admit of this relationship, we can see how a 'genuine epistemology' can be: "built on knowledge of the social conditions under which scientific schemata actually function" and autonomy "does not come without the social conditions of autonomy; and these conditions cannot be obtained on an individual basis" (Bourdieu in Bourdieu and Wacquant 1992: 178, 183). It is for these reasons that we have written about the importance of understanding the varying degrees of 'epistemic permeability' that exist between and within institutions and disciplines in order to understand the enabling and constraining conditions associated with institutional boundaries (May with Perry 2011).

Boundaries, analysis and democracy

The institutional boundaries of scientific practice given by the university cannot be assumed in the current age. Further, through insulation, scholastic reasoning can lay claim to expertise and the associated recognition among peers and those urban elites who accord their knowledge with status. It is a powerful attractor for those who wish to amplify recognition for their exceptionality. Indeed, it is from within universities that ideas often emerge that only serve to feed the insatiable appetite for knowledge which knows no bounds. In current circumstances, therefore, to look towards academic positions as a basis for engaged critique is problematic without an examination of those contexts from which the critique is constructed and its relationship to how it is produced and for whom. When we raise these questions we find a reflexive paradox: as critique gets close to the familiar, it activates a strong reaction that often leads to the preservation of the status quo (May and Perry 2013; 2017).

As universities promote their place in the global economy, academics that are apparently critical of such aspirations easily reproduce exactly those same ones in celebration of their own expertise through a simple separation between content and context. Indeed, there is much to be gained from this activity for those busy empiricists whose work is divorced from overt discussions of purpose and value. A technicism divorcing content from context, which characterises the knowledge economy, exists in the university with a resulting change in the locus of control. As a quote from this study indicates, this much was apparent as the beginning of the 21st century and it has increased in intensity since that time: "Greater stress on data recording, on procedures and systems, and on the formal appraisal of academic work meant that this work was more open to scrutiny by administrators as well as by senior academic management and academics' own heads of department" (Henkel 2000: 253). What is added to here is the supposed neutrality of organisational measures in which values are assumed to be displaced; all of which is ably assisted by the assumption that they are trans-local (Smith 1999) and thus feed into the constant comparisons in global league tables of 'excellence'.

As with the practices of the knowledge economy, these forms of objectivism become their own justification with criticism being denounced for it questions the very presuppositions upon which mundane, institutional decision-making processes are based. It also questions the prerogatives of those who hold 'strategic positions' in these institutions and whose rewards are measured in their salaries based upon an exceptionality manifest in 'executive' decision-making. Academic practitioners are often bewildered in the face of these organisational politics in which administrative practices work to depoliticise issues and withdrawal, denial and retreat are frequent reactions. At the same time as these organisational knowledges are produced, researchers opt, consciously or by default, for schools of thought, thinkers and techniques of investigation in order to frame issues that enable explanations to arise for particular phenomena. Indeed, entire careers are built upon the investigation of highly specific and narrow fields of interest. What we then see is a 'generative dance' (Cook and Brown 1999) embodied in a separation in universities between organisational knowing and the knowledge produced by academics about the world beyond its institutional boundaries.

By not thinking about these ways of thinking, a researcher constitutes objects of investigation within frames of justification that enable particular explanations and outcomes. Yet the effort of understanding this process and the relations between the content of work and the contexts of its production is part of an intellectual disposition to excavate taken-for-granted assumptions in order to generate new ways of framing and explaining. Ultimately, it seems, research is caught between a dynamic conservatism that reproduces itself through the actions of individual researchers who claim to be at the cutting edge of knowledge production and a critical disposition that refuses to regurgitate supposed truisms and opts, instead, to problematise dominant modes of working in the name of positive transformations. Separating the content of what is produced from the context in which it occurs is a frequent occurrence through a celebration of an insulated expertise that perpetuates an abstract individualism.

We have argued that the promise of the knowledge economy is driven by an image that is real in its effects for the development of cities, but which benefits a few to the detriment of the majority. Particular types of practice, combined with forms of knowledge, are selective in framing views of the economy and the trajectory of urban development. Our focus has been not only upon the political climate that has led to this, with an emphasis upon an increasing encroachment into all areas of life, but also the ubiquity of the promise leading to both its persuasive power and associated benefits to those who gain from this process. The discourse is thus significant in its omnipresence as it signifies a container for potentiality that mobilises particular interests. Like all ideals, therefore, it possesses an allure to business, city politicians and policymakers and acts as a panacea for contemporary problems whose solutions are assumed to be contained in some future state. It is through allusion to such potentiality that concerted efforts to ameliorate the issues of the present can easily be suspended, or avoided. The attributed power to knowledge tends to be focussed upon the economic and technological as if these were separate spheres of activity from the social, cultural and political whilst, simultaneously, seeking to populate and colonise those spheres of life their name. That results in a particular framing of issues bolstered by an army of experts producing justifications.

In this context, to produce work for urban elites can easily feed an antidemocratic impulse. Whilst it is not within the domain of research to confuse the content of research with its consequences for how others might live, we need different forums to discuss and debate ideas, as well as examine their implications for actions beyond the narrow confines of policymakers and academics. That means taking the relations between analysis and deliberation seriously by using the university as a 'third space' whose distinction lies in bringing together different voices and forms of knowledge. To practise a radical agenda of this type within a university is highly problematic and requires different forms of working and organisation. When those do occur, institutional absorption is a typical response when faced with anomalous practices or innovative programmes of work (see, for example, Messer-Davidow 2002; Perry and May 2015), as well as censorship if perceived as a threat (Price 2004).

The challenge needs to be directed at the circuits perpetuated by environmental expectations of particular forms of knowledge. We have also argued that for reflexivity to flourish, institutional and occupational practices can be improved to enable a diversity of roles within supportive cultures. If pushed too far, however, the results will be counter-productive. Reducing everything to its utility in terms of performing an operation on the world undermines the importance of the status of knowledge produced in a distance from that world. It is for this and other reasons that the distinction of what is produced in universities, in diverse ways, is so important for their future and that of societies as a whole. The issue is not to collapse them, nor to assume that they are simply separated through sealed boundaries. As we have said, a great deal of boundary work goes on, consciously and otherwise, to create this distance from particular forces. How forms of knowledge interact and learn from one another, how we learn in terms of taking our background assumptions into an object for contemplation and seeing how things and people are connected, are central to a general understanding of ourselves through others and in the environments we inhabit.

Disciplinary consequences ensue from these discussions. We have used 'science' so far in its broadest sense without disciplinary specification, to incorporate the social sciences, arts and humanities. Yet differential value is attached to types of knowledge and expertise in the context of the pressures we have described. Practices within the physical sciences have tended to be more greatly valued in terms of their potential economic benefits thus far, despite recognition of their intangible and uncertain outcomes at different time frames. Doubt remains over the proportion of viable spin-outs that can be created in the life sciences vis-à-vis the huge investments needed, whilst issues of what are called market failures necessitate public financing (Nightingale and Martin 2004; Department for Business, Innovation and Skills 2010). The potential contributions of the social sciences, arts and humanities cannot be ignored, despite the assumption that they are on the 'softer' side of innovation processes, for they demonstrate the need for context-sensitivity and the importance of tacit and embodied knowledge as well as that which is codified and explicit. Not only disciplines, but broader epistemologies are at stake in terms of the value attached to different forms of knowing. In the meantime, models triumph over the mundane; the tangible over the intangible; outputs over understanding processes and outcomes; and narrow ideas of measurement over the generation of understanding.

We can move back to the 17th century to find insights that assist our contemporary understanding. Giambattista Vico was critical of those who take particular methods and insights and overextend them into domains in which they are inapplicable. He was not against science, but scientism. Disciplinary specialism was of importance, but when specialism was applied to areas that were foreign to understanding this was due to: "weakness of our nature, which prompts us to take inordinate delight in ourselves and in our own pursuits" (Vico 1990: 80). Excessive attention to the supply of information and the feeding of particular aspirations in the current political climate works to relieve politicians and experts who benefit from processes that should be part of public, political discourse, not disguised as technical-instrumental modes of reasoning. As Vico put it: "We neglect that discipline which deals with the differential features of the virtues and vices, with good and bad behaviour-patterns, with the typical characteristics of the various ages of man, of the two sexes, of social and economic class, race and nation, and with the art of seemly conduct in life, the most difficult of all arts. As a consequence of this neglect, a noble and important branch of studies, i.e., the science of politics, lies almost abandoned and untended" (Vico 1990: 33).

Excellence and relevance in the game of scales

Universities are often typified as pursuing some medieval conception of their role in present times. Whilst an inaccurate characterisation, it is born of the idea that universities should be measured by the usefulness of their outcomes to business in terms of exploitable products, their abilities to attract the praise of the rich and to add to the stock of human capital to enhance competitiveness. Here we find the language of academic 'excellence' as part of the same pursuit we find in the knowledge economy: "excellence is an attempt to redefine and reconstruct the economic/cultural terrain, and to 'win' social subjects to new conceptions of themselves – to turn them into 'winners', 'champions' and 'everyday heroes'" (du Gay 1996: 67). It is part of the same 'dream work' we found earlier, because it is not just the deployment of technical knowledge, but seeks to connect with everyday experience in organisations and works as an idea that can appeal across different motivations. Who would not want to be 'excellent'! "Through deployment of the vocabulary of enterprise, excellence appears to have established a 'translatability' between the economic objectives of employers and managers of capital, changing political rationalities, and the capacities of the self" (du Gay 1996: 68). In the face of such pressures the lure of institutional insulation can appear enticing.

Despite this lure, realities are often different. A frenetic journal output mentality informs the pursuit of advancement up the academic career ladder; all of which takes place in cultures that exhibit differing forms of support that, in turn, are informed by the degrees of institutional shelter provided from immediate wider forces. Such forces include not only changes in funding, but profound shifts in how knowledge has been conceptualised and treated and the assumptions made for its potential transformative effects on modes of understanding and production. Occupational cultures promoting excellence then appear to sit at odds with the demand for immediate relevance. A focus on relevance, after all, appears to sit at odds with excellence-driven basic research. The latter is taken to be one-step removed from the varying constructions of 'necessity' and 'usefulness'. Research funding, whether through national research council systems or otherwise, practises forms of justification on the basis of supporting the 'best research' with quality control assessed through peer review accompanied, where necessary, by statements of worth and impact. 'Excellence', within an international community of scholars, has formed the criteria for justifying whether research should be funded in any given area with accompanying evaluation mechanisms for assessing its 'impact' and merit.

Within the excellence paradigm other criteria for the justification or application of knowledge are not deemed to be so significant compared to relevance. A by-product of research may be economic or social relevance, but it has certainly not normally been the dominant funding rationale itself. With changes in this trend, however, the impartiality of knowledge is at risk. Whilst critique has been levelled at the biases in peer review systems, based on personal networks and entrenched cultural prejudices, or the extent to which objective knowledge is itself a realistic ambition, a widespread acceptance of peer review as the best available means of guaranteeing scientific excellence still prevails (see Lamont 2009). A connection between *relevant* and *relative* knowledge is often made in academic cultures. That works to devalue the former by rendering it more contestable than knowledge produced through the excellence mode informed by being of international quality which itself is far from unproblematic: for example, who is to judge the merit of translating cross-national research – domestic or foreign peers? (Fuller 2002).

Blurring these boundaries, can also have its effects. Bringing different judgements together for the purpose of demonstrating consensus regarding the importance of research can easily go against innovative work, thereby reproducing the status quo. Such processes themselves, whilst also boundaries to protect research, are not immune from the idea of reproduction that we have outlined. As the demands for relevance through such measurements as 'impact' increase, criteria stem from a range of possible sources: the strategic-military interests of states; attributed economic interests of commerce; the political interests of parties or the social interests of various groups. The view that relevance implies the involvement of different interests in the research process and therefore a 'contamination' may be commonly held. At the same time, concerns for relevance, along with recognition of its inherent contestability, involves a greater degree of preparedness to enter into a domain of uncertainty with its corresponding challenges to the attributed value of expertise bounded within particular disciplines, groups and organisations.

The trends in environmental pressures we have outlined drive, fund, shape and validate work. That requires reflection not only between and within academic communities, but also the individual researcher and assumptions concerning what is constituted as the 'outside world' according to the contexts in which they work. As relevance criteria grow in importance, the disjuncture between content and context becomes ever more problematic for an academic identity that is based on the pursuit of excellence as judged by particular peers. Context increasingly informs not only what work is funded, but how it is performed, the increasing number of organisational processes through which it is attempted to be captured and the conditions in which value judgements about its ultimate worth are made. Although not within the control of particular researchers, processes that lose sight or ignore these issues only exacerbate the problems.

Questions that define the boundaries of work are not only what research, but how, why, with whom and where? Within the bounds of relevance, problems can be set and solved in the context of application, widely understood as being outside the university. Within the excellence paradigm, practices of professionally defined closure are taken to operate that enable degrees of separation between justification and application. Yet contexts of knowledge production are spatial. Indeed, it is at the local or regional level that the dynamics of different knowledge capitalisms, from policy conceptualisation to conditions of production, are most apparent.

Whilst regions and cities are devoting increasing resources to participating in the knowledge economy, the aspiration here is that excellence and relevance can come together in particular contexts; in other words, the 'embedding' of academic institutions and scientific expertise can occur in particular places. In the face of these pressures, context becomes a conduit in which issues of politico-economic, institutional and disciplinary affiliations react and collide.

As context shapes content, so the reverse is true. The increased economic and social relevance attached to knowledge leads a plethora of actors, whether within national states, regional or local environments or university governance structures, to consider the relative strengths and weaknesses of the preexisting knowledge base. Across Europe we see efforts to reshape regional and local identities through harnessing the 'brand' power of science and technology both for the purpose of local economic development and crisis management (Brenner 2004). We can draw a contrast between a neoliberal acceptance of the spatial consequences of excellence-driven investments in science and technology and a social-democratic approach to managing out conflicts that arise between potentially conflicting policy objectives. If we find short-circuits between expert analysis and policy formulation in the absence of democratic deliberation, the reproduction of the status quo is a likely outcome.

The conditions we have charted lead to differing dimensions in the excellence-relevance relationship. Those dimensions, in turn, affect the contexts in which urban research is produced. Parallels are evident between the aspiration to be globally excellent in research terms through the development of typologies of urban comparison and the trend in urban benchmarking. In the latter, think tanks, media, university communications divisions and business interests can all work together to produce reports on competitiveness and quality of life indices. Of course, we are dealing with trends. These are tendencies that lead to particular effects and those, in turn, produce conflicting results. One way in which these are manifest lies in the dimension between excellent and relevant knowledge. To understand this in more detail, we can identify five dimensions whose dynamics shadow the knowledge city through, in particular, the interactions that take place between space and place and content and context.

First, we can identify a *disembedded excellence*. This may be seen as traditionally non-spatial with the idea of place being firmly in the background through amenability to the idea of global logics through international comparison. It is frequently manifest in dispositions towards both theoreticism and empiricism. The 'scholastic fallacy' in knowledge production (Bourdieu 2000) consists of conflating practical with theoretical reason (Bourdieu 1998). Empiricist-based allusions are also evident in international indices through which cities are placed in hierarchies according to their abilities to exhibit particular characteristics according to their ability to live up to particular visions. This process of knowledge production divorces content from context and such admission would be assumed to undermine the universal applicability of what is produced. Those residing in so-called 'world leading' institutions find themselves in positions that enable this route to be deployed more easily as they often perpetuate, or generate, the ideas upon which the promise itself is based – as centres of excellence for others to emulate. Distributive issues become secondary to quality as judged by peer review for which recognition is explicitly sought. Many academics have a clear stake in the reproduction of this form of practice as it celebrates content and the mobility of expertise with less concern for context. A relational understanding easily evaporates in the process and the idea of an absolute space in which excellence flourishes, reigns. Contextual experiences are admitted only insofar as they fit a more general standard of the promise of expertise-objectivism-scientism. Reflexive concerns regarding limits, values and other forms of knowing are relatively absent, ignored or sidelined as 'local' matters.

Second, there is *competitive relevance*. Here we find some parallels with the above in terms of the idea of space – particularly when it comes to the production of indicators of urban competitive success. However, this is manifest through a decontextualised interpretation of relevance that places emphasis upon application to specific socio-economic issues and strategic priorities as a precondition for global success. Therefore, it is the attributed value to the content of success which is prioritised over the context of its application, which is left to frequently bemused practitioners to tackle in the face of the aspirations and expectations of their political masters. A focus on technological innovation is symptomatic: research may be 'applied' but does not have a direct advantage to any particular community or group. Once again, context evaporates in favour of an exemplary politics that privileges the transferable model in a marketplace of ideas with a resulting: "nexus of media, public opinion and portable urban policy oriented around the competitive threat from other cities, and a discursive uniformity of intuitive urban comparability" (Gleeson 2014: 368). Any general talk of local implementation gaps easily lapses into an issue of local deficiency which is judged as insufficient by global aspirations. What is then required is a 'game-change' in attitudes and certainly not a questioning of the values of the entire enterprise.

Third, there is *relevant excellence*. Here we have a highlighting of the indirect benefits of science and technology to particular places and spaces. It does not relate to changes in processes of knowledge production, rather it seeks to exploit, extract and attract knowledge products and institutions for territorial benefit. Universities who position themselves as, or are seen as, significant economic actors in their own right in their localities can capture and exploit the product of research process through the construction of spin-offs or patents. The local or regional becomes a space of funding, with the consequence that it becomes a place that benefits through an indirect consequence of research activity. The promise is less an explicit spur to original action, but deployed to justify actions in the name of potential. Lower degrees of ambivalence are evident in the relations between the content of knowledge and the contexts of its enactment, but the expertise, as with our earlier forms, is 'contributory' and this: "enables those who have acquired it to *contribute* to the domain to which the expertise pertains: contributory experts have the ability to *do* things within the domain of expertise" (Collins and Evans 2009: 24. Original italics). It may tend towards the propositional end of knowledge, but is enabled through the attribution of promise to remould the contextual in the name of the imaginary of the global.

Fourth, *excellent relevance* is concerned with the generation of co-produced research priorities and agendas through linking content with context. The distinction between relevant-excellence and excellent-relevance is subtle but important: it is not the criteria of excellence that is at stake, rather the extent of interpenetration into processes of knowledge production itself and how it is understood among different parties that the benefits may be obtained. Issues associated with the integrity of process, divorced from product are taken seriously in this scenario. However, it is also the consequences of knowledge for significant actors/organisations that inform the impetus for the research itself. The type of expertise that exists here tends towards 'interactional' as the ground between the propositional contained in data sets and books: "Interactional expertise is, however, nearer to the informal than to the formal view. Interactional expertise is far from a set of propositions. Interactional expertise is mastery of the language of a domain, and mastery of any language, naturally occurring or specialist, requires enculturation within a linguistic community" (Collins and Evans 2009: 30). Knowledge is translated in taking context seriously, but without simply reflecting it, or being amenable to some supply and demand calculation. For all parties concerned, it is a challenge to the normal ways of production, reception and transmission in situations of 'active intermediation' between researchers and other communities (May and Perry 2017).

Finally, there *is contextual relevance*. Here we find research investments being driven by narrow political or economic objectives, with less concern for the quality or content of the work. An articulation of the relationship between science and regional economic development can only be found at the periphery of policy opinion. It is not a clearly expressed or implicitly held view, rather it works to inform a negative fear among certain epistemic communities that the growth of a regional dimension to science policy will lead to 'second-rate' science. Equally, it can lead to the capability to capture and mobilise resources at different spatial scales for the purposes of reproducing excellence in terms of the idea of 'untainted' interference from outside forces as a result of the mobilisation of institutional power. It is a preoccupation with contextual relevance that provokes a response from the scientific community regarding the importance of excellence and impartiality, as well as important discoveries that have been made through serendipity.

Disembedded excellence and competitive relevance frame the contours of the emerging neoliberal knowledge economy. They converge around an aspatial politics whereby we see a conjunction between commodification and the production of models of reality, as well as a distance from the urban realm and its communities. The dominant view is that place is of secondary value in the search for global success and any understanding of the contexts within which excellence or relevance can be built is limited and partial. In the face of these pressures, shelter is provided to urban research by those institutions who can position themselves as being relevant in the pursuit of excellence. Whilst clear intra-institutional differences exist between disciplines and where they are positioned within faculties as captured in the idea of 'degrees of epistemic permeability' (May with Perry 2011), particularly when it comes to levels of resource allocation, inter-institutional differences also play a significant role. Concern with the recognition of contingency within a city can be read as destiny and constructed as a threat to the pursuit of excellence. All have a stake in this pursuit if the institution provides a shelter from what are regarded as contaminants that derive from unwanted outside forces. The power of attributed value to activities may then work to inform a shelter for those disciplines and institutions whose relevance is taken to be derived from their excellence.

In traditional modes of knowledge production, justification is characterised as taking place within bounded communities with values being attributed to varying forms of knowledge and activities on the basis of norms and practices. Whilst epistemic permeability varies between disciplines, application can be absent, accidental or delegated but, importantly, not necessarily a direct part of the justification process itself. Increased pressures for relevant knowledge challenge these practices as concerns with application move into justification with implications for the reflexive practices that contribute to the distinction of the knowledge produced (May 2005). Those who move into the terrain of relevance, without due concern for the content and context in which knowledge is produced, can end up in a state of capitulation to the assumption that knowledge is a one-way street to be judged according to its contexts of application. The context-revising nature of knowledge and the efforts needed to make it work in those contexts are then bracketed and with that the potential for learning.

Increased demands for relevance and the importance of reflexivity point to the need to re-examine the relationship between the content and context of knowledge production (May and Perry 2017). Here, matters of institutional, spatial or socio-political contexts have often not been considered relevant factors in discussion on urban knowledge. It is perfectly possible to produce insightful discussions concerning epistemic cultures, but say relatively little about the institutional conditions, vis-à-vis the university and its environment, which shape the attribution of value to different knowledges (Knorr-Cetina 1999; May and Perry 2016). Equally, within the science, technology and society (STS) community, a situation can appear where context becomes everything, leading to a relativisation of knowledge claims the result of which is to collapse the justification for knowledge into the context of its discovery (Norris 2014). An understanding of why and how knowledge is taken up and translated in different contexts according to its content, then evaporates. In both of these cases, the content and context of knowledge has been divorced. Preoccupations have focussed either on micro-level analyses of processes of knowledge production or else on ideas of content without consideration of *what* knowledge is produced and *how* its reception is shaped and informed by particular conditions.

Excellence easily becomes a game in its own right, manifest in an emphasis on positioning in international league tables, emblematic science investments and the pursuit of prestige. The global is invoked as necessity by those within institutions who operate more like sport teams, seeking position as an indicator and demonstrator of capability. The result is a competitive situation in which an increasing concentration of research excellence in particular localities leads to a 'survival of the fittest' mentality, without due regard to the actual concentration of expertise, or even the benefits that places may derive from such an existence. The logic of the global finally meets the pursuit of excellence and this informs a pervasive managerialism within universities whose power can be bolstered by academic cultures seeking the same end (May and Perry 2013). The dominance of the disembedded excellence or competitive relevance discourse gives rise to assumptions about connections between research, teaching and third mission activities that dictate 'appropriate' measures of success for the university. Matters of organisational accountability are set according to targets; performance is judged by the ability to attract resources; economic impact is mediated through the production of spin-out companies, patents and the attraction of inward investment, whilst research and teaching scores are taken as demonstrable indicators of success. The resulting epistemic hierarchies have their benefits for individuals seeking to obtain recognition for their good works. However, a series of dynamic tensions in the current international political economy highlights the importance of forging alternative pathways to a more just and sustainable urbanism.

Academic preoccupations with matters of relativism and relevance have their effects upon occupational cultures of knowledge production, and one casualty is learning. As cities shape urban research, so research shapes cities (May and Perry 2011). City officials practice anticipatory decision-making: that is, fear of having no voice or influence unless conforming to particular political priorities. That means prioritising knowledge around particular areas of development. These practices of epistemic framing, found in both academia and the city, are born of a distance, not acquaintance. Understanding values, the relations between knowledge and practice and how and why particular issues come into the framing of urban processes and problems, are left in the wake of these practices. To open up alternatives, other forms of analysis, framing, values and processes are needed.

Summary: Knowledge, context and action

The relationship between knowledge, context and action is informed by the changing forces we have charted and these lead to a set of 'devilish dichotomies' (Perry and May 2010) and ambivalence about the relations of knowledge to action and those between context and content. As critiques of instrumentalism in urban development arose in the 1960s and 70s, the possibility of change reared its head. The same developments that were forging the urban, however, came to rest in the site of activity from which most of these critiques were launched: the university. As global forces shaped the urban, so they shaped the means of knowledge production with the desire for academic excellence according to aspatial views finding its parallels in the pursuit of world-city hierarchies.

In the face of the pressures we have examined, the idea of the disinterested pursuit of knowledge can easily become indifference to its consequence. The propensity to believe that you can dance with data without owning an interpretation and at least an anticipation of its consequence is part of a disposition that feeds knowledge for the economy. Equally, to be a spectator at the periphery of what is occurring can be limited, especially when those places which are thought to enable this to occur are themselves being reconfigured in a particular image of what counts as 'valid' knowledge. What we argue is that a partiality exists which saturates context in the name of an apparent necessity and in so doing, renders the political as the administration of techniques in its name. Its promise is given in a combination of means, rationale and the framing of horizons of opportunity formulated in its image. Politics expressed as a claim, cry or possibility of bringing into being alternative conceptions, is marginalised in this process in favour of constructing individuals as consumers, rather than political subjects, through the consumption of goods and services.

The geography of the knowledge-practice relationship is varied. Relevance and excellence exist in a dynamic tension which may be both productive and negative. It can be productive in the sense that parties recognise not only the strengths of their knowledge and practice, but also their limitations and how each can learn from the other. It can be negative in the sense that practice remains impervious to change, whilst knowledge production is geared to the demands of agencies that are only marginally connected to the knowledge needs of different communities. To tackle this means stressing the importance of understanding the relationship between content, context and consequence and that is a challenge for all concerned.

The need for the integration of what is already known in cities is now greater than ever and in the search for the new, we must not forget the past. Disparate knowledges can be integrated, seen alongside each other and re-contextualised. Sharing individual understandings can generate new social learning. Only then does it become possible to know when and how knowledge has had particular outcomes that are seen, by different parties, to have had benefits or contain potentials. Considerable effort is needed in order to learn from processes and there are no quick routes towards this end. This implies taking lessons from the past and not ignoring them in the name of slogans such as 'innovation' and 'enterprise'. It also means sharing an understanding of orientations and institutional positions and what is valuable about those, as well as their limits.

In our age of climate change, resource constraint, income and wealth inequality, knowledge needs to be owned and understood. Findings will be contestable and uncomfortable for many. They will meet with denial or a refusal to recognise, let alone understand, the content of what is produced and its implications. Active translation enables research to resonate with experiences and issues in order that they are intelligible to urban communities. To tackle a resulting ambivalence, models are moved across contexts as if they were a panacea for social and environmental problems, thereby relieving their recipients of the efforts needed to reach mutual understanding, let alone coordinate their actions. We face different and common challenges. They may be common in their origin, but contestable in their effects and consequences. Placing this at the feet of those who have different capacities and capabilities to respond is not only ineffective, it is unjust.

References

Archer, M., Bhaskar, R., Collier, A., Lawson, T. and Norrie, A. (eds.) (2013), *Critical Realism: Essential Readings*, London: Routledge.

Bourdieu, P. (1992), *The Logic of Practice*, translated by Nice, R., originally published in 1980 as *Le sens pratique*, Cambridge: Polity.

Bourdieu, P. (1998), *Practical Reason: On the Theory of Action*, Cambridge: Polity.

Bourdieu, P. (2000), *Pascalian Meditations*, translated by Nice, R., Cambridge: Polity.

Bourdieu, P. and Wacquant, L.J. (1992), *An Invitation to Reflexive Sociology*, Cambridge: Polity.

Brenner, N. (2004), *New State Spaces: Urban Governance and the Rescaling of Statehood*, Oxford: Oxford University Press.

Brenner, N. (ed.) (2014), *Implosions/Explosions: Towards a Study of Planetary Urbanization*, Berlin: Jovis Verlag.

Butler, J. (2006), 'Israel/Palestine and the paradoxes of academic freedom', *Radical Philosophy*, 135: 8–17.

Cairney, P. (2015), *The Politics of Evidence-based Policymaking*, London: Palgrave Macmillan.

Cohen, S. (1985), *Visions of Social Control*, Cambridge: Polity.

Collins, H. and Evans, R. (2009), *Rethinking Expertise*, Chicago: University of Chicago Press.

Cook, D.N. and Brown, J.S. (1999), 'Bridging epistemologies: the generative dance between organizational knowledge and organizational knowing', *Organizational Science*, 10 (4): 381–400.

Department for Business, Innovation and Skills (2010), 'Life sciences 2010: delivering the blueprint', *BIS Economics Paper 2*, London: Department for Business, Innovation and Skills, https://www.biocity.co.uk/file-manager/Group/reports2010/2010-bis-economics-paper-02.pdf (accessed May 2017).

Dorling, D. (2014), *Inequality and the 1%*, London: Verso.

du Gay, P. (1996), *Consumption and Identity at Work*, London: Sage.

Dunne, S., Harney, S., Parker, M. and Tinker, T. (2008), 'Discussing the role of the business school', *Ephemera: Theory and Politics in Organization*, 8 (3): 271–293.

Etzioni, A. (1990), *The Moral Dimension: Towards a New Economics*, New York: Free Press.

Etzkowitz, H. (2008), *The Triple Helix: University-Industry-Government Innovation in Action*, Oxford: Routledge.

Fuller, S. (2002), *Knowledge Management Foundations*, Woburn, Mass: Butterworth-Heinemann.

Garvey, J. (2008), *The Ethics of Climate Change: Right and Wrong in a Warming World*, London: Continuum.

Gibbons, M., Limoges, C., Nowotny, H., Schwartaman, S., Scott, P. and Trow, M. (1994), *The New Production of Knowledge: The Dynamics of Science and Research in Contemporary Societies*, London: Sage.

Gleeson, B. (2014), 'What Role for Social Science in the "Urban Age"?', in Brenner, N. (ed.) *Implosions/Explosions: Towards a Study of Planetary Urbanization*, Berlin: Jovis Verlag.

Graham, G. (2005), *The Institution of Intellectual Values*, Exeter, UK: Imprint Academic.

Gurvitch, G. (1971), *The Social Frameworks of Knowledge*, translated by Thompson, M. and Thompson, K., London: Harper and Row.

Habermas, J. (1981), 'Towards a reconstruction of historical materialism', in Knorr-Cetina, K. and Cicourel, A. (eds.) *Advances in Social Theory and Methodology: Towards an Integration of Micro and Macro Theories*, London: Routledge and Kegan Paul.

Harding, S. (1996), 'European expansion and the organization of modern science: isolated or linked historical processes?', *Organization*, 3 (4): 497–509.

Harloe, M. and Perry, B. (2005), 'Rethinking or hollowing out the university? external engagement and internal transformation in the knowledge economy', *Higher Education Management and Policy*, 17 (2): 11–16.

Henkel, M. (2000), *Academic Identities and Policy Change in Higher Education*, London: Jessica Kingsley.

Jameson, F. (2013 [1983]), *The Political Unconscious: Narrative as a Socially Symbolic Act*, London: Routledge.

Kenway, J., Bullen, E., Fahey, J. and Robb, S. (2006), *Haunting the Knowledge Economy* (Vol. 6), New York: Routledge.

Knorr-Cetina, K. (1999), *Epistemic Cultures: How the Sciences Make Knowledge*, Harvard: Harvard University Press.

Knorr-Cetina, K. and Cicourel, A. (eds.) (1981), *Advances in Social Theory and Methodology: Towards an Integration of Micro and Macro Theories*, London: Routledge and Kegan Paul.

Lamont, M. (2009), *How Professors Think: Inside the Curious World of Academic Judgement*, Harvard: Harvard University Press.

Lanham, R.A. (2007), *The Economics of Attention: Style and Substance in the Age of Information*, Chicago: University of Chicago Press.

Latouche, S. (2009), *Farewell to Growth*, translated by Macey, D., Cambridge: Polity.

Lawson, T. (1998), 'Economic science without experimentation', in Archer, M. et al. (eds.) *Critical Realism: Essential Readings*, London: Routledge.

May, T. (2001), 'Power, knowledge and organizational transformation: administration as depoliticisation', Special Issue 'Social epistemology and knowledge management', *Social Epistemology*, 15 (3): 171–186.

May, T. (2005), 'Transformations in academic production: context, content and consequences', *European Journal of Social Theory*, 8 (2): 193–209.

May, T. and Marvin, S. (2009), 'Elected regional assemblies: lessons for better policy making', in Sandford, M. (ed.) *The Northern Veto*, Manchester: Manchester University Press.

May, T. and Perry, B. (2006), 'Cities, knowledge and universities: transformations in the image of the intangible', *Social Epistemology*, 20 (3–4): 259–282.

May, T. and Perry, B. (2011), 'Urban research in the knowledge economy: content, context and outlook', *Built Environment*, 37 (3): 352–368.

May, T. and Perry, B. (2013), 'Universities, reflexivity and critique: uneasy parallels in practice', *Policy Futures in Education*, 11 (5): 505–514.

May, T. and Perry, B. (2016), 'Knowledge for just urban sustainability', *Local Environment*, http://www.tandfonline.com/eprint/iE9gQiruc4ahFAzFcnFF/full (accessed May 2017).

May, T. and Perry, B. (2017), *Reflexivity: The Essential Guide*, London: Sage.

May, T. with Perry, B. (2011), *Social Research and Reflexivity: Content, Consequences and Context*, London: Sage.

Menand, L. (2010), *The Marketplace of Ideas*, London: W.W. Norton and Company.

Messer-Davidow, E. (2002), *Disciplining Feminism: From Social Activism to Academic Discourse*, Durham, NC: Duke University Press.

Miao, J.T., Benneworth, P. and Phelps, N. (eds.) (2015), *Making 21ˢᵗ Century Knowledge Complexes: Technopoles of the World 20 Years After*, London: Routledge.

Nightingale, P. and Martin, P. (2004), 'The myth of the biotech revolution', *TRENDS in Biotechnology*, 22 (11): 564–569.

Norris, C. (2014), 'What strong sociologists can learn from critical realism: Bloor on the history of aerodynamics', *Journal of Critical Realism*, 13 (1): 3–37.

Nowotny, H., Scott, P. and Gibbons, M. (2003), 'Introduction: Mode 2 revisited: the new production of knowledge', *Minerva*, 41 (3): 179–194.

Perry, B. and May, T. (2010), 'Urban knowledge exchange: devilish dichotomies and active intermediation', *International Journal of Knowledge-Based Development*, 1 (1–2): 6–24.

Perry, B. and May, T. (2015), 'Context matters: the English science cities and visions for knowledge-based urbanism', in Miao, J., Benneworth, P. and Phelps, N. (eds.) *Making 21st Century Knowledge Complexes: Technopoles of the World Revisited*, London: Routledge, pp. 105–127.

Pratten, S. (ed.) (2014), *Social Ontology and Modern Economics*, London: Routledge.

Price, D.H. (2004), *Threatening Anthropology: McCarthyism and the FBI's Surveillance of Activist Anthropologists*, Durham: Duke University Press.

Romer, P.M. (1986), 'Increasing returns and long-run growth', *Journal of Political Economy*, 94 (5): 1002–1037.

Russell, B. (2004 [1935]), *In Praise of Idleness*, London: Routledge.

Sayer, A. (2015), *Why We Can't Afford the Rich*, Bristol: Policy Press.

Shore, C. and Wright, S. (2000), 'Coercive accountability: the rise of audit culture in higher education', in Strathern, M. (ed.) *Audit Cultures: Anthropological Studies in Accountability, Ethics and the Academy*, London: Routledge.

Siedentop, L. (2015), *Inventing the Individual: The Origins of Western Liberalism*, London: Penguin Books.

Slaughter, S. and Leslie, L. (1997), *Academic Capitalism: Politics, Policies and the Entrepreneurial University*, Baltimore, Maryland: Johns Hopkins University Press.

Smith, D.E. (1999), *Writing the Social: Critique, Theory and Investigations*, Toronto: Toronto University Press.

Soros, G. (1998), *The Crisis of Global Capitalism (Open Society Endangered)*, London: Little, Brown and Company.

Strathern, M. (ed.) (2000), *Audit Cultures: Anthropological Studies in Accountability, Ethics and the Academy*, London: Routledge.

Turner, S. (2003), *Liberal Democracy 3.0: Civil Society in an Age of Experts*, London: Sage.

Vico, G. (1990 [1709]), *On the Study Methods of Our Time*, translated and introduced by Gianturco, E., Ithaca, New York: Cornell University Press.

Wilkinson, R. and Pickett, K. (2010), *The Spirit Level: Why Equality is Better for Everyone*, London: Penguin.

Žižek, S. (2014), *Trouble in Paradise: From the End of History to the End of Capitalism*, London: Allen Lane.

PART III

Possibilities

6

EXCAVATING ALTERNATIVES IN THE SHADOWS OF THE KNOWLEDGE ECONOMY

Introduction

A 'knowledge economy' discourse has become pervasive. Across Europe it is reflected in a focus on knowledge, creativity and skills underpinning smart growth (European Commission 2010). 'Network' models of governance have become hegemonic (Davies 2011) embodied in 'growth coalitions' particularly prevalent at the urban level (Harvey, 1989; Logan and Molotch 2007). These bring together and transform a range of knowledges to create place-specific strategic interventions in pursuit of elusive goals. Growth coalitions value academic, technical and professional knowledge highly for justifying more 'evidence-based' or 'consensual' decision-making (Moser 2013). Regular partner contact within urban coalitions generates knowledge networks which, over time, acquire systemic properties creating 'urban knowledge architectures' (cf. Komninos 2013) and regulating knowledge transformations. Despite the apparent diversity of aims, which include sustainable and inclusive futures, it is a neoliberal imagination that tends to inform urban futures (Purcell 2008).

We have seen how the discourse of the knowledge economy is significant in its omnipresence throughout the end of the 20th and beginning of the 21st centuries, manifest in an irresistible allure to city policymakers, professionals and planners. The promise tends to focus upon the economic and technological as if these were separate spheres of activity from the social and political. Urban growth coalitions are increasingly adept at presenting consensus-driven grand narratives around 'smart', 'green' or 'creative' cities as uncontested representations of a homogeneous urban psyche (Swyngedouw 2009). Mediated through issues of scale, institutional design and dominant assumptions about whose knowledge matters, urban knowledge is marshalled to support existing pathways and palatable prescriptions within already inscribed processes (Mitchell et al. 2015). Marginal knowledge claims become obscured behind 'cleansed' accounts of stakeholder engagement, despite contestation being a part of democratic politics (Purcell 2008; Mouffe 2005). A gap is emerging between the values attributed to elite forms of knowledge/expertise and the knowledge that resides within civil society. There is a growing disconnection between these informal ways of knowing and acting in the urban and formalised urban policy development and implementation. Forms of 'epistemic injustice' (Fricker 2007) prevent both voices and alternative perspectives from being heard.

How can it be otherwise? What possibilities exist for challenging dominant ways of knowing and valuing expertise in our increasingly urbanised societies? Local community groups and movements, loosely networked across different scales of activity, are articulating alternatives to mainstream urban policy to advocate for a more socially inclusive, economically viable and ecologically sound urbanism (Brenner et al. 2012). Individuals and groups seek to reclaim their 'right to the city' and bring about 'just' urban transformations (Marcuse 2009). Whilst often implicit, what we see in these alternatives are different epistemological assumptions about the relationships between knowledge, action and place, which take democracy and the role of the citizen expert and communities of practice seriously. Knowledge of and approaches towards urban problems is increasingly produced and circulated in non-formalised circuits, operating in parallel to the mainstream. The task, therefore, is: "to excavate the possibilities for alternative, radically emancipatory forms of urbanism" (Brenner 2012: 19).

This chapter sets out to examine these alternative possibilities. These are ones which have emerged in urban places for various reasons and among different communities. They all share in common an emergence in parallel to what we have described and also in opposition to its rationale and trajectory. They are, therefore, counter-hegemonic visions of urban futures. To consider these, we first provide an overview of alternative urban imaginaries and visions from the Global South and North. We then move on to outline the key characteristics of these and finally, suggest how they collectively prefigure an alternative urban epistemology that positions the citizen as active agent and lay expert in relation to the reconstitution of urban futures.

Forging alternative urban imaginaries

As urban researchers concerned to formulate just and sustainable urban futures, we also have an idea of a possible within the present. Without imagination of how cities and city-regions could be configured and run differently, where would we be? Where do we look to nurture our imaginations of how things could be otherwise? After all: "Explicit alternative scenarios for the future are fundamental to any kind of democratic debate" (Levitas 2013: xviii). So we need to: "become open to possibility rather than limits on the possible" (Gibson-Graham 2008: 14). Yet we have also spoken about recognition of ambivalence for we hold out an image of the future that is more open to including different voices and what is revealed is a difficult journey, not one named and contained for the few. That opens up a 'negative dialectic of ambivalence' where there is a questioning of oneself, including our expectations of the relations between knowledge, action and aspiration: "For the critical irony expressed in utopias is the complex attitude of those who are able to let go of what human beings cling to – namely, the status quo *as well as* the dreams, but without betraying the latter" (Frost 2014: 190. Original emphasis). Free from seeing lock-in and path dependency, we can refer to resistance and spaces of possibility. Local actors draw on alternative traditions, knowledge and memories to resist policies (Bevir and Rhodes 2010) and neoliberalisation has 'cracks' that can be exploited by new coalitions of democratic movements (Purcell 2008).

The knowledge economy has been developed as a Westernised concept informed by a neoliberal ideology. That is perhaps unsurprising given the epistemological dominance of the West and the systematic suppression of other philosophical traditions. The origins of philosophical thought are often attributed to the Greeks, yet this is a problematic claim. There is evidence of extensive visits of early Greek scholars to Egypt in search of wisdom, but the result was denial and a denigration of African capability (Asante 2004). Whilst efforts to ground alternative epistemologies are increasing, through valorising endogenous ways of being and knowing (see Nkulu-N'Sengha 2005; Nyamnjoh 2012), these often rely on non-written oral traditions, giving rise to ethno-philosophical studies. The dominance of European, male, white writings in most histories of reflexive thought is readily apparent, not only to the exclusion of African, but also Asian or South American perspectives. Those traditions, coupled with the ability of neoliberalism to deploy knowledge in its name and translate difference into matters of administrative-technical means raises a challenge: "how to reanimate resistance to the contemporary neoliberal urban context by connecting with the hopes and desires of those women that form the majority urban group, the working poor, by situating demands for gender justice not only within a critique of contemporary capitalism but also within the context of women's right to the city" (Peake 2017: 91).

Global cities in the West are often seen as 'models' for the world and megacities, mainly in the third world, are often seen as 'in crisis' (Roy 2005), whilst the forces of globalisation and uneven urban development shape cities in countries such as Brazil (Vicino 2017). Although there is a great deal of development and innovation in the Global South and Latin America (for example, see Ciccariello-Maher 2016), models developed in the West are frequently assumed to be appropriate. What are neglected are the opportunities for understanding from initiatives developed elsewhere in the spirit of forging learning cities (McFarlane 2011). Instead, the knowledge economy discourse has been infused in the language, policies and practices of international development organisations, in an uncomfortable fusion between economic growth and social development goals. On the one hand, in governmental and formal top-down initiatives the goals of net wealth creation are not separated from wealth distribution, in so far as they are accompanied by efforts to support capacity-building and poverty alleviation.

The Cities Alliance was established in 1999 as a global partnership for urban poverty reduction and the promotion of the role of cities in sustainable urban development. The main stakeholders are national governments, multilateral institutions, associations of local governments, international non-governmental organisations, the private sector and foundations and universities and knowledge networks. The focus for them is on inclusive strategy development, capacity-building to improve services for the urban poor and developing mechanisms to engage citizens in city or urban governance. This is enshrined in the Cities Without Slums Action Plan which proposed a target of improving the lives of 100 million slum dwellers by the year 2020. The Global Partnership for Social Accountability (GPSA) is another example focussed on bridging the gap between 'what citizens want and what governments actually do'. Here the emphasis, following Couldry (2010), is not only to enhance citizens' voices, but to support the capacity of governments to respond effectively.

The extent to which top-down initiatives challenge hegemonic visions of knowledge-based growth needs to be subject to analysis, especially as they have developed in the long shadow of institutions such as the World Bank. In the work of the GPSA, the development of 'knowledge platforms' to support this is reminiscent of the discourse of the knowledge economy in a commitment to learning, networking, knowledge exchange and the development of a knowledge repository. A critical view would posit that the goal of poverty alleviation is of at least equal importance to wealth creation and would take limits to the continued reproduction of global flows and finance seriously. Global institutions committed to address inequalities do so in the name of mopping up the worst excesses of unfettered global economic growth and removing barriers to its further consolidation. Moreover, organisations speak on behalf of the poor within formal partnership governance structures, with citizen sharing variable and sometimes limited, influence and power within decision-making structures.

These tensions are illustrated in initiatives such as the Global Pulse Labs. Global Pulse works through a network of labs which: "brings together government experts, UN agencies, academia and the private sector to pioneer new methods and frameworks for using Big Data to support development goals. Pulse Labs tap into local knowledge and innovation, establish key partnerships, test and pilot real-time monitoring approaches at the country level and support the adoption of proven approaches" (www.unglobalpulse.org). With headquarters in New York, Pulse Labs exist in cities such as Kampala and Jakarta. On the one hand an emphasis on education and skills development supports a far broader conception of the knowledge society in which the benefits from knowledge-based development are shared more widely with those living in the worst conditions. Yet a strong linear input-output model may prevail within such those (more education and skills = better economic growth), echoing those that rely on particular interpretations of data ('Big') and a top-down perspective in which citizens themselves are positioned as the beneficiaries of, rather than agents in, knowledge-based development. Organisations such as United Nations Educational, Scientific and Cultural Organization can, in this respect, produce cultural products and ideas that may unwittingly produce new inequalities. Declarations of tolerance, whilst laudable, rely upon access to public platforms and spheres which are not uniform

(Madanipour 2011). Policies can easily become echo-chambers and amplifiers for dominant practices.

Control, participation and coproduction

Alternative approaches are suggested through bottom-up initiatives from citizens and those living in poverty. The Urban Poor Fund International is a subsidiary of the Slum Dwellers International (SDI) which provides capital to support savings federations undertaking urban improvements and housing projects. The fund is established on the basis of the idea that: "the poor are central actors in urban devel-opment and poverty eradication and are best able to decide and co-manage their own urban improvement programs" (http://upfi.info/about/). The idea is to give direct control of capital to those living in poverty to enable them to negotiate and deal with other, more formal partners and bodies. Such funds have enabled water and sanitation upgrading in Omusati, Namibia (http://upfi.info/projects/namibia -share/) and a Community Urban Planning Studio in Kampala. Similar values and approaches can be seen across countries in the Global South with the Indian Alliance (between the Society for the Promotion of Area Resource Centres, the National Slum Dwellers Federation and Mahila Milan) stating: "If Indian cities are to grow in a healthy or sustainable way, we must learn how to partner and engage with informality and the urban poor. The Alliance of SPARC, NSDF and MM is currently working with 750,000 households across India and has built or is building housing for over 8500 families" (http://www.sparcindia.org/housing.php). Their programmes engage communities in exploring land tenures and building houses and participating in the design and construction of facilities.

What sits behind many of these initiatives is a call not just for taking control back into communities, but processes of 'coproduction' in the redesign of public poli-cies and services, involving implementing and delivery services in equal relations between different stakeholders in the process (Boyle and Harris 2009; Durose and Richardson 2015). In terms of the production of a knowledge commons for this purpose, Ostrom's work (1996) is often seen as seminal, drawing first on work with colleagues in the United States and later on cases in Brazil and in Nigeria related to the relative encouragement/discouragement of citizen engagement in urban infrastructure and primary education. Initiatives have focussed on inclusive sanita-tion and coproduction as an empowerment strategy for low-income marginalised groups (Banana et al. 2015) which can be state- or society-initiated (Watson 2014).

Coproduction may be seen as a rather nebulous concept, but one which has traction and roots in designing and delivering better public services (Osborne et al. 2016). Although many initiatives focus on specific areas of policy develop-ment – for example, education and sanitation – others, such as the Abuja Town Hall Meetings are focussed more on the democratic spaces to facilitate dialogue between political leaders and citizens (see: http://participedia.net/en/cases/abuja-town-hall-meetings). This was part of a concerted effort to shift the city's demo-cratic culture away from a militaristic mentality and draw on Nigeria's tradition of communitarian decision-making. Extensive works on civil society capacity building have also pointed to how coproduction is increasingly not only about service delivery, but chosen as a strategy for the urban poor to consolidate their local organisational base and negotiate with the state (Mitlin 2008). If the coproduction paradigm draws attention to forms of sharing and citizen participation, then experiences in Latin America point to the importance of continued struggle and social and grassroots movements. Lessons from Brazil highlight development being a tool for social justice with a variety of urban forms strengthening public voices, along with participatory democracy in planning processes (Vicino 2017).

Caution is needed when replacing one elite imaginary with another popular panacea, for that does not mean development then results in genuine power-sharing between participants. It is a process that takes a great deal of energy and organisation with potentially two-edged outcomes. This may be seen in the case of the communes in Venezuela: "The construction and consolidation of grassroots power from below in Venezuela has been a long and arduous process, stretching across decades. Today, this alternative power emerging from below, this dual power, is seeking out an alternative space in the communes in which to make the long promised revolution a concrete reality. But this power does not escape the imperative Lenin once assigned to it: it must tip eventually to one side or the other. As time runs out, the tipping point rushes to greet us" (Ciccariello-Maher 2016: 134).

Latin Americans have generated a level of social and political creativity that has caught the imagination of many parts of the world. It is perhaps best known for giving us participatory budgeting – or 'PB' (Allegretti 2003; Baiocchi 2005; Gret and Sintomer 2005). PB requires not only financial control, but the active involvement of city-level or decentralised districts and elected bodies, a repeated process, public deliberation and accountability for the outcomes. Whilst acknowledged as the first and most documented case, other Latin American cities were developing participatory budgeting at the same time as Porto Alegre (for example, Guayana, Caracas and Montevideo). Here we find a process which mobilises citizens from groups who have been difficult to engage with and does so within a degree of far greater transparency. Despite this, issues remain: "In Porto Alegre, the administration has ensured that the process is highly transparent and the public has good access to information. Even with a highly supportive administration, there remains a danger that the professional standing of officials (whether intentionally or not) unduly influences decisions of citizens" (Smith 2009: 71).

Despite such issues, participatory budgeting spread from Latin America around the world, mostly under the leadership of left-wing governments. These include Grottamare and Pieve Emanuela in Italy; Albacete and Seville in Spain; Berlin in Germany; Płock in Poland and Bradford, Manchester, Salford and Newcastle in the UK. However, it is not clear that the value and outcomes of PB in Latin America have translated into Europe (Sintomer et al. 2012). PB in Latin America is attributed with largely positive outcomes in terms of reducing cronyism, establishing civil society as a countervailing power and supporting more emancipatory processes involving lower socio-economic groups. Equally, there is a concern that it can serve as an instrument to justify budget cuts or reform services according to a preconceived agenda. As we have argued, the idea of transferring models from one place to another without any link to existing histories or cultures is problematic: "A process that can be combined with certain existing traditions of participation might lead to more transformative results than an 'artificial' process with no links to existing structures. On the other hand, radical innovations seem necessary to challenge the present asymmetric power relations within most common participatory devices and in society. This dilemma is not easy to resolve, and it is one of the reasons why there are multiple ways towards more just and more democratic urban development in the world, depending on the situation, rather than one 'royal road'"(Sintomer et al. 2012: 29).

Whilst much can be learnt from comparisons through an 'import-mirror' and 'difference' view (May and Perry 2018), the above reflects our view of the political, economic and structural processes of reproduction outlined in chapters 3–5. Such inspirations need to be set alongside efforts to rethink the possible in the context of already existing initiatives and ideas. These might include democratic experiments such as the different approach to municipal governance in Bologna, Italy. There, 'pacts of collaboration' have been formed between the city authorities and citizens as formal contracts supporting a range of projects around collaborative services, ventures and working practices. The results include a nursery, agricultural cooperative and social streets initiative (www.participedia.net). Parallels can be seen in the UK with projects such as Participatory City in Lambeth, an experimental initiative to co-develop a participatory demonstration environment supporting local people's ideas. Within this ethos we find the 'transition movement'. Started in Kinsale, Ireland, by Rob Hopkins, it developed in Totnes, England and is now an international network underpinned by six principles: inclusion; awareness raising; resilience; psychological insights and credible and appropriate solutions (Hopkins 2008).

In contrast to the deliberate attempts of policymakers to transplant best practice around the world in the export industry of a Westernised concept of the knowledge economy, alternative circuits and global-local relationships of learning and solidarity are emerging. The growth of Transition Towns is one example, in which an international movement has developed based on the sharing and replication of local actions. Similarly we can cite the enthusiasm, albeit without sufficient contextual understanding, to emulate the PB model across Europe. Skills-sharing and local networks connect grassroots activists and community entrepreneurs in the exchange of ideas and practices. In work on an experimental vertical farm established in Salford, England, the local embeddedness of the project was only possible through drawing on practice-networks and insights in the US, East Africa and Eastern Europe (Perry et al. 2017). Local action, embedded within global networks of solidarity, is well illustrated through the example of urban food experimentation, as well as new forms of housing, eco-homes and alternative economic frameworks.

Learning from alternatives

In search of possibilities, we can identify a range of initiatives springing up to challenge dominant responses to the siren call of the knowledge economy from which we can learn. These differ not only in their objectives but in the criteria they judge themselves by, the scales at which they operate, the processes they work through and the social interests involved (Table 6.1, reproduced from Perry et al. 2013).

Whilst these initiatives may suggest a set of common characteristics, there are also important lines of differentiation. In particular, the extent to which initiatives suggest a *real* alternative to the knowledge economy differs according to whether and how they challenge economic models, reframe global-local relationships and adopt different radical or incremental change processes. This is important given that: "The knowledge economy is a grasping economy, its only obligation is to acquire without constraint and reciprocity, and, therefore, it ignores the gift-like qualities of knowledge. Knowledge is not a gift freely given, it is buoyant with powerful obligations" (Kenway et al. 2006: 122). The proposition of these authors is that 'spectral economies' haunt the knowledge economy and demonstrate its priorities, limitations and exclusions, along with contradictions.

Increasingly, movements and campaigns are emerging to fight to bring alternative economic frameworks into being. Examples here include ideas about the blue economy, sharing economy, foundational and circular economy, the de-growth and steady state movements and new systems of exchange and sharing. Complementary currencies such as the Bartercard network (De La Rosa I Esteva 2011) and the Bristol pound have emerged, whilst Timebanking is rising in popularity in East Amsterdam where residents get credits for helping neighbours or doing community work. Similarly, Ithaca Hours, an initiative in New York state, acts as a currency system to: "promote local economic strength and community self-reliance in ways

TABLE 6.1 Alternative responses to the knowledge economy

	Dominant Responses	*Alternative Responses*
Objectives	Econo-centric	Varied: triple line of sustainability
Measurements	Tangible	Intangible
Scales	Global excellence	Glocal 'excellent relevance' and 'relevant excellence'
Processes	Linear, products, supply/demand, push/pull models	Ecosystems, networks and flows
Knowledges	Narrow; disciplinary; sectoral; codified	Broad; interdisciplinary; cross-sectoral; tacit
Mechanisms	Technological, mechanistic solutions	Multiple interventions and mechanisms
Learning	Transferable models	Context-sensitive approaches
Social Interests	Elites and experts: corporate, governments, major institutions	Wide stakeholders, potential beneficiaries and participants

which will support economic and social justice, ecology, community participation and human aspirations in and around Ithaca" (http://www.alternatives.org/ithaca hours.html).

In terms of self-proclaimed alternatives propping up the status quo, in the case of urban agriculture questions are raised concerning whether so-called 'Alternative Food Initiatives' are bolstering existing systems. Some argue that there are contradictions in urban agriculture with initiatives being both 'interstitial and subversive' insofar as they attempt to subvert commodity forms by seeing food as a public good, but also, inadvertently, filling gaps left by the rolling back of social security in times of austerity. Therefore, it is suggested that: "urban agriculture, in its many forms, is not radical *or* neoliberal, but may exemplify *both* a form of actually existing neoliberalism *and* a simultaneous radical counter-movement arising in dialectical tension" (McClintock 2004: 148).

At this point we come to the issue of whether localism is a progressive or regressive phenomenon (Featherstone et al. 2012). There are different kinds of urban activism and they vary in their relationship to scale. Local neighbourhood activists may not aim to speak on behalf of those outside a particular area, whilst globally oriented activists recognise the need to link up with others to make transformative change. Stronger links are needed in international movements to avoid the backlash against the global in reducing actions to parochial affairs. Simple celebrations of the local are thereby avoided as they can produce both positive and negative results: "Movements that pursue only localisation will not only run the risk of getting counter-productive results, but they will also miss scalar-strategies that might be more effective for them. Resisting neoliberalisation requires movements to pursue political initiatives at a range of scale, and to do so flexibly and strategically. Different temporal and spatial contexts will require different scalar strategies. A right to the city limited to the urban or even the neighbourhood scale would undermine that necessary flexibility" (Pearce 2013: 101).

If we consider the idea of community-led 'grassroots innovations' (Seyfang and Smith 2007) there is the possibility of this level being a source for more radical change: "Change within the regime tends to be incremental and path-dependent ... 'revolutionary' change originates in 'niches'" (Smith et al. 2010: 440). Multiple niches, networked together, have the potential to change the system. Here the concept of the 'information society' can play a different role in forging a non-proprietorial knowledge commons (Hess and Ostrom 2007). Instead of intellectual property, knowledge as a public good is shared via digital platforms and social practices that are enabled by information technology. Counter-austerity movements in Greece, for example, rely on social media to allow direct communication between societal actors (Arampatzi 2016).

The realisation of possibilities depends on the strategies adopted and the social, economic and political conditions in which they emerge. Here we find a distinction between those that advocate radical change from below and those that believe that change is possible from within existing institutions (Perry and Atherton 2017). Some argue that the project of governance has 'failed' requiring new democratic movements, forms of politics and institutions (Purcell 2013). In terms of practical purchase on issues, there is a need to move from abstract discussions on the just city, to the right to the city, drawing intellectually on Lefebvre and on the ground-swell of counter-publics and counter-claims that are being made about the right to occupy urban space (Marcuse et al. 2009). In terms of the conditions for achieving this possibility, there are those who suggest change needs to be conceptualised and achieved within the existing capitalist systems (Fainstein 2010; Hay and Payne 2015). What is held here is a gradual transformation of existing institutions that support capitalism will eventually provide a pressure to bring about change. In considering these views, Nancy Fraser (2003) makes a distinction between 'affirmative' and 'transformational' strategies, with the former concerned to correct unequal outcomes and the latter transforming the social framework that gives rise to these in the first instance. Affirmative strategies seek 'non-reformist' reforms from within existing frameworks, whilst setting in motion a trajectory of change over time in which more radical reforms become practicable. A key element of the non-reformist incremental agenda, often ignored by more radical perspectives, is to focus on actually existing rather than imagined institutions (Young 1990: 22). Even here, ethnographic accounts of urban life under conditions of threat and fear can reveal the construction of moral worlds where people can find honour, dignity and respect (Goffman 2015).

Learning for change includes an understanding of the relations and reasons for consensus and protest. In her analysis of scale, Pearce (2013) contrasts the willingness to engage in confrontation by the global activists with those at a neighbourhood level. Gramsci's crisis of authority or hegemony is relevant here: "a condition of awareness and distrust of existing forms of power and ideology, which provides room for an assessment of agency, conflict and the production of alternatives from below" (Gramsci, 1971: 275–276). In producing alternatives from below, different strategies of change are being undertaken – from the radical to incremental, the consensus-oriented or protest-based. These strategies may be multi-present. The case of the Orlando 'Food Not Bombs' project is one in which local activists worked to feed vulnerable people and sought to deploy existing governmental processes to contest urban decisions and finally, were forced to break the law in order to pressure authorities into enacting change (Sbicci 2014). This supports Purcell's invocation to focus on the spaces of resistance and the doors still left open by neoliberalism: "If they are alert and organised, oppositional movements can take advantage of those opportunities to destabilise existing logics and advocate for alternatives" (2008: 3).

Challenging dominant frames

There are a range of initiatives emerging around the world and at the grassroots level that suggest a growing movement committed to exploring, testing and developing alternative approaches to neoliberal forms of knowledge capitalism. The examples above suggest that dominant economic models, as outlined in earlier chapters, are perpetuated through particular knowledge circuits. They embody potential alternative mixtures of knowledge architectures and practices and ideas of global-local relationships and strategies for change. The extent to which such initiatives can live up to their claims to be 'radical' or 'progressive' requires a reflexive process in which original values and intentions are realised in practice and if not, for what reasons? However, the plethora of initiatives bubbling in niches of experimentalism and collective endeavour at the micro-scale, sometimes linked through international networks of equivalence (Purcell 2008) does point to possibilities of other ways of organising urban life through the broadening of urban epistemologies (Pieterse 2017).

We have argued that social epistemological framing explains a great deal concerning the current climate. The above may possess different epistemological assumptions about the relationships between knowledge, action and place, which take democracy and the role of the citizen expert and varying communities of practice seriously. Knowledge of and approaches towards urban problems is increasingly produced and circulated in non-formalised ways, operating in parallel to the mainstream. If knowledge capitalism embodies the commodification of knowledge as a private good, it is challenged by the possibility of forging the knowledge commons defined as: "knowledge as a shared resource, a complex ecosystem that is a *commons* – a resource shared by a group of people that is subject to social dilemmas" (Hess and Ostrom 2007: 3. Original italics). Instead of narrow, privatised, codified knowledge, operating in circuits of sectoral closure, a different urban epistemology is suggested.

We can see evidence of the active reshaping of boundaries in order to allow multiple voices and varying forms of expertise into policy and governance processes. Citizen participation and direct action is demanded not only as a fundamental right, but because the dominant justifications of the knowledge economy need to be contested. The value of citizen knowledge and expertise is at the heart of these initiatives, with a strong rejection of the patriarchal omniscience suggested by an apparently benevolent educating state: "The fundamental deficit in neoliberal democracies is, then, not one of voice but of ways of valuing voice, of putting voice to work within processes of social cooperation" (Couldry 2010: 144). That concerns institutional change to support transformation through the inclusion of different voices and to recognise those as legitimate. That challenges the speed of change and the lack of time and requires public consultation to be valued as a process of enrichment. Citizens are demanding to be recognised as knowledge bearers in their own right, with understanding, skills and expertise that confronts and exposes the self-evident truths of the global economic elite. Drawing on examples outside a Western context, we can see the epistemological underpinnings of alternative knowledge claims stemming from neighbourhoods and communities, squats, favelas and barrios that propose greater citizen participation in the definition, construction and ownership of cities. Counter-movements and international networks of practice and activism provide circuits through which knowledge can be shared in the spirit of transformation.

Governmental efforts exist on a spectrum from a naive, reluctant and instrumental approach to seeing citizen knowledge as an input to better efficiencies and decision-making to genuine power-sharing efforts based on recognition of the value and diversity of expertise. The Global Partnership for Social Accountability (GPSA) bases itself on: "constructive engagement between governments and civil society in order to create an enabling environment in which citizen feedback is *used to solve fundamental problems in service delivery and to strengthen the performance of public institutions.*" (http://www.thegpsa.org/sa/. Emphasis added). Crowd sourcing is deployed as a tool for e-participation in local government in order to take advantage of citizen knowledge to find solutions to municipal problems. However, this can easily be framed in an instrumental way in order to deal with 'wicked problems' and "generate, introduce and implement innovations more quickly" (Royo and Yetano 2015: 324). It is suggested that local authorities will increasingly turn to new technologies, particularly in the context of economic pressures. A tension thus exists between the facilitation of an extractive relationship in which citizen knowledge is turned into a process input and the potential of alternative forms of engagement and participation that may include digital technologies.

Such initiatives are contrasted with those where genuine co-productive power-sharing forums are created in which citizens are involved, not as 'inputs' but as 'owners' of the process. For Cahn (2008) coproduction needs to be at the heart of a manifesto for a new economy in light of the failure of representative democracy and the need for new models. It does not mean coproduction as a means of inviting citizens into predetermined agendas, but rather creating spaces for struggle and contestation over who sets the agenda in the first place: "hell-raising is a critical part of coproduction and of the labour that it entails and must value. Those with wealth, power, authority and credentials hold those assets as stewards for those who came before and in trust for those yet unborn. They must be held accountable – and sometimes that requires the creation of new vehicles that give rise to scrutiny, to questioning, to criticism, and to social protest" (Cahn 2008: 4).

The idea of participative vehicles needs to be seen against the reproduction of existing formal civic organisational practices in cities. As we have said, urban responses are framed in particular ways that allow for a sense-making that leaves learning and participation in its wake. To guard against this, reflexive considerations need to be built into practices in order that the idea of coproduction and meaningful consultation process do not combine with a managerial or professional power that blunts them as instruments of change. Here, we can also draw on the work of Janet Newman and John Clarke (2010: 149–150) in terms of what it means to engage publics in situations where models of participation abound and are produced not only by consultants and those who self-define as facilitators, but also academics. As the model or reality so easily become the reality of the model, a technical and procedural focus becomes antithetical to what is needed in terms of a political reframing of participation. Participation fatigue and tokenism can be avoided through the production of meaningful and tangible outcomes that are seen as legitimate by urban citizens. In addition, it is important to avoid particular framing through a 'sectorsemia' (May and Perry 2016): that is, a form that divides up the urban according to organisational rationales focussed upon particular sectors such as health, social care, schools and environment. If such organisational rational-ities predominate it means that participation is not only localised, but particularised. The result is not relational thinking in terms of the realities of the experiences of urban life, but a framing that makes sense in terms of meeting organisational imper-atives – these are not the same thing.

We have noted the construction of the urban subject as an abstraction of everyday practice that is governed by consumption and exchange. That does not take the voice and views of people as political subjects, but consumers of ser-vices whose opinions are solicited through the numerous techniques deployed by marketing companies and those whose positions and revenues depend on these limited ideas of participation. We are not suggesting that e-polls and such forms may not contribute to transformative effects, but they may easily by-pass active and deliberative forms due to their design around consumers, rather than participants and shapers of, public services. After all, with service-based forums: "power is rarely shared: decision-making tends to remain firmly in managerial hands, and service users tend to be involved individually and fleetingly, despite some exceptions, and so have little opportunity to develop a collective voice" (Newman and Clarke 2010: 150). Such propensity to depoliticisation may be equally evident in the routines of political cycles of decision-making that expect participation at particular moments in time, as well as the kind of outsourcing that we have seen under neoliberalism where the state invests responsibility for obtaining participation within civil organisations, but not the power of resource allocation.

Participation can open up citizen knowledge so it can inform and shape agendas and policymaking within a new urban epistemology. Moving away from an elite-based policy community to connect with an urban citizenry means recognising how that is now structured and going from the promotion of a discourse to further governance by elites to a more participatory relationship that facilitates public dis-course (Fischer 2000). Such action requires consideration of predominant ration-alities in organisations and the boundaries that both enable their distinction, but also constrain the capabilities to undertake work that challenges those. Set up in 2012, Greeniversity received a grant from the Cabinet Office which is managed by National Endowment for Science, Technology and the Arts (NESTA) to roll the scheme out nationally. Greeniversity helps people get together and learn prac-tical skills and information for sustainable communities of the future. Whether it's cooking, growing, making or mending – the emphasis is on activities that con-tribute to building community spirit. The basic premise is that knowledge and skills-sharing is an essential prerequisite to challenging unsustainable neoliberal models of economic growth. The search for 'new' knowledge and technological fixes can result in overlooking the value of existing understanding and skills. Rather than assuming that people need to be 'taught' about climate change or told about carbon reduction, this approach values the cultural activities that make up the fabric of everyday lives. A sharing city is one in which people learn from each other, through volunteering their time to teach life skills across a range of areas, contributing to a wider cultural shift. Whilst the initiative itself had its last year in 2016 due to the availability of alternative online skill sharing sites, examples such as these recognise that many grassroots initiatives have limited resources and are reliant on volunteers, making more general alternative forms of interaction between ideas, knowledge and skills, critical.

Organised forms of social protest and movements in the urban setting represent not just alternative articulations of current trajectories, but contain within them imaginaries that do not simply ignore the present in the name of elite-based visions, but build upon it through the mobilisation of what resides in localities, often hidden from more general public view. Such movements can be seen as struggles in defence of the idea of the public sphere and whilst some may be explicitly anti-capitalist, those which are not may be in the effects they produce through exposing the absence of these spaces of possibility. These forms of action frequently need to share understanding as a precondition to transformation. New social movements are represented as conflicts at the seams between what has been termed the system and lifeworld (Habermas 1981) through a process of decolonisation and re-building of the public sphere. There have been critiques of this thesis (see Calhoun 1992; Fraser 1997), but more recent work indicates the continuing relevance of these ideas (Schlosberg 2006; Schlembach 2015). 'Colonisation' is relevant in understanding global capitalism and neoliberal policies (Edwards 2009). In the exercise of the imaginary, the practices and movements charted here can be seen as 'experimental anticipations of empowered democracy' (Unger 2004). At the other end of the spectrum in terms of government power, efforts by local governments to open up spaces for citizens' knowledges to inform governance and policy may be seen in terms of an emphasis on self-determination and emancipation. Yet as we have argued, that needs reflexive monitoring in order not to replicate the very rationalities that exclude the implications of these processes. As part of the path to this end, the ways in which urban knowledge architectures inform dominant practices should itself be subject to critique and opened up in a deliberative, public space and not closed down within elite orders of narrow, normative justification.

As citizens concerned with the possibility of more inclusive and just urban development, we are all caught in varying spheres and levels of power. In the spaces between trance and struggle (Unger 2004), self-determination and participation, 'active subjects' can shape and influence new spaces (Taylor 2007) and question the consensus that degrades rights and justice (Tyler 2013). The possibilities of citizen knowledge activism rest in liminal spaces between the formal and informal. On the one hand transformative action may be achieved: "by focussing on strategies from below which aim to resist governmental ambitions, this emphasises that subjects are reflexive and can accommodate, adapt, contest or resist top-down endeavours to govern them if they so wish" (McKee 2009: 479). On the other hand, it is important to avoid '*trasformismo*' (Gramsci 1971) whereby there is absorption of opposition into the state apparatus. Therefore, those engaging with participatory networks need to be prepared to move 'outside and against' the state – to have an " 'exit-action' strategy, becoming separate and insurgent, challenging the network itself, rather than finding ways to make it work better" (Davies 2011: 136).

Summary: The search for just and sustainable possibilities

Cities are caught in the dominant dynamics and logics of a Westernised model of knowledge capitalism. The knowledge economy casts a long shadow over efforts to imagine different possibilities and options. Governments recognise that education, skills and capacity-building are essential to address poverty, but turning that into a consumerist, human capital logic means an increasing inability to pay, whilst a linear input-output model pervades discourses of the knowledge society in which the end goal of unfettered economic growth and development remains the same. In this chapter, however, we set out on a search for alternatives. These exist across the Global North and South and share similar characteristics. Whilst there are constraints and limits on the extent to which they challenge dominant models, they provide fuel for imaginative responses that inform alternative futures.

Grassroots initiatives, social movements, struggles, experiences and experiments promise an alternative insofar as they aim at producing social, cultural and ecological benefits rather than narrow economic ones, are open and participatory, emphasise nonlinear ecologies of practice, see knowledge as a common good and promote collective values over the individualism that pervades the contemporary landscape. How these possibilities may be more generally realised in practice depends on the relationships between initiatives and institutions and dominant economic models and those between localism and global networks of solidarity. Here, spaces and processes of learning and exchange become important, along with a critique and exposure of the cracks in dominant ways of framing urban development. With this in mind, we turn to the role of the university and academic practices in supporting the emergence of alternative urban futures.

References

Allegretti, G. (2003), 'L'insegnamento di Porto Alegre. Autoprogettualità come paradigm urbano [The lesson of Porto Alegre. Self-managed project as urban pardigm]', Florence: Alinea.

Arampatzi, A. (2016), 'The spatiality of counter-austerity politics in Athens, Greece: emergent "urban solidarity spaces"', *Urban Studies*, 54 (9): 2155–2171.

Asante, M.K. (2004), *An African Origin of Philosophy: Myth or Reality?* City Press, July, http://www.asante.net/articles/26/afrocentricity/ (accessed May 2017).

Asante, M.K. and Mazama, A. (eds.) (2005), *Encyclopaedia of Black Studies*, Thousand Oaks, CA: Sage.

Baiocchi, G. (2005), *Militants and Citizens: The Politics of Participatory Democracy in Porto Alegre*, Stanford, CA: Stanford University Press.

Banana, E., Chikoti, P., Harawa, C., McGranahan, G., Mitlin, D., Stephen, S., Schermbrucker, N., Shumba, F. and Walnycki, A. (2015), 'Sharing reflections on inclusive sanitation', *Environment and Urbanisation*, 27 (1): 19–34.

Bevir, M. and Rhodes, R.A. (2010), *The State as Cultural Practice*, Oxford University Press.

Boyle, D. and Harris, M. (2009), *The Challenge of Co-production: How Equal Partnership between Professionals and the Public are Crucial to Improving Public Services*, London: NESTA.

Brenner, N. (2012), 'What is critical urban theory?', in Brenner, N., Marcuse, P. and Mayer, M. (eds.) (2012), *Cities for People, not for Profit: Critical Urban Theory and the Right to the City*, London: Routledge.

Brenner, N., Marcuse, P. and Mayer, M. (eds.) (2012), *Cities for People, not for Profit: Critical Urban Theory and the Right to the City*, London: Routledge.

Cahn, E. (2008), Foreword to *Co-production: A Manifesto for Growing the Core Economy*, London: New Economics Foundation, available at: http://b.3cdn.net/nefound ation/5abec531b2a775dc8d_qjm6bqzpt.pdf

Calhoun, C. (ed.) (1992), *Habermas and the Public Sphere*, Cambridge, Massachusetts: MIT Press.

Ciccariello-Maher, G. (2016), *Building the Commune: Radical Democracy in Venezuela*, London: Verso.

Couldry, N. (2010), *Why Voice Matters: Culture and Politics and Neoliberalism*, London: Sage.

Davies, J. (2011), *Challenging Governance Theory: From Networks to Hegemony*, Bristol: Policy Press.

De La Rosa I Esteva, J.L. (2011), 'Wits: complementary currencies backed by knowledge', paper presented to the International Conference on Community and Complementary Currencies, Lyon, 15–18 February.

Durose, C. and Richardson, L. (2015), *Designing Public Policy Through Coproduction: Theory, Practice and Change*, Bristol: Policy.

Edwards, G. (2009), 'Habermas and social movement theory', *Sociology Compass*, 3 (3): 381–393.

European Commission (2010), *Europe 2020: A Strategy for Smart, Sustainable and Inclusive Growth COM (2010), 2020 Final*, Brussels: Commission of the European Communities.

Fainstein, S.S. (2010), *The Just City*, Ithaca, New York: Cornell University Press.

Featherstone, D., Ince, A., Mackinnon, D., Strauss, K. and Cumbers, A. (2012), 'Progressive localism and the construction of political alternatives', *Transactions of the Institute of British Geographers*, 37 (2): 77–182.

Fischer, F. (2000), *Citizens, Experts, and the Environment: The Politics of Local Knowledge*, Durham: Duke University.

Fraser, N. (1997), *Justice Interruptus: Critical Reflections on the 'Postsocialist' Condition*, London: Routledge.

Fraser, N. (2003), 'Social justice in an age of identity politics', in Fraser, N. and Honneth, A. *Redistribution or Recognition: A Political-Philosophical Exchange*, translated by Golb, J., Ingram, J. and Wilke, C., New York: Verso.

Fraser, N. and Honneth, A. (2003), *Redistribution or Recognition: A Political-Philosophical Exchange*, translated by Golb, J., Ingram, J. and Wilke, C., New York: Verso.

Fricker, M. (2007), *Epistemic Injustice: Power and the Ethics of Knowing*, Oxford: Oxford University Press

Frost, R. (2014), *Justification and Critique*, translated by Cronin, C., Cambridge: Polity.

Gibson-Graham, J.K. (2008), 'Diverse economies: performative practices for other worlds', *Progress in Human Geography*, 32 (5): 613–632.

Goffman, A. (2015), *On the Run: Fugitive Life in an American City*, New York: Picador.

Gramsci, A. (1971), *Prison Notebooks: Selections*, translated by Hoare, Q. and Smith, G.N., London: Lawrence and Wishart.

Gret, M. and Sintomer, Y. (2005), *The Porto Alegre Experiment: Learning Lessons for a Better Democracy*, Zed Books: London.

Habermas, J. (1981), 'Towards a reconstruction of historical materialism', in Knorr-Cetina, K. and Cicourel, A. (eds.) *Advances in Social Theory and Methodology: Towards an Integration of Micro and Macro Theories*, London: Routledge and Kegan Paul.

Harvey, D. (1989), 'From managerialism to entrepreneurialism: the transformation in urban governance in late capitalism', *Geografiska Annaler*, 71 (B): 3–17.

Hay, C. and Payne, A. (2015), *Civic Capitalism*, Cambridge: Polity Press.

Henneberry, J. (ed) (2017), *Transience and Permanence in Urban Development*, Oxford: Wiley-Blackwell.

Hess, C. and Ostrom, E. (eds.) (2007), *Understanding Knowledge as a Commons: From Theory to Practice*, MIT Press.

Hopkins, R. (2008), *The Transition Handbook: From Oil Dependency to Local Resilience*, Totnes: Green Books.

Kenway, J., Bullen, E., Fahey, J. and Robb, S. (2006), *Haunting the Knowledge Economy* (Vol. 6), New York: Routledge.

Knorr-Cetina, K. and Cicourel, A. (eds.) (1981), *Advances in Social Theory and Methodology: Towards an Integration of Micro and Macro Theories*, London: Routledge and Kegan Paul.

Komninos, N. (2013), *The Age of Intelligent Cities: Smart Environments and Innovation for All Strategies*, London: Routledge.

Levitas, R. (2013), *Utopia as Method: The Imaginary Reconstitution of Society*, Basingstoke, Hampshire: Palgrave Macmillan.

Logan, J. and Molotch, H. (2007 [1987]), *Urban Fortunes: The Political Economy of Place*, Berkeley: University of California Press.

Madanipour, A. (2011), *Knowledge Economy and the City: Spaces of Knowledge*, London: Routledge.

Marcuse, P. (2009), 'From critical urban theory to the right to the city', *City*, 13 (2–3): 185–197.

Marcuse, P., Connolly, J., Novy, J., Olivo, I., Potter, C. and Steil, J. (eds.) (2009), *Searching for the just city: debates in urban theory and practice*, Routledge.

May, T. and Perry, B. (2016), 'Knowledge for just urban sustainability', *Local Environment*, http://www.tandfonline.com/eprint/iE9gQiruc4ahFAzFcnFF/full (accessed May 2017).

May, T. and Perry, B. (2018), *Social Research: Issues, Methods and Process*, 5th edition, London: McGraw-Hill.

McClintock, N. (2014), 'Radical, reformist, and garden-variety neoliberal: coming to terms with urban agriculture's contradictions', *Local Environment*, 19 (2): 147–171.

McFarlane, C. (2011), *Learning the City: Knowledge and Translocal Assemblage*, Oxford: Wiley-Blackwell.

McKee, K. (2009), 'Post-Foucauldian governmentality: what does it offer critical social policy analysis?', *Critical Social Policy*, 29 (3): 465–486.

Mitchell, D., Attoh, K. and Staeheli, L. (2015), 'Whose city? What politics? Contentious and non-contentious spaces on Colorado's front range' *Urban Studies*, 52 (14): 2633–2648.

Mitlin, D. (2008), 'With and beyond the state', *Environment and Urbanization*, 20 (2): 339–360.

Moser, P. (2013), 'Integrating Urban Knowledge', in Anderson, H.T. and Atkinson, R. (eds.) *Production and Use of Urban Knowledge*, Netherlands: Springer, pp. 17–34.

Mouffe, C. (2005), *On the Political*, London: Routledge.

NEF (2008), *Coproduction: A Manifesto for Growing the Core Economy*, New Economics Foundation: London.

Newman, J. and Clarke, J. (2010), *Publics, Politics and Power: Remaking the Public in Public Services*, London: Sage.

Nkulu-N'Sengha, M. (2005), 'African epistemology', in Asante, M.K. and Mazama, A. (eds.) (2005), *Encyclopaedia of Black Studies*, Thousand Oaks, CA: Sage.

Nyamnjoh, F. (2012), 'Blinded by sight: divining the future of anthropology in Africa', *Africa Spectrum*, 47 (2–3): 63–92.

Osborne, S.P., Radnor, Z. and Strokosch, K. (2016), 'Co-production and the co-creation of value in public services: a suitable case for treatment?', *Public Management Review*, 18 (5): 639–653.

Ostrom, E. (1996), 'Crossing the great divide: coproduction, synergy, and development', *World Development*, 24 (6): 1073–1087.

Peake, L. (2017), 'Feminism and the urban', in Short, J.R. (ed) *A Research Agenda for Cities*, Cheltenham, UK: Edward Elgar, pp. 82–97.

Pearce, J. (2013), 'Power and the twenty-first century activist: from the neighbourhood to the square', *Development and Change*, 44 (3): 639–663.

Perry, B. and Atherton, M. (2017), 'Beyond critique: the value of coproduction in realising just cities?', *Local Environment*, Available at: http://www.tandfonline.com/doi/full/10.1080/13549839.2017.1297389.

Perry, B., May, T., Hodson, M. and Marvin, S. (2013), 'Re-thinking sustainable knowledge-based urbanism through active intermediation', in Anderson, H.T. and Atkinson, R. (eds.) *The Production and Use of Urban Knowledge: European Experiences*, Dordrecht: Springer.

Perry, B., Walsh, V. and Barlow, C. (2017), 'Navigating the rapids of urban development: lessons from the Biospheric Foundation, Salford', in Henneberry, J. (ed.) *Transience and Permanence in Urban Development*, Oxford: Wiley-Blackwell, pp. 85–101.

Pieterse, E. (2017), 'The city in sub-Saharan Africa', in Short, J.R. (ed.) (2017), *A Research Agenda for Cities*, Cheltenham, UK: Edward Elgar.

Purcell, M. (2008), *Recapturing Democracy: Neoliberalization and the Struggle for Alternative Urban Futures*, New York: Routledge.

Purcell, M. (2013), 'The right to the city: the struggle for democracy in the urban public realm', *Policy and Politics*, 41 (3): 311–328.

Roy, A. (2005), 'Urban informality: toward an epistemology of planning', *Journal of the American Planning Association*, 71 (2): 147–158.

Royo, S. and Yetano, A. (2015), ' "Crowdsourcing" as a tool for e-participation: two experiences regarding CO_2 emissions at municipal level', *Electronic Commerce Research*, 15 (3): 323–348.

Sbicca, J. (2014), 'The need to feed: Urban metabolic struggles of actually existing radical projects', *Critical Sociology*, 40 (6): 817–834.

Schlembach, R. (2015), 'Negation, refusal and co-optation: the Frankfurt School and social movement theory', *Sociology Compass*, 9 (11): 987–999.

Schlosberg, D. (2006), 'Communicative action in practice: intersubjectivity and new social movements', *Political Studies*, 43 (2): 291–311.

Seyfang, G. and Smith, A. (2007), 'Grassroots innovations for sustainable development: towards a new research and policy agenda', *Environmental Politics*, 16 (4): 584–603.

Short, J.R. (ed.) (2017), *A Research Agenda for Cities*, Cheltenham, UK: Edward Elgar.

Sintomer, Y., Potsdam, H., Röcke, A. and Allegretti, G. (2012), 'Transnational models of citizen participation: the case of participatory budgeting', *Journal of Public Deliberation*, 8 (2).

Smith, A., Voß, J.P. and Grin, J. (2010), 'Innovation studies and sustainability transitions: The allure of the multi-level perspective and its challenges', *Research Policy*, 39 (4): 435–448.

Smith, G. (2009), *Democratic Innovations: Designing Institutions for Citizen Participation*, Cambridge: Cambridge University Press.

Swyngedouw, E. (2009), 'The antinomies of the postpolitical city: in search of a democratic politics of environmental production', *International Journal of Urban and Regional Research*, 33 (3): 601–620.

Taylor, M. (2007), 'Community participation in the real world: opportunities and pitfalls in new governance spaces', *Urban Studies*, 44 (2): 297–317.

Tyler, I. (2013), *Revolting Subjects: Social Abjection and Resistance in Neoliberal Britain*, London: Zed.

Unger, R.M. (2004), *False Necessity: Anti-Necessitarian Social Theory in the Service of Radical Democracy*, London: Verso.

Vicino, T.J. (2017), 'The city in Brazil', in Short, J.R. (ed.) *A Research Agenda for Cities*, Cheltenham, UK: Edward Elgar, pp. 182–194.

Watson, V. (2014), 'Co-production and collaboration in planning – the difference', *Planning Theory and Practice*, 15 (1): 62–76.

Young, I. (1990), *Justice and the Politics of Difference*, Princeton: Princeton University Press.

7

CRITIQUE AND TRANSFORMATION IN THE 'REAL' UNIVERSITY

Introduction

The desire for recognition among consultants and academics and how that reproduces mainstream discourses is a central ingredient in the reproduction of the configurations we have described between knowledge and power in neoliberal development. Process triumphs over purpose, which is a political terrain, through the tendency to allude to impersonal forms of knowledge in the relations between science and the public imagination (Ezrahi 2004). The gap between the imaginary and the real is one between a passive scientific gaze and the active post-Kantian self in which ideas cannot and should not be squashed, but explored and interrogated in a collaborative confrontation with the realities of the world itself (May and Perry 2017). In the history of science and experimentation there was an: "opposition between allegedly passive observation and active experimentation and a split within the scientist's own self" (Daston and Galison 2010: 242). That split, rather than the subject of reflexive consideration, can be manifest not only through an empiricist focus on the technical aspects of method, but also by withdrawal in theoreticism.

In view of the elitist retrenchment in higher education under the neoliberal gamble with universities (McGettigan 2013), tackling the above issues is important for knowledge production. Here, however, it is easy to provoke reaction. After all: "there are many intellectuals who call the world into question, but there are very few intellectuals who call the intellectual world into question" (Bourdieu 2007: 23). The expectation that critique and more just transformation will arrive without considerable political mobilisation against prevailing forces is, to put it mildly, unlikely. As it stands, the motivations of those who feed these views come in the form of reward through recognition and a profound ambivalence concerning the relations between critical, reflexive and engaged practice in the 'split' we referred to above. Yet individual responses are linked to contexts that reward certain behaviours manifest in what we already referred to as 'journal list fetishism' (Willmott 2011). As for those employed in urban development, the effects of institutional pressures on their practices cannot be readily dismissed.

With these points in mind, we continue our exploration of possibilities that might fuel alternative conceptualisations and realisations of our futures. As with chapter 6, we do not contend that these alternatives have been realised, nor are we ignorant as to the limits and barriers that lie before them. However, we do maintain that it is only through actively confronting, exploring and learning from efforts to transform the conditions and cultures of knowledge production and reception that we can hope to transcend existing limits. We seek to do this by examining the institutions and practices that we elaborated in chapters 4 and 5 in our critique of universities and dominant forms of knowing. Our journey into the world of higher education and its practices seeks to draw out progressive ideals and actions which unsettle an easy sideswipe at the so-called ivory tower. It is all too easy to support homogenising discourses that position universities as elitist bastions of disengaged intellectual fervour and academics as self-interested scholars in pursuit of higher journal rankings. As is clear so far, we are not suggesting this is not a clear facet of university life, but all organisations have a structuring effect on their employees. Culture and context matter, but they do not simply saturate practices (Bauman and May 2018). Therefore, we start with alternative ideas of the university and then turn to examine critical, urban research practices. We end by concluding that new epistemic practices are needed that contribute to an alternative knowledge commons.

Searching for the 'real' university

There is a call from within critical urban studies to appeal to the 'real' as a counterpoint to the urban imaginaries and visions promised by neoliberal growth co-alitions (Chatterton 2000; Hollands 2008; Perry et al. 2015). Such a call challenges forms of justification deployed in mainstream knowledge production as a stage in the constitution of more just relations (Forst 2014; Fricker 2007). In the process, dominant representations and trajectories are questioned through the incorporation of experiences of urban communities excluded from the promise of the knowledge economy. Systematic, comparative and collaborative research agendas may then focus on identifying and critically assessing 'real' examples of alternatives and generating transformative knowledge practices that inform and forge more inclusive and sustainable futures.

Paradoxically, the university is perhaps the institution most challenged by the knowledge economy as the traditional semi-monopoly of the university and its authority in large areas of knowledge production is increasingly under question. On the one hand, in the market of knowledge one would expect competition in knowledge production and provision to increase. On the other hand, the problem may be seen as partly 'self-inflicted' (Gibbons et al. 1994: 10). As universities have succeeded in producing skilled graduates, in response to demands for a mass higher education system, they move out of the university and create new sites for research and knowledge production. New knowledge producers include the role of 'knowledge officers' and those companies become knowledge organisations themselves (Barnett 2000). The rapid development of ICT and of e-learning also facilitates new providers that include so-called 'corporate universities' as well as various commercial, online, 'e-universities' and those selling expertise to write essays for students who can afford it.

As the university centres itself within the development of the knowledge economy, a process of 'self-infliction' is accompanied by attempts to occupy a terrain in which it becomes indispensable to its promulgation. A belief in the rational administration of complex societies meant the education of elites for this purpose. That was accompanied by particular views of knowledge and objectivism that came with a doubt concerning the capacity of ordinary citizens to participate in expert decisions (Noveck 2015). Knowledge formed its boundaries through a route in which it sought to short-circuit alternatives in its desire to legislate for what counts as valid knowledge, who may pronounce upon it and who should be included in its production. These tactics of knowledge short-circuiting may be situated within a broader process in terms of the contextualisation of science whereby science and society increasingly enter the domain of the other (Jasanoff 2012). Those involved in areas of basic research find themselves having to negotiate not just the support for their work, but even the very definition of research problems and content in a wider social arena. In so doing, science moves beyond valid knowledge production to the production of socially robust knowledge, sensitive to a much wider range of social factors and implications. In this sense, the authority of the university to determine what is researched and how, is weakened, but that does not necessarily weaken attempts to then re-draw the boundaries.

Aside from consultancies, universities are challenged by new forms of provision outside their walls which re-appropriate the term 'university' away from traditional institutions in the spirit of learning and pedagogy. In the UK, Ragged University, for instance, is about the free exchange of knowledge and skills in social spaces. It contends that knowledge should be 'enjoyed' and that people are about more than CVs, certificates and economic gain (https://www.raggeduniversity.co.uk/). The project is non-commercial, based on philanthropic values and runs learning events and meetings for anyone to attend, arguing for 'free education and valuing knowledge wherever it may lay'. Other examples come from the Free University Movement, such as the IF, a free university in London or the Free University Brighton. The Free University Brighton was founded by a Green Party activist who worked in organisational change. Here, students meet lecturers in free meeting places provided by libraries, community centres, or in caravans and trailers (http://freeuniversitybrighton.org).

Free universities may be seen as a protest against the growing marketisation of education and inspired by the free school movement of the late 18th and 19th centuries. They aim to create democratic educational experiences where learning is two-way and free educational events are run across an urban context. Whilst there is doubt about the extent to which they replicate existing tensions in the higher education sector, they have an explicit intent to reach excluded and disenfranchised groups – both as students and as citizens. Sperlinger (2014) quotes the poet and essayist Adrienne Rich, in her 1974 essay 'Towards a female-centred university' that it would be: "naïve to imagine that the university can of itself be a vanguard for change" and that there was power in the "unrecognised, unofficial university-without-walls" (https://www.theguardian.com). Such developments are suggestive of the power and bureaucratic freedom that exists outside the university in the creation of the knowledge commons.

Universities seek distinctiveness in the context of a much wider terrain of knowledge providers with whom they cannot and perhaps should not, compete. These institutions must be different contexts and cultures from other sites in order to be distinctive. Some place the uniqueness of the university in a: " 'lack of haste', its relative stress-freeness, or its socially sanctioned withdrawal from the swift pace of everyday life and alternative professional cultures" (Pels 2003: 2). What is needed is not participation in the freneticism of the reproduction of dominant views. Instead, we should find: "the preservation of a place of quiet, stillness and unhastened reflection, which must be incessantly negotiated for and demarcated against the speedy cultures of the 'outside' world" (Pels 2003: 2–3). Of course, the university is not immune to the pressures of speed and how time and power become implicated in the construction of organisational 'necessity' bolstered by particular appraisal and performance measures. Recovering time for the cultivation of contemplation informs those who seek to resist the trend of corporatisation in universities (Berg and Seeber 2016).

Universities do need to change their institutional cultures and develop comprehensive, realistic strategies (Benson, Harkavy and Puckett 2000) if social or community activities are not to be relegated to the realm of "non-essential, secondary and naturally-occurring activities" (PACEC/CBR 2010: 26). Considering universities as 'participatory learning organisations' (Levin and Greenwood 2016) by focussing on their social contribution, enables a longer-term developmental role in building capacity among different groups (Gunasekara 2006). As Amartya Sen puts it: "Individuals live and operate in a world of institutions. Our opportunities and prospects depend crucially on what institutions exist and how they function. Not only do institutions contribute to our freedom, their roles can be sensibly evaluated in the light of their contributions to our freedom" (2001: 142). Thus, to transform the urban context we can turn to the university as a place where frenetic activity is tempered, change is subject to critique and we find an alternative space for the incubation of ideas and knowledge whose generation is more inclusive.

Difference, resistance and transformation

In looking towards this possibility, to rewrite the history of universities as one of insulation from society is inaccurate. Equally, for them to become a simple reflection of the so-called imperatives of the knowledge economy, undermines them as institutions. As Steve Fuller expresses it: "It should become the clearing house for all the voices that would otherwise be silent or muted beyond recognition, with the understanding that these will change as the power relations in society change … Only in this way will the university continue to play a necessary role in the process of social reproduction – by reproducing dissent and difference – whilst retaining its independence" (2000: 78). For such reasons those concerned with understanding knowledge as a commons have urged that the exercise of the imagination of researchers turn to a world of potential colleagues, rather than passive recipients of knowledge (Boyle 2007). Universities must reclaim their position as civic and learning institutions.

In terms of context, the city has also been characterised as core to the creation of a civic university that brings together the global and local (Goddard, Kempton and Vallance 2012). Whilst this is sometimes expressed through a focus on the role of universities in the cultural economy, community engagement or as living laboratories for socio-ecological experimentation as affirmative rather than transformative, we see here the potential to refocus the boundaries and interactions between the university and society. Thus, the Alternative University Project, which developed in Montreal after a series of student protests, is based around the ideal of non-hierarchical, consensus-based learning. Their manifesto speaks of creative exploration, active learning and community involvement to show that 'a university can be a place without gates around it' and 'by giving as much as it receives' (http://participedia.net/en/cases/alternative-university-project-montreal-canada). Whilst this appeals to the localisation of higher education, with a strong emphasis on community engagement, free global online access is the goal of other initiatives. The University of the People (UoP) proclaims itself as the world's first nonprofit, tuition-free, accredited, online academic institution (http://uopeople.edu).

The promise of technology is embraced in an effort to open access to knowledge. However, changes such as these do not penetrate into the core of the university itself and are frequently mobilised to accelerate, rather than question and alter, the tendencies apparent in the development of the knowledge economy. It is not just external engagements, but internal transformations at the heart of the university that matter (Harloe and Perry 2004; 2005). Observers of changes have made a direct link between the endangered state of public universities and the decline of social democratic values in society as a whole (Levin and Greenwood 2016). They are sceptical of existing university engagement strategies in the US and elsewhere: "policy makers and most higher education administrators articulate some kind of democratic and economic mission for public universities in their public relations campaigns, and then rain down budget cuts and coercive assessment and ranking schemes on their institutions" (2016: 3). Such practices are inconsistent with the aim to recreate *public* universities for a participatory social democracy.

Morten Levin and Davydd Greenwood allude to examples to support these type of institutions. Sabanci and Ozyegin universities in Turkey were established as self-sufficient and sustainable participatory institutions. Mondragan University in Spain is part of a broader system and managed as a labour cooperative with students, faculty and administrators working together. They operate without lectures, with participatory methods of teaching, collaborative working groups and minimal hierarchical administrative costs. In the UK, the Social Science Centre in Lincoln aspires to follow a similar model, funded by subscriptions from staff according to the level of their salaries and managed by a cooperative system whereby students and staff collaborate to design and deliver courses. Their response is to advocate action research projects within the university to engage staff, students and professional support staff in redesigning more democratic civic institutions. Inspired by the Humboldtian idea of the university, they set out an agenda for 'Neue Bildung' by which they mean: "authentically integrated, system-based and interconnected courses put together in an education process aimed at behavioural change and the promotion of civic values and practices" (Levin and Greenwood 2016: 5). In the meantime, conflict between students and universities in reaction to the marketisation of higher education are apparent: for example, at the London School of Economics (http://occupylse.tumblr.com/), School of Oriental and African Studies in London (http://www.cherwell.org/2017/02/01/the-campaign-for-curriculum-decolonisation-in-soas/) or protests at the University of Cape Town over race and exclusions in higher education. All of this is accompanied by a questioning of curricula and their applicability to the world as, for example, in the case of the teaching of mainstream economics (Earle, Moran and Ward-Perkins 2017).

In terms of formulating a position on change and resistance within universities, in order to find the spaces of possibility for circumstances to be otherwise, it is worth noting that we should: "doubt the reality of a resistance which ignores the resistance of reality" (Bourdieu 2000: 108). There are movements and experiments emerging that point to different ideas about knowledge hierarchies not only outwith but inside the academy, relations between students and professions and citizens and educators. Therefore, the call is for greater dialogue. Such a dialogue would also need to have its expression within the university itself through breaking out of silos and forging new 'academic tribes' (Becher 1989) bound by stronger ties than disciplinary affiliation. For some, academics should be required to justify their own proposals and work in open forums in the presence of those from different fields in a 'democratic science policy regime', in which: "institutionalised forms of cognitive euthanasia extend the principles governing science to society itself" (Fuller 2000: 136).

Changes have led to calls to 'open' disciplines (Wallerstein 1996) through challenging the 'habits of thought' among academics (Strober 2010). Indeed, in the last ten years there has been a body of forward-looking studies that come from a range of disciplines: political science, geography, economics, sociology, comparative literature, planning, anthropology and architecture (see Cameron and Palan 2004; Drennan 2002; Gibson-Graham, Cameron and Healy 2013; Leyshon, Lee and Williams 2003; Madsen and Plunz 2002; Massey 2005; Watson 2006). We can see this as due, in large part, to how changing concepts have been generated through the global to an examination of action in context. The question for the social sciences is how to rise to these challenges?

Forging a critical, engaged research practice

There are those who have argued for a re-education of both society and the university itself as to its values via a form of 'pragmatic action research' that links an understanding of needs with the environment in which researchers operate (Levin and Greenwood 2016). Echoes are found here with allusions to a 'pragmatic social science' and attention to the conditions that enable its production (Stehr 1992). The Gulbenkian Commission (1996) to 'Open the Social Sciences' similarly drew attention to the responsibility of social scientists themselves for shaping the parameters of debate, as well as defining, through action, the types of activities that might characterise a revised relationship between social research and the outside world. Social scientists should: "take a hard look at their present structures and try to bring their revised intellectual perceptions of a useful division of labour into line with the organisational framework they necessarily construct" (Wallerstein 1996: 96).

There are difficulties in positions that contradict received wisdom as it leaves one open to charges of 'ideological bias' or 'political axe-grinding'. The result is that the social sciences must work harder to provide: "infinitely more proof than is asked of the 'spokesmen' of common sense" (Bourdieu 1993: 11). A movement away from narrowly conceived agendas in favour of pursuing transformative engagement is seen to be possible. As the editorial team of the World Social Science Report 'Challenging Inequalities: Pathways to a Just World' put it: "Transformative pathways, we suggest, require transformative knowledge; transformative in what it covers, how and by whom it is produced and communicated, and how it interlinks with action and change. There are key opportunities for a transformative knowledge agenda that is co-constructed with those who are experiencing inequalities and are in a position to influence change through policies, practices and politics" (UNESCO 2016: 274).

Taking the relations between the content of knowledge and the context of its production seriously, we find a paradox at work in relations between the university and society. Its distance constitutes a way of seeing that marks out the distinction and value of the work that it produces. Yet that same distance can enable that knowledge production to become implicated in relations of dominance. If we take the issues that are said to matter to cities as a condition of relevance, as mediated by officials within the discourse of the knowledge economy that easily translates into a problem because: "preconstructed objects … impose themselves as scientific objects" (Bourdieu 1991: 249). The process of the production and reception of knowledge – its interpretation and deployment – are framed within the status quo and with that departs the possibility for circumstances to be otherwise. To inform these dynamics we need a better understanding of how societies organise the production of sciences to better: "understand how sciences organize societies" (Harding 1996: 506).

Co-constructing research is seen as one way to overcome this paradox. However, whilst such knowledge may clarify what is needed, it is within collective practice that transformation is achieved. All forms of practice, in turn, need to be reflexive in orientation to remind itself of the values that inform its orientation and desired outcomes, as well as to guard against succumbing to a continuation of what already exists by turning means into ends (May and Perry 2017). These are clearly political issues associated with the need for greater inclusion and public deliberation concerning what matters outside of the narrow confines of the circuits that make up the knowledge economy. Critique, to inform this possibility, needs to first gain a purchase on this reproduction: "An understanding of contemporary relations of power, and of the Western intellectual's role within them, requires an examination of the intersection of a theory of representation and of the political economy of global capitalism. A theory of representation points, on the one hand, to the domain of ideology, meaning, and subjectivity, and, on the other hand, to the domain of politics, the state, and the law" (Spivak 2010: 237).

When it comes to taking these insights on board within the university, it depends not just on organisational rationalities and institutional conditions, but the cultures that inform the gaze and approach of the researcher. From this point of view, the city has fluctuated between being the subject, object and location of study: a crucible in which broader socio-economic, cultural and political dynamics could be examined; a lens through which a route from the particular to the general can be traced in pursuit of comparison and generalisation, or a terrain that is contested, complex and infinitely re-imaginable. Yet the relationship between urban research production and the city has been treated as a second-order question. Reflexivity concerning the relationship between research, policy and practice has been one-way, via a *dyadic* concern with individual academics and the external world. Differential levels of detachment, engagement, critique and complicity shape these relationships resulting in more nuanced accounts of the dynamic interactions between research, policy and practice worlds. Responses may contribute to the spectator view (see chapter 8), but also to a conflation that produces a distance from the world that easily spills over into a denial of the reality of the world via, for example, indifference, arrogance or displays of: "irresponsible utopianism and irrealist radicalism" (Bourdieu 2007: 9). It is a Janus-faced phenomenon as both distance and anticipation of what will be acceptable are continually at play.

For those concerned with critically engaged practices, the relations between organisational contexts and the content of work cannot be taken for granted. This means that: "urbanists must work to clarify and continually redefine the 'critical' character of their theoretical engagements, orientations and commitments in light of early 21st century processes of urban restructuring" (Brenner 2009: 206). Where a climate exists in which particular forms of knowledge have an attributed value, there is a strong temptation and perhaps even requirement, to feed its insatiable appetite. To avoid this means finding the other side of these processes to inform practices: "a secondary definition of the city of knowledge, operating somewhat in tension with the first, that a scholarly community should use its scientific knowledge to improve society in general and urban life in particular" (O'Mara 2005: 234). Critical academics may not get the oxygen of recognition that comes from producing the next recipe for success in the quiet and concerned activity of reproducing presuppositions of self-evidence. Alternative framings may easily be dismissed as falsehoods or the idealisations of those who fail to see the idea of necessity as given by the institution and economy. Feeding its imaginaries from within the university bolsters its epistemic authority and can contribute to a deficit view concerning those whose knowledge is excluded. This is particularly important to counter given that: "In all societies – democratic and nondemocratic ones – people live surrounded by epistemic injustices that call for resistance. But the difference is that in democratic societies, given their commitment to free and equal epistemic participation, there is a prima facie obligation to correct and detect the systematic disparities in the epistemic agency that different members of society can enjoy and the inequalities associated with them" (Medina 2013: 4).

We have seen the paradoxes in the selectivity of particular forms of framing. Resistance from within the university has to encounter the fact that its reproduction is not just outside the university and so readily identifiable at a distance, but that it works in proximity through rationales that work hard to produce their self-evidences (May and Perry 2013). A commitment to try to balance critique and engagement draws not only on different academic traditions and schools of thought, but also on the commitments of those who seek alternatives. Here, the tradition of critical theory plays its part through a reflexive process of knowledge production related to critique and social emancipation (May and Perry 2017).

Knowledge is not simply a mirror of reality, but a form of social criticism that recognises that it is embedded in social processes. Relations of domination inform not just systems, but meanings, claims and demands. The task is to seek alternatives to forms of oppression and control via understanding oppositional cultures and insisting: "that another, more democratic, socially just and sustainable form of urbanisation is possible, even if such possibilities are currently being suppressed through dominant institutional arrangements, practices and ideologies" (Brenner 2012: 11). A critical urban practice would reflect the legacies of the Frankfurt School in several key ways through insisting on: the need for abstraction and theoretical arguments about urbanisation under capitalism; the contextual and historical situatedness of knowledge; the rejection of instrumental, technocratic and market-driven forms of urban analysis and the desire to excavate the alternative, radical, emancipatory, latent yet suppressed possibilities for urban transformation (Brenner 2012: 19). In terms of the relations between theoretical and practical reason, we find theory in that it abstracts and falls short of suggesting what actions ought to be undertaken or providing route maps for change. It may be seen as practical in that it deconstructs and theoretically reconstructs modern cities; it does not offer a formula for social change. It critiques instrumental reason by focussing on how practice informs theory and provides a place from which to see the: "basic form of the historically given commodity economy on which modern history rests contains in itself the internal and external tensions of the modern era; it generates these tensions over and over again in an increasingly heightened form; and after a period of progress, development of human power, and emancipation for the individual, after an enormous extension of human control over nature, it finally hinders further development and drives humanity into a new barbarism" (Horkheimer 1972: 227).

What is opened up is a gap between the actual and possible. It is in this process that alternatives are revealed with implications for practice through recognition of and engagement with those forms of knowledge that are marginalised. In itself, this is not sufficient because in terms of the relations between knowledge and action: "there is no theory that can overcome this divide, because, by definition, it cannot be overcome theoretically; it can only be overcome in practice" (Brenner 2012: 18). The reflexive underpinnings of the project of urban research are explicit: all social knowledge is embedded and there can be no standpoint outside the time/space of history. Critical urban scholars must locate themselves in the city, in relation to the evolution of modern capitalism and consider what enables their own critique. In this respect, the central task is to understand what makes understanding possible: "the meanings and modalities of critique can never be held constant; they must, on the contrary, be continually reinvented in relation to the unevenly evolving political – economic geographies of this process and the diverse conflicts it engenders" (Brenner 2012: 19).

Participation and possibility: Ambivalence in action

We have reflected on the issues that arise in urban engagement that take matters of context and content and the pursuit of critique and insights of critical theory and pragmatism on board (May and Perry 2013; 2017; Perry and May 2015). In a classic statement of pragmatism, George Herbert Mead asked what if philosophy was to take itself out of the ivory tower of its existence and turn: "from its subjective and transcendental idealisms" into "the world in which we live and move and have our being" (Mead 1938: 514–515). His work was part of a tradition which does not see reality 'out there', but as actively created as we act in and towards the world. John Dewey then developed ideas on cooperative democracy whose relevance remains in the 21st century (Honneth 2007). Jane Addams (1860–1925) was a philosopher and social reformer. As women were often excluded from university careers, struggling to gain credibility and legitimacy for their work, alternative sites for social action and reform were developed. Addams converted her own house, Hull House, into a hub for local activities and community organising, supporting diverse immigrant groups in Chicago's poorest areas in her efforts to become "a symbol of the 'real' world – a world of work and of people that I longed to reach but could not" (Seigfried 1996: 56).

We can find the intellectual resources and historical examples of those who have moved across epistemic boundaries. Those who self-identify as scholar-activists engage from the academy to bring about the kinds of transformations that we outlined in chapter 6. The aim is to both embrace critique and learn to 'walk with others': "Speaking our moral truths to each other is a starting point for understanding each others' realities and for developing a wider consciousness. Learning to walk together on common ground is about negotiating the tricky line between universalism (what is best done for distant others) and particularism (how can we best improve our patch). Some level of wider judgement and cognitive reasoning is needed to stop the rule of the mob and a lapse into particularism and relativism" (Chatterton 2006: 276). Such research has found a role in relation to housing cooperatives (Chatterton 2008), migration (Huschke 2014) and climate change (Russell 2014). The task is to reimagine the university as a machine for not only the imagination but the active production of alternatives. In a similar vein O'Flynn and Panayiotopoulos (2015) see the role of the scholar-activist to bridge the gap between movements of social justice, developing counter-hegemonic narratives and a collective strategy for social justice. There are multiple challenges and difficulties in undertaking scholar-activist research, especially for those earlier in their careers (Suzuki and Mayorga 2014), whilst a range of writings and sharing approaches and learning have arisen (Flood et al. 2013).

Maintaining these different roles in the modern universities is no easy task and ossifications of affiliation between one and the other do nothing to recognise the ambivalence that is inevitable and is a condition of reflexive practice (May and Perry 2017). Gaze and position may combine in the absence of reflexivity leaving academia to be: "a velvet cage that makes it extremely difficult for individuals to make meaningful contributions to social movement efforts" (Croteau 2005: 20). Working at the boundaries of academia and other forms of practice is rife with issues. As we outlined in chapter 6, how certain forms of citizen engagement in local decision-making risks treating citizens' knowledges as inputs to an otherwise exclusionary set of practices, so this applies to the process of societal engagement in research, whatever its form may be. 'PUS' – public understanding of science – may easily lapse into a 'deficit model' in which the transmission of scientific understanding aims to address ignorance among the public. We can see this tendency in multi-disciplinary studies in which social science joins science as the means through which application is addressed among stakeholders, leaving justification unquestioned.

We need to be aware that we do not constitute scientific communities as coherent entities from which flow facts to the domain of lay knowledge. If we take a nuanced view, what implications does it have for the governance of science? The following factors are a start to the creation of better interactions between forms of knowledge. First, scientific communication is about different issues and groups at different moments in time. That requires a willingness to understand the dynamics of these processes outside of the normal realms of activity accorded to government and its manifestation in cities. Second, science, society and citizenship are all bound up together. Therefore, welfare and social development – domains often outside of the narrowness of scientific considerations – need to be taken into account. Third, understandings of risk, uncertainty and ignorance have conceptions that are worthy of consideration in their own right, rather than being forced into narrow frames that can easily dismiss 'local' knowledge as false. Fourth, instead of public engagement being after the event and perhaps even leading to suspicion, there should be forward, inclusive thinking and forms of public scrutiny that take on board the social contexts in which expected applications occur. Fifth, in the absence of single pathways for successful engagement, there should be a combination of experimentation and critical reflection to enable wider issues to be taken on board. Sixth, there is a need to encompass what are called industrial activities as inseparable from issues associated with scientific governance and social contexts and finally, alternative ethno-epistemic assemblages should be seen as part of the route to political influence and transformation, not regarded as diversions from narrow preoccupations (adapted from Irwin and Michael 2003: 150–151).

The idea of science as pure representation through an idea of mechanical objectivism is not necessarily openly defended in scientific communities, but in the spaces between science and publics and science and the techno-economic practices we have discussed, it is played out (Restivo, Weiss and Stingl 2014). If some forms of public understanding and inclusion in science are at the end of a spectrum, this contrasts with a range of more transformative methods where the aim is to: "engage the researched at the problem definition stage and to actively alter the social conditions in which they find themselves" (Robinson and Tansey 2006: 152). This research moves away from the subjectification of the researched towards a conceptualisation of people as active agents (Heron and Reason 2001). Participatory research, for instance, is a process which combines three activities: research, education and action (Hall 1979; 1981).

Participatory inquiry is sometimes seen as a way for researchers and oppressed people to join in solidarity to take collective action for radical social change leading to locally determined and controlled action. Key principles include the liberation of knowledge and political power within a continuous process of life and work (Fals-Borda and Rahman 1991); breaking down the distinctions between the researchers and the researched and involving people-for-themselves in the process of gaining and creating knowledge and in mobilising action (Gaventa 1988). Participatory action research offers a challenge to the epistemological hierarchies evident in both the knowledge economy and the academy through acknowledging the legitimacy of different knowledge claims and the right for individuals to use this knowledge as a guide in actions. Such approaches are contested and subject to critique, especially insofar as they may involve the insertion of researchers into other people's lives. Some have seen participatory research as a means to legitimise the personal convictions of academics concerning the oppression of the poor and to push for social change (Fideres 1992). Such efforts can be construed as patronising if the labels of marginalised or vulnerable end up undermining individuals' potential for human agency and extend institutional influence over people's psychological and emotional well-being (Ecclestone 2004).

These debates take place against a broader intellectual concern with the changing relationship between science and society. In 'States of Knowledge', Sheila Jasanoff (2004) considers whether coproduction 'loops back' and is reorganising the way we think about the relations of knowledge, power and culture. The co-producing society proposition concerns changes in the world and as such provides an analysis of how the relationship between science and society is changing under the confluence of pressures in the 21st century. It has given rise to a related idiom:

co-producing research. Research-initiated coproduction (Polk and Kain 2015) can be seen as the latest manifestation of a long lineage in participatory research (Facer and Enright 2016), drawing on a rich vein of action research and cooperative inquiry (see Greenwood and Levin 1998; Reason and Bradbury 2001; May and Perry 2018).

The factors influencing these trends come from the alignment of perspectives between endogenous and exogenous concerns. In the context of risk and the increasing complexity of society, global challenges are such that they cannot be addressed by any single discipline. Epistemic boundaries work against, not for, the production of social scientific knowledge that must combine with other forms of expertise to be relevant in the world. That is reinforced by an endogenous drive that the most interesting questions are at the intersections between disciplinary boundaries. Inter- or transdisciplinary knowledge production combines knowledge and makes new areas of inquiry. Accompanying this are conditions of uncertainty and increasing contestability of knowledge claims in which not only the authority, but sufficiency of expertise, is questioned according to: whose knowledge matters, whose knowledge counts and towards what ends? Attention is thereby drawn to forms of expertise that have been traditionally excluded from the knowledge production process. In these contexts, coproduction is heralded as a more ethical or even democratic way to produce research. Drawing on the traditions of participatory action research, many welcome coproduction as part of a more open and democratic process of knowledge production (Brock and McGee 2002; Durose et al. 2011).

Coproduction in research might be seen as lying on a continuum between collapse and questioning of epistemic boundaries between research and other forms of practice: "coproduction of knowledge requires that contributions from specific disciplines and social actors are not privileged over what other disciplines and social actors contribute" (Pohl et al. 2010: 271). Across multiple definitions there is a general consensus that coproduction means valuing different kinds of expertise in the research process from the definition of questions through to the analysis and representation of findings. End stage impact, 'knowledge transfer' and dissemination are dethroned in favour of an interactive, reflexive, learning and dialogic process of research which dismisses the juxtaposition between a: "knowing subject to a supposedly ignorant one" (Pohl et al. 2010: 271). Accounts are largely positive and optimistic about both the quality and impact of coproduction. Our emphasis on excellence and relevance as mutually compatible and achievable goals of a mature and reflexive social science has been more recently echoed in the insistence that, through coproduction, both 'social relevance' and 'scientific reliability' (Polk and Kain 2015) or 'intellectual insight' and 'wider public benefit' (Campbell and Vanderhoven 2016) are possible. Studies report positive effects and experiences with a focus on trust, reciprocity and commitment as key factors in building successful relationships (Facer and Enright 2016).

The claim being evaluated through both pilot studies (Campbell and Vanderhoven 2016) or large-scale international programmes (Mistra Urban Futures 2016; see: http://www.mistraurbanfutures.org/en) is that coproduction leads to 'better' knowledge that is more immediately useful and usable in practice. Yet studies equally report challenges and issues relating to the institutional power and strength of the university, funding constraints and continued hierarchies that impact on the degrees of equality within participants in projects. Whilst universities may not be homogeneous organisations, they strategically position themselves as agents of the knowledge-based state. Faced with such positioning, coproduction offers no quick fix or panacea and its practice raises questions concerning silences and exclusions within different research spaces and places. Power is fundamental: on the one hand, producing imbalances wrought by the bureaucratic weight of the university and on the other, raising the spectre of co-optation and silencing critique, to ensure that research does not capitulate to the 'technocratic demand for evidence' (Durose and Richardson 2015).

Challenges emerge throughout the research process, from design to implementation and the communication of results. Some have noted a negative qualitative shift in this research journey in the move from conception to analysis and writing up which accelerates the process of de-participation and exclusion (Bain and Payne 2016). What is sought to be avoided is a 'symptomatic social science' and how the processes of co-optation, to which we are all subject, should be open to analysis within supportive environments that seek to avoid individualisation of social problems (May 2015). Academic careers are often made on the back of reproducing conventional wisdom, moving across disciplinary boundaries to forget the histories on which innovations are claimed and producing neologisms that are attributed with insight by those who benefit from them. The parallels between these practices and those in the knowledge economy are clear.

Coproduction is said to be qualitatively different from other research experiences. The reasons it is qualitatively different relate to the arguments we have revisited in this book – a questioning of a simple subject/object dichotomy, the embrace of context as fundamental to the conduct and value of the research and the positioning of the research in epistemologies of reception to open up forms of justification to deliberation. However, coproduction is not new, nor is it another panacea to the issues we have identified. What is distinctive is how coproduction in the 21st century has been mobilised as a backlash against narrow economic-driven impact agenda, working as a call to action for a more engaged and critical social science. It is becoming a receptacle into which all aspirations and hopes for a better social science are currently being poured and thus any distinctiveness may evaporate. Yet critical analysis of its promise, politics and possibilities can only be achieved by interrogating its political, methodological and ethical dimensions, underpinned by a reflexive ethos and disposition. Indeed, coproduction centres the need, now more than ever, for a reflexive, critical and engaged social scientific practice (May and Perry 2017).

Summary: Spaces of mediating relations

A reflexive approach to urban research and engagement with the mission to create a civic university requires navigation between the paths of scientism and relativism and deconstruction and reconstruction. It is concerned with how to recognise different viewpoints and ways of knowing without undermining the sites of knowledge production that enable a critical distance that does not give itself over to 'scholastic slumbers' (Bourdieu 2000). That brings the disposition and position of the researcher within the remit of reflexivity in social inquiry, along with those who enter these spaces of engagement and learning. For all concerned, it becomes a continual process of seeking to understand what is seen, the manner in which it is constructed and its place within social relations and forging futures. During the process, it is necessary to take varying insights on board and translate them into a collaborative research practice. The process of research itself is not regarded as valid by virtue of being constituted by the reflexive attitude of the points of view of each participant. Research becomes a dialogic process whereby the views of participants are incorporated into the findings (Cook and Fonow 1990). Rooting actual experiences within contexts brings to light similarities in experiences, but also demonstrates disjunctures that require analytic attention, as opposed to being glossed over in favour of formulaic neatness as determined by models.

Given what we have said about contemporary dynamics, we offered no models in this chapter. Whilst a critical orientation to work, in terms of its processes, purpose and potential is needed, it is support for practices informed by the ethos we have outlined that is also required. As the army of 'doxosophers' (Bourdieu 2003), both inside and outside the university, benefit from current arrangements, frustrated ambitions may align to unrealisable expectations whereby attempts from different parties might lead to cynical resignation. Those outside of the confines of research communities need to be more involved and that means moving away from the very institutions that can provide varying degrees of shelter from contemporary pressures and being attentive to relations of power. That necessitates high degrees of effort from all those concerned, but whose capabilities to act are variable. It is not an easy task. Yet it is equal in effort to the work that goes into what already exists, but remains hidden in presuppositions and the frenetic efforts directed towards its reproduction. Change is a collective act. It is to an elaboration of its possible organisation, along with a final examination of the issues we have examined so far, that we now turn.

References

Bain, A.L. and Payne, W.J. (2016), 'Queer de-participation: reframing the coproduction of scholarly knowledge', *Qualitative Research*, 16 (3): 330–340.

Barnett, R. (2000), *Realizing the University in an Age of Supercomplexity,* Buckingham: Open University Press.

Bauman, Z. and May, T. (2018), *Thinking Sociologically*, 3rd edition, Oxford: Blackwell-Wiley.

Becher, T. (1989), *Academic Tribes and Territories: Intellectual Enquiry and the Cultures of Discipline*, Milton Keynes: Society for Research into Higher Education and Oxford University Press.

Benson, L., Harkavy, I. and Puckett, J. (2000), 'An implementation revolution as a strategy for fulfilling the democratic promise of university-community partnerships: Penn-West

Philadelphia as an experiment in progress', *Nonprofit and Voluntary Sector Quarterly*, *29* (1): 24–45.

Berg, M. and Seeber, B.K. (2016), *The Slow Professor: Challenging the Culture of Speed in the Academy*, Toronto: University of Toronto Press.

Bourdieu, P. (1991), 'Meanwhile, I have come to know all the diseases of sociological understanding: an interview', conducted by Krais, B., in Bourdieu, P., Chamboredon, J-C. and Passeron, J-C. *The Craft of Sociology: Epistemological Preliminaries*, edited by Krais, B., translated by Nice, R., New York: Walter de Gruyter.

Bourdieu, P. (1993), *Sociology in Question*, translated by Nice, R., London: Sage.

Bourdieu, P. (2000), *Pascalian Meditations*, translated by Nice, R., Cambridge: Polity.

Bourdieu, P. (2003), *Firing Back: Against the Tyranny of the Market 2*, translated by Wacquant, L., London: Verso.

Bourdieu, P. (2007), *Sketch for a Self Analysis*, translated by Nice, R., originally published in 2004 as *Esquisse pour une auto-analyse*, Cambridge: Polity.

Bourdieu, P., Chamboredon, J-C. and Passeron, J-C. (1991), *The Craft of Sociology: Epistemological Preliminaries*, edited by Krais, B., translated by Nice, R., New York: Walter de Gruyter.

Boyle, J. (2007), 'Mertonianism unbound? Imagining free, decentralized access to most cultural and scientific material', in Hess, C. and Ostrom, E. (eds.) *Understanding Knowledge as Commons: From Theory to Practice*, MIT Press.

Brenner, N. (2009), 'What is critical urban theory?', *City*, 13 (2–3): 198–207.

Brenner. N. (2012), 'What is critical urban theory?' in Brenner, N., Marcuse, P. and Mayer, M. (eds.) (2012), *Cities for People, not for Profit: Critical Urban Theory and the Right to the City*, London: Routledge.

Brenner, N., Marcuse, P. and Mayer, M. (eds.) (2012), *Cities for People, not for Profit: Critical Urban Theory and the Right to the City*, London: Routledge.

Brock, K. and McGee, R. (2002), *Knowing Poverty: Critical Reflections on Participatory Research and Policy*, London: Earthscan.

Cameron, A. and Palan, R. (2004), *The Imagined Economies of Globalization*, London: Sage.

Campbell, H. and Vanderhoven, D. (2016*), Knowledge that Matters: Realising the Potential of Co-Production*, ESRC, http://www.n8research.org.uk/media/Final-Report-Co-Production-2016-01-20.pdf (accessed May 2017).

Capello, R., Olechnicka, A. and Gorzelak, G. (eds.) (2012), *Universities, Cities and Regions: Loci for Knowledge and Innovation Creation*, Oxford: Routledge.

Chatterton, P. (2000), 'Will the real creative city please stand up?', *City*, 4 (3): 390–397.

Chatterton, P. (2006), 'Give up activism and change the world in unknown ways: or, learning to walk with others on uncommon ground', *Antipode*, 38 (2): 259–281.

Chatterton, P. (2008), 'Demand the possible: journeys in changing our world as a public activist-scholar', *Antipode*, 40 (3): 421–427.

Cook, J. and Fonow, M. (1990), 'Knowledge and women's interests: issues of epistemology and methodology in sociological research', in McCarl Nielsen, J. (ed.) *Feminist Research Methods: Exemplary Readings in the Social Sciences*, London: Westview.

Croteau, D. (2005), 'Which side are you on? The tensions between movement scholarship and activism', in Croteau, D., Hoynes, W. and Ryan, C. (eds.) *Rhyming Hope and History: Activists, Academics and Scholarship*, Minneapolis: University of Minnesota Press.

Croteau, D., Hoynes, W. and Ryan, C. (eds.) (2005), *Rhyming Hope and History: Activists, Academics and Scholarship*, Minneapolis: University of Minnesota Press.

Daston, L. and Galison, P. (2010 [2007]), *Objectivity*, New York: Zone Books.

Drennan, M.P. (2002), *Information Economy and American Cities*, Baltimore: John Hopkins University Press.

Durose, C. and Richardson, L. (2015), *Designing Public Policy Through Coproduction: Theory, Practice and Change*, Bristol: Policy.

Durose, C., Beebeejaun, Y., Rees, J., Richardson, J. and Richardson, L. (2011), *Towards Co-Production in Research with Communities*, http://www.ahrc.ac.uk/documents/project-reports-and-reviews/connected-communities/towards-co-production-in-research-with-communities/ (accessed May 2017).

Earle, J., Moran, C. and Ward-Perkins, Z. (2017), *The Econocracy: The Perils of Leaving Economics to the Experts*, Manchester: Manchester University Press.

Ecclestone, K. (2004), 'Learning or therapy? The demoralisation of education', *British Journal of Educational Studies*, 52 (2): 112–137.

Ezrahi, Y. (2004), 'Science and the political imagination in contemporary democracies', in Jasanoff, S. (ed.) *States of Knowledge: The Co-production of Science and Social Order*, London: Routledge.

Facer, K. and Enright, B. (2016), *Creating Living Knowledge: The Connected Communities Programme: Community-University Relationships and the Participatory Turn in the Production of Knowledge*, https://connected-communities.org/wp-content/uploads/2016/04/Creating-Living-Knowledge.Final_.pdf (accessed May 2017).

Fals-Borda, O. and Rahman, M.A. (eds.) (1991), *Action and Knowledge: Breaking the Monopoly with Participatory Action Research*, New York: Apex Press.

Fideres, J. (1992), *A World of Communities: Participatory Research Perspectives*, North York, Ontario: Captus University Publications.

Flood, M., Martin, B. and Dreher, T. (2013), 'Combining academia and activism: common obstacles and useful tools', *Australian Universities Review,* 55 (1): 17–26.

Forst, R. (2014 [2007]), *The Right to Justification*, translated by Flynn, J., New York: Columbia University Press.

Fricker, M. (2007), *Epistemic Injustice: Power and the Ethics of Knowing*, Oxford: Oxford University Press.

Fuller, S. (2000), *The Governance of Science: Ideology and the Future of the Open Society*, Buckingham: Open University Press.

Gaventa, J. (1988), 'Participatory research in North America', *Convergence*, 21 (2): 19.

Gibbons, M., Limoges, C., Nowotny, H., Schwartaman, S., Scott, P. and Trow, M. (1994), *The New Production of Knowledge: The Dynamics of Science and Research in Contemporary Societies*, London: Sage.

Gibson-Graham, J.K., Cameron, J. and Healy, S. (2013), *Take Back the Economy: An Ethical Guide for Transforming our Communities*, Minneapolis: University of Minnesota Press.

Goddard, J., Kempton, L. and Vallance, P. (2012), 'The Civic University: Connecting the Global and the Local', in Capello, R., Olechnicka, A. and Gorzelak, G. (eds.) (2012), *Universities, Cities and Regions: Loci for Knowledge and Innovation Creation*, Oxford: Routledge.

Greenwood, D. and Levin, M. (1998), *Introduction to Action Research: Social Research for Social Change*, London: Sage.

Gunasekara, C. (2006), 'Reframing the role of universities in the development of regional innovation systems', *The Journal of Technology Transfer*, 31 (1): 101–113.

Hall, B. (1979), 'Knowledge as a commodity and participatory research', *Prospects: Quarterly Review of Education*, 9 (4): 393–408.

Hall, B. (1981), 'Participatory research, popular knowledge and power', *Convergence*, 14 (3): 6.

Harding, S. (1996), 'European expansion and the organization of modern science: isolated or linked historical processes?', *Organization*, 3 (4): 497–509.

Harloe, M. and Perry, B. (2004), 'Universities, localities and regional development: the emergence of the Mode 2 university?', *International Journal of Urban and Regional Research*, 28 (1):212–223.

Harloe, M. and Perry, B. (2005), 'Rethinking or hollowing out the university? External engagement and internal transformation in the knowledge economy', *Higher Education Management and Policy*, 17 (2): 11–16.

Heron, J. and Reason, P. (2001), 'The practice of co-operative inquiry: research with rather than on people', in Reason, P. and Bradbury, H. (eds.) *Handbook of Action Research: Participative Inquiry and Practice*, London: Sage, pp. 179–188.

Hess, C. and Ostrom, E. (eds.) (2007), *Understanding Knowledge as a Commons: From Theory to Practice*, MIT Press.

Hollands, R. (2008), 'Will the real smart city please stand up? Intelligent, progressive or entrepreneurial?', *City*, 12 (3): 303–320.

Honneth, A. (2007), *Disrespect: The Normative Foundations of Critical Theory*, Cambridge: Polity.

Horkheimer, M. (1972), *Critical Theory: Selected Essays*, translated by O'Connell, M.J. and. others, New York: Herder and Herder.

Huschke, S. (2014), 'Performing deservingness: humanitarian health care provision for migrants in Germany', *Social Science and Medicine*, 120: 352–359.

Irwin, A. and Michael, M. (2003), *Science, Social Theory and Public Knowledge*, Maidenhead, Berkshire: Open University Press/McGraw-Hill.

Jasanoff, S. (2012), *Science and Public Reason*, London: Earthscan, Routledge.

Jasanoff, S. (ed.) (2004), *States of Knowledge: The Co-production of Science and Social Order*, London: Routledge.

Levin, M. and Greenwood, D. (2016), *Creating a New Public University and Reviving Democracy: Action Research in Higher Education*, Oxford: Berghahn.

Leyshon, A., Lee, R. and Williams, C. (eds.) (2003), *Alternative Economic Spaces*, London: Sage.

Madsen, P. and Plunz, R. (eds.) (2002), *The Urban Lifeworld: Formation, Perception, Representation*, London: Routledge.

Massey, D. (2005), *For Space*, London: Sage.

May, T. (2015), 'Symptomatic social science: reflexivity, recognition and redistribution in the Great British Class Survey', *Sociological Review*, 63 (2): 400–414.

May, T. and Perry, B. (2013), 'Universities, reflexivity and critique: uneasy parallels in practice', *Policy Futures In Education*, 11 (5): 505–514.

May, T. and Perry, B. (2017), *Reflexivity: The Essential Guide*, London: Sage.

May, T. and Perry, B. (2018), *Social Research: Issues, Methods and Process*, 5th edition, London: McGraw-Hill.

McCarl Nielsen, J. (ed.) (1990), *Feminist Research Methods: Exemplary Readings in the Social Sciences*, London: Westview.

McGettigan, A. (2013), *The Great University Gamble: Money, Markets and the Future of Higher Education*, London: Pluto Press.

Mead, G.H. (1938), *The Philosophy of the Act: Works of George Herbert Mead, Volume 3*, edited and introduced by Morris, C.W., Chicago: University of Chicago Press.

Medina, J. (2013), *The Epistemology of Resistance: Gender and Racial Oppression, Epistemic Injustice, and Resistant Imaginations,* Oxford: Oxford University Press.

Miao, J.T., Benneworth, P. and Phelps, N. (eds.) (2015), *Making 21st Century Knowledge Complexes: Technopoles of the World 20 Years After*, London: Routledge.

Morris, R.C. (ed.) (2010), *Can the Subaltern Speak? Reflections on the History of an Idea*, New York: Columbia University Press.

Noveck, B.S. (2015), *Smart Citizens, Smarter State: The Technologies of Expertise and the Future of Governing*, Cambridge, Mass: Harvard University Press.

O'Flynn, M. and Panayiotopoulos, A. (2015), 'Activism and the academy in Ireland: a bridge for social justice', *Studies in Social Justice*, 9 (1).

O'Mara, M.P. (2005), *Cities of Knowledge: Cold War Science and the Search for the Next Silicon Valley*, Princeton: Princeton University Press.

PACEC/CBR (2010), *Knowledge Exchange and the Generation of Civic and Community Impacts: A Draft Report to HEFCE*, https://www.cbr.cam.ac.uk/fileadmin/user_upload/centre-for-business-research/downloads/special-reports/specialreport-highereducationknowledge.pdf (accessed May 2017).

Pels, D. (2003), *Unhastening Science: Autonomy and Reflexivity in the Social Theory of Knowledge*, Liverpool: Liverpool University Press.

Perry, B. and May, T. (2015), 'Context matters: the English science cities and visions for knowledge-based urbanism', in Miao, J., Benneworth, P. and Phelps, N. (eds.) *Making 21st Century Knowledge Complexes: Technopoles of the World Revisited*, London: Routledge, pp. 105–127.

Perry, B., Smith, K. and Warren, S. (2015), 'Revealing and re-valuing cultural intermediaries in the "real" creative city: Insights from a diary-keeping exercise', *European Journal of Cultural Studies*, 18 (6): 724–740.

Pohl, C., Rist, S., Zimmermann, A., Fry, P., Gurung, G.S., Schneider, F., Speranza, C.I., Kiteme, B., Boillat, S., Serrano, E., Hadorn, G.H. and Wiesmann, U. (2010), 'Researchers' roles in knowledge co-production: experience from sustainability research in Kenya, Switzerland, Bolivia and Nepal', *Science and Public Policy*, 37 (4): 267–281.

Polk, M. (ed.) (2015), *Co-producing Knowledge for Sustainable Cities: Joining Forces for Change*, Abingdon: Routledge.

Polk, M. and Kain, J.H. (2015), 'Co-producing knowledge for sustainable futures', in Polk, M. (ed.) (2015), *Co-producing Knowledge for Sustainable Cities: Joining Forces for Change*, Abingdon: Routledge.

Reason, P. and Bradbury, H. (eds.) (2001), *Handbook of Action Research: Participative Inquiry and Practice*, London: Sage.

Restivo, S., Weiss, S.M. and Stingl, A.I. (2014), *Worlds of ScienceCraft: New Horizons in Sociology, Philosophy, and Science Studies*, Farnham, Surrey: Ashgate.

Robinson, J. and Tansey, J. (2006), 'Co-production, emergent properties and strong interactive social research: the Georgia Basin Futures Project', *Science and Public Policy*, 33 (2): 151–160.

Russell, B. (2014), 'Beyond activism/academia: militant research in the radical climate and climate justice movement(s)', Special Issue 'Practising participatory geographies: potentials, problems and politics', *Area*, 47 (3): 222–229.

Seigfried, C.H. (1996), *Pragmatism and Feminism: Reweaving the Social Fabric*, London: University of Chicago Press.

Sen, A. (2001), *Development as Freedom*, Oxford: Oxford University Press.

Sperlinger, T. (2014), 'Is a co-operative university model a sustainable alternative?' *The Guardian*, https://www.theguardian.com/higher-education-network/blog/2014/mar/26/free-university-cooperative-model-sustainable-alternative (accessed May 2017).

Spivak, G.C. (2010), 'Appendix: can the subaltern speak?', in Morris, R.C. (ed.), *Can the Subaltern Speak? Reflections on the History of an Idea*, New York: Columbia University Press.

Stehr, N. (1992), *Practical Knowledge: Applying the Social Sciences*, London: Sage.

Strober, M. (2010), *Interdisciplinary Conversations: Challenging Habits of Thought*, Stanford, California: University of Stanford Press.

Suzuki, D. and Mayorga, E. (2014), 'Scholar-activism: a twice told tale', *Multicultural Perspectives*, 16 (1): 16–20.

UNESCO (2016), *World Social Science Report: Challenging Inequalities, Pathways to a Just World*. Paris: UNESCO Publishing, http://unesdoc.unesco.org/images/0024/002458/245825e.pdf (accessed May 2017).

Wallerstein, I. (1996), *Open the Social Sciences: Report of the Gulbenkian Commission on the Restructuring of the Social Sciences,* Stanford, California: Stanford University Press.

Watson, S. (2006), *City Publics: The (Dis)Enchantments of Urban Encounters,* London: Routledge.

Willmott, H. (2011), 'Journal list fetishism and the perversion of scholarship: reactivity and the ABS list', *Organization* 18 (4): 429–442.

8

ORGANISING FOR PARTICIPATIVE FUTURES

Introduction

The future is not set, nor is it singular in its direction. Urban futures are sets of potentials for how we might live together in cities and it is the 'we' that is at stake in forging them. The promise of the knowledge economy will never be delivered if cities compete for global advantage and universities join them in the search; nor if urban strategic and decision-making processes are based on narrow, technical and elitist forms of expertise. The weight of expectations of knowledge *for* the economy is considerable but, as we have seen, pockets of alternatives are apparent and they harness the potential for more democratic change. Seeing this does not mean embracing naive optimism, nor a poor grasp of structural constraints, rather a belief in progressive alternatives forged in imaginative political spaces. That means reframing the economy away from governance by supposed mechanical and immutable laws, to seeing its dimensions in terms of power, regulations, distortions, distributions and effects.

Overcoming the idea that the economy is beyond human reach and design is one of the: "principal impediments to taking back the economy for people and the planet" (Gibson-Graham, Cameron and Healy 2013: 190). An acknowledgement of markets as neither being self-regulating nor self-equilibrating is required along with the notion that: "market conformity is not so much the key to growth as the guarantor that any such growth is ultimately unsustainable" (Hay and Payne 2015: 12). Thus, in this final chapter we first reprise our critique, but then ask how we can move and then organise for more participative futures. We consider what it would mean to focus on the knowledge needed for more sustainable urban futures in terms of who governs and whose knowledge matters and how research might be practised? We conclude by suggesting that more mediating spaces and practices are required in the messy, complex interstices of urban space that refuse to capitulate to a knowledge-based instrumentalism. The spirit is one of transformation and a consideration of how research can contribute to more progressive urban futures (Conti 2005).

Beyond knowledge for the 'economy'

Science has become ever more deeply integrated into the fabric of modern societies and is bound up in decisions about the environment, health, welfare and security (de la Mothe 2001; Scambler 2002; Stehr 2004; Strydom 2002). This has given rise to societies that: "run on expert processes and expert systems that are epitomised by science but are structured into all areas of social life" (Knorr-Cetina 1999: 1). Such is this process that it has altered the nature of democratic society, providing unambiguous and disinterested technocratic 'solutions' to multiple areas of public policy. In recent times we have seen a wave of politics that alludes to democracy being governed by expert bodies thereby playing a populist move by those who have benefited from the arrangements they now critique. When linked to forces that are indifferent to their consequences, this can easily form justifications for ignoring, denying or being indifferent to context, leaving one with the overall impression that: "the flows of capital would willingly dispatch themselves to the moon if the capitalist State were not there to bring them back to earth" (Deleuze and Guattari 1984: 258).

Whilst we have noted variations in the actions of states in terms of their gravitational pull on capital, we have also seen politicians allude to the control of experts over everyday life. What these populist sentiments often achieve is a displacement of the importance of values outside of the narrow terrain between knowledge, the economy and promise. In the process, other values about what our lives might become are impoverished. The market, after all, is a value created by the models of economists and the practices of daily business and political justification and reproduction, enabled through the isolation of factors within complex systems. It is framed and bounded through values attributed to forms of knowledge and in so doing, regulates what is known and thus admissible by omission and exclusion. What is needed is a transformation in this process, but one which: "takes seriously the capacity, intelligence, and expertise of all people and forges institutions that know how to marshal and use that human capital" (Noveck 2015: xvi).

With the dominance of a neoliberal ideology, a move takes place that seeks to naturalise some boundaries, whilst demolishing others. There are a number of ways in which this takes place. We have a sleight of hand from the construction of a public realm which is seen to comprise individualised consumption to a private one in which freedom takes a 'negative' form (Berlin 1979). Core to the development of an alternative conception, are the issues that arise in the support that negative conceptions (freedom 'from') require from positive ones (freedom 'to') and a need to curtail the negative freedom of some to enable the continuation of cultural communities (Honneth 2007: 240–253). However, we cannot overlook the power of the simplicity of arguments that naturalise the economy and link together desire, human nature and an idea of the operation of society: "The fact that in all these areas the argument is so simplistic as to be full of holes is, for ideological purposes, of almost no significance, particularly if one is proposing a more coherent alternative" (Graeber 2001: 257).

Boundaries: The why, how and what of knowledge

The point of the above is that the 'why' in the deployment of knowledge for economic gain in contemporary discourse takes on a similar move: it supplants 'what' (for) with the supposed technicalities of 'how' (to) in terms of the efficient use of knowledge according to a particular idea of abstract value: "In other words, talking about rational efficiency becomes a way of avoiding talking about what the efficiency is actually for: that is, the ultimately irrational aims that are assumed to be the ultimate ends of human behaviour" (Graeber 2015: 15). The how of knowledge, in terms of its assumed fit in fulfilling the promise, takes priority over what values knowledge is expected to serve. Such values are simply given and placed in the realm of the taken-for-granted through a naturalisation of global competition, the desires for urban development in its name and the eradication of context through an alignment between global excellence and competitive relevance. Hayek's epistemic defence of the market as a mechanism that fosters local and practical knowledge is then turned on its head: "the growth of global markets is associated with the disappearance of knowledge that is local and practical, and the growth of abstract codifiable information. Hence, there is something at the least paradoxical about Hayek's epistemic defence of the market, for the market as a mode of coordination appears to foster forms of abstract codifiable knowledge at the expense of knowledge that is local and practical" (O'Neill 2007: 192). Knowledge content becomes context-revising in an image whose very sensitivity to context would entail recognition outside of the bounds of its rationale thereby bringing light to its tensions and contradictions.

The sheer effort that goes into the boundary work to prevent this outcome needs to be taken seriously to inform alternatives. It becomes part of the habitual forms through which the institutions of urban governance select and deploy knowledge as part of contemporary political regimes of 'twofold legitimacy': on the one hand, appealing to the virtue of the populace during times of voting to choose those who will find solutions to their problems and on the other, once elected, to deploy the solutions given by an 'objective' analysis of the state of things derived from expert knowledge: "There was a time when harmony between the expert knowledge that legitimates the action of governments and the free popular choice that legitimates their actions was presupposed. Today these two principles tend to dissociate themselves, albeit without being able to divorce. And it is to fill this gap that the electoral process adopts this strange aspect of being a pedagogical test and a therapeutic process" (Rancière 2010: 143).

A concern with competitive success fed by 'expert' knowledge exceeds the realm of understanding among the urban population, with the naturalisation of the economy enabling this disjuncture to continue. That situation is not helped by the observation that social scientists who study alternative, common pool resources often end up adding to centralised forms of political authority (Ostrom 2015). The absence of such understanding has led those with whom we have worked over the years in cities bemused at the speed of changes, dissatisfied with the lack of time to reflect and silenced unless engaged in a self-fulfilling anticipation of the reproduction of the status quo. Freneticism – being and working at being busy with little time to stop and reflect – rules at the expense of reflexive, participatory learning. Those feelings should not be easily discounted for, as in organisations of urban governance and universities, this has social-psychological advantages and acts to displace alternatives: "Habitus of necessity operate as a defence mechanism against necessity, which tends, paradoxically, to escape the rigours of necessity by anticipating it and so contributing to its efficacy" (Bourdieu 2000: 232–233). Time and knowledge are implicated in power or, more accurately, in a relation that relieves participants of engagement with alternatives through the power of a spectator view of the world.

In speaking to officials, politicians and academics over a period of twenty years of research in different contexts, there is a sense of what Barbara Adam terms the 'window ethic'. It is one which: "belongs to the instrumental world of measurement. Located in the linear-perspective vision, it presents a reality independent of the specific, contextual vantage-point of observation" (Adam 1995: 152). We have argued elsewhere that a spectator view relieves oneself of the reflexive relations to knowledge that exists in recognition of contexts, embeddedness and an active role in sense-making and can also be found in critical practices (May and Perry 2013; 2017; May with Perry 2011). The spectator view is not 'philosophical' as if such a term places it within the speculative and beyond the 'real'; it works as the life blood of the practices we have charted and like the supposed 'laws' of supply and demand, acts not only as a transcendental regulator, but a contextual justificatory mechanism. After all, who can be against knowledge? One can, it seems, only be against the consequences of its application but, if that is placed in the future, it is seen to be beyond responsibility through allusion to permanent potential.

We have seen a great deal of this type of justification by managerial elites who assume that grateful masses or employees will eventually become enlightened as to the efficacy of their actions. Whilst there are those who suggest that history will have its revenge (Milne 2012), upon examination it frequently ends up being nothing more than framed by the interests of multinational capital (Crouch 2011) and a corresponding diminution of social democratic principles (Marquand 2004). To feed this requires not only a symptomatic politics that frames causes according to individualistic explanations, but a scientism satisfying its appetite. A constant hastening brings with it the view that territory is something to be reconstituted in a process in which the intangible goes in search of the unattainable. As Paul Virilio expresses it in an essay on speed and politics: "The final power would thus be less one of imagination than of anticipation, so much that to govern would be *no more than* to foresee, simulate, memorise the simulations; that the present 'Research

Institute' could appear to be the blueprint of this final power, the power of utopia" (1986: 141. Original italics).

The agonism between knowledge and belief, needed for democratic vibrancy, is collapsed once knowledge is instrumentalised and becomes a means to an end which, if not simply accepted, is adhered to in the face of the absence of time to consider alternatives. The 'performative' is replaced by the 'constative' (Bourdieu 2000) as ambiguity is turned into the symbolic power of the organisation of the urban in the name of political organisation over the expressions of politics in civil society. It is part of a displacement in which effort goes into avoiding the problems of the present in modern democratic societies: "in which power, law and knowledge are exposed to a radical indetermination, a society that has become the theatre of an uncontrollable adventure, so that what is instituted never becomes established, the known remains undermined by the unknown, the present proves to be undefinable, covering many different social times which are staggered in relation to one another within simultaneity – or definable only in terms of some fictitious future" (Lefort 1986: 305).

Here we have a process in which knowledge is framed and deployed where the capacity and capability to act upon the present is unevenly distributed, whilst the future is suspended through the armies of technicians engaged in prediction. Degrees of acquaintance with contemporary issues are mediated through descriptions and explanations born in the combinations of global excellence and competitive relevance. Engagement to challenge these processes is far from easy as the texts that describe them are not just objects, but possess rhetorical powers of persuasion that bring with them reductions in associated uncertainties regarding the justification for actions. Recognition of the ambivalence between knowledge and action meets a celebration of expertise born of a distance to context which, paradoxically, explains its attributed power. Context cannot speak back as it is structured by the content of knowledge as part of the apparatus of the political, leaving the 'how' through reflections on practice and the process of sense-making in context to be a residual activity. Indeed, to speak of actually existing conditions is a rude and irresponsible interruption to dream work. A consequence is that the content of expertise is not challenged and so the democratic sphere of deliberation is impoverished through technocratic and economic promise: "Ideologies are justifications of relations of rule or domination that insulate themselves from critical challenge by distorting the space of reasons and presenting relations of rule or domination as 'natural' (unalterable), 'God-given', or in some way falsely, as sufficiently justified" (Forst 2014: 104).

We have argued that there is clear tendency to use particular sources of knowledge to simply read off actions according to environmental 'necessities'. Equally, the relations between denial and knowledge cannot be underestimated (May with Perry 2011). Frequently: "scientific discourse misses the fact that the ability to deny is an amazing human phenomenon, largely unexplained and often inexplicable, a product of the sheer complexity of our emotional, linguistic, moral and intellectual lives" (Cohen 2001: 50). The sphere of intelligence – the application of knowledge to context in action – is supplanted by the 'model of reality becoming the reality of the model' (Marx) which has to be dealt with as part of the satisfaction of the reification of the economy. Texts then become part of the imaginary of the instruments of political institutions, leaving the terrains of politics to be enacted, in varying ways, within civil society. There is no speaking back to that process, only recognition if willing to be configured in its name. The 'new spirit of capitalism' (Boltanski and Chiapello 2005) has the ability to absorb and utilise critique, as well as escape through displacement to other locations (Chiapello 2014).

Whilst concerted efforts go into framing visions and their means to place them beyond doubt in the policy realm, another process is at work in the public realm to structure views of the economy: agnotology. This refers not to: "the study of ignorance and doubt under all their manifestations, as sometimes mistakenly asserted, but rather the focused study of the intentional manufacture of doubt and uncertainty in the general populace for specific political motives" (Mirowski 2014: 226). Think tanks and consultancies, often fed by the academic wares of university employees, produce the certainty, whilst the: "promotion of doubt over 'what orthodox economists really believe' has proven a convenient smokescreen behind which the procession can evade the pitchfork-wielding populace, all the while pursuing its conventional practice of telling its patrons what they want to hear" (Mirowski 2014: 230). This connects knowledge to an idea of being and prevents forms of action through the paralysis of doubt due to permanent suspicion, leaving the terrain of the future devoid of democratic participation and a field of endeavour for elites and the technicians of their visions (Mirowski 2014). Whilst it depends on the absence of questioning for its naturalisation, if justification for such a gap is needed, the 'doxosophers' are happy to be its apologists and there is always the neoliberal short-circuit we discussed: from the abstract idea of the market to its personification in individual freedom (also see Bourdieu 2005: Appendix II).

Doubt and scepticism mix with certainty with the former feeding the latter. There have been many critiques of attempts to improve the public understanding of science that emphasise the limits of a deficit model and the need for a two-way process of communication between science and society (Irwin and Michael 2003). Yet despite this mixture, science remains a black box for many societal actors and a "mutually tolerable ignorance" (Fuller 2000: 8) persists. Time frames then enter to displace a focus on the present whereby, despite what has been known for a long time about the problems of prediction, it is a source of epistemic reproduction. The attribution of value to what are taken to be universal methods readily permits scientism to saturate the realm of political responsibility for context, the result of which indicates willingness for the city to be a place of continual adaptation to the demands of abstract forces. A technicism of method based on aspatial indifference and tempering of 'extraneous' values in the constitution of facts, mixes with political justifications. What this all demonstrates is the circuits of receptiveness of the aspirant city to become a vibrant site for global futures. The indifferent method mixes with desire that seeks to place decisions beyond doubt and renders places ever more flexible in their attraction to capital.

All that is solid has not just 'melted into air' (Marx), but the air breathed by the promulgators of promise have created their own micro-climates. You are not permitted to breathe that air when critiquing its content by allusion to consequence, for that is seen as synonymous with a denial of willingness to participate in its realisation. It might be argued that knowledge is anchored to time and scale, but those are things to be reconfigured. There is no history to this, for that is to be eradicated and innovation itself can become nothing more than the forgetting of history that is convenient to those who wish to claim novelty. It is a project, fed by those seeking status in satisfying its insatiable appetite that contributes to bracketing of relations between the past, present and future. What becomes inhibited is an: "understanding of selves and societies *being* their pasts and futures, of mutual implication, of coevalness, of unity and relatedness with difference. Finally, the future is conceived as a realm to be conquered and colonised. It is considered to be a calculable realm of potential, a world amenable to prediction and control on the basis of past experiences" (Adam 1995: 169. Original italics). The dream is realised by removing recognition of its dystopian dimension.

Changing contexts: Contextualisation, uncertainty and complexity

The ideological circuits we have characterised are manifest in the speed, intensity and complexity of change. The reasons for this state of affairs have been attributed to advances in information technology, globalisation and capitalism and this new epoch brings with it fragmentation, disaggregation and feelings of a loss of control, along with a turn to the apparent certainties of fundamentalist beliefs. Towards the end of the 20th century, writers turned to consider how these vast changes in society were having considerable implications for recasting the relationship between science and society, driven by science and technology in the context of first industrialisation and then post-industrialisation.

Increasing complexity, uncertainty and dialogue between science and society has led to the 'contextualisation' of a more socially accountable science which itself requires a different reflexive relation to work on the part of the researcher. For some, the social distribution of expertise and the fragmentation of established linkages between expertise and institutional structures are fundamental in informing degrees of reflexivity (Nowotny et al. 2001). The result is not only shifting boundaries between the public and science, but also intellectual property and public and private forms of knowledge (Harvey and McMeekin 2007; Dreyfuss, Zimmerman and First 2001). For Sheila Jasanoff (2004), this gives rise to a new 'idiom of coproduction': that is, the proposition that the ways in which we know and represent the world (both nature and society) are inseparable from the ways we choose to live in it: "Scientific knowledge is not a transcendent mirror of reality. It both embeds and is embedded in social practices, identities, norms, conventions, discourses, instruments and institutions" (2004: 3).Coproduction is an *idiom* rather than a theory, a way of interpreting and accounting for complex phenomena that can be applied to how knowledge-making has been incorporated into processes of state making and how, in turn, the practices of governance influence the making and use of knowledge. To this extent, knowledge becomes the object of study itself as it is: "crystallizing in certain ontological states – organisational, material, embodied" (Jasanoff 2004: 3).

As social and technological problems have become larger, so the search for certainty has become more challenging for social scientists faced with complexity and interdependence. In efforts to manage this complexity we have already seen how boundaries have been constituted to deal with and avoid the encounter with ambivalence. For Bruno Latour, a nature/culture divide pervades us and we should put aside the state of nature: "The world is young, the sciences are recent, history has barely begun, and as for ecology, it is barely in its infancy. Why should we have finished exploring the institutions of public life?" (Latour 2004a: 228). Latour (1993) takes the non-human elements in the world on a par with the human through a network approach in which the domains of nature, society and language become integrated and subject to a process of 'hybridisation'. What is avoided is the subject–object duality in which humans not only stand at the centre of the universe, but through which the objective is approached as exteriorised and the subject interiorised.

If the quest for certainty moved us from an understanding of 'argumentation' in Renaissance humanism, towards a concern with 'proof', critique needs to attend to matters of concern (Latour 2004b). Matters of concern are not just about discrete fields of endeavour that support the aspirations of scientism, but those things that have also now become part of the everyday practices of life. Those changes that informed Descartes' time and fuel the search for certainty at a distance are now part of constitution of the contemporary world. Whereas there was a belief that a rationally organised world of scientism would produce outcomes that could be universalised, we see an increasing disenchantment that requires a process of "perpetual reorientation" (Bauman 2014: 54). Thus, the search for certainty and the impossibility of its attainment rears its head once more. Yet, now, changes in the relationship between science and society remove that goal even more clearly from vision. A more reflexive social science concerns the replacement of certainty with the relations between knowledge, uncertainty and choice (Morgan 1983). This means a: "new discursive culture of perception, communication and collective attempts to define and resolve an unprecedented problem turned into a public and political issue" (Strydom 2002: 5).

To inform change, we need a broader understanding of: "the more pervasive cognitive dimension that embraces acts of recognition and knowledge, processes of the generation of knowledge and the micro, meso and macro cognitive structures shaping, forming and containing knowledge from the outset and throughout" (Strydom 2002: 148). For Piet Strydom, the work of Jürgen Habermas is central to this development (also see Strydom 2000). We can see this in Habermas' remarks on Dewey: "The question for certainty is the obverse side of a consciousness of risk which is aware of the fact that enduring 'adaptive' behavioural patterns can develop only through productive coping with disappointments and the progressive mastering of problems. What sets human being[s] apart as active beings is precisely this problem-solving behaviour" (Habermas 2006: 134–135). Taking us away from contemporary circuits and images as societies become more complex and inter-connected in the context of forces of globalisation and technological development, also means recognition of knowledge producing certainty receding. Such recognition takes place against a background in which the effects of these changes are negative: an increasing encroachment of instrumental rationality into the lifeworld with a resulting diminution in freedom; dehumanisation and the shifting emphasis from a sphere of reflexive understanding to the calculation of particular means to secure predetermined ends (Ritzer 2015). For those who have sought to explain the crises endemic to contemporary capitalism, this is characteristic of dialectic relations between helplessness and omnipotence in societies which are: "dominated by the wage form of labor and commodity form of need satisfaction" (O'Connor 1987: 167).

In turning towards science to seek certainty, we find a body of knowledge open to continual revision. The idea of a 'risk society' (Beck 1992) is central here, mixing with recognition that forces have been unleashed whose control depends upon a global effort (Giddens 2009; Koch 2012). Here was the first of many works examining the relationship between structures and agency in the era of 'reflexive modernisation' (Beck, Giddens and Lash 1994). There is so much to know and so little possibility of doing so: "Where is the line between prudent concern and crippling fear and hysteria? And who defines it? Scientists, whose findings often contradict each other, who change their minds so fundamentally, that what was judged 'safe' to swallow today, may be a 'cancer risk' in two years' time? Can we believe the politicians and the mass media, when the former declare there are no risks, while the latter dramatise the risks in order to maintain circulation and viewing figures? Let me end with an ironic confession of non-knowledge. I know that I, too, simply do not know" (Beck 2006: 345). The idea of a risk society is one in which ecological disasters mix with an increasing circulation of knowledge and a micro-ethics of responsibility that heightens uncertainty. Such conditions increase the need for reflexivity about the strengths and limitations of our knowledge claims.

Post-normal science is another way of framing what informs the developments we have charted. Developed by Silvio Funtowicz and Jerome Ravetz (1993), it mirrors a need for new modes of knowledge production where there is uncertainty, disputation, urgency and high stakes. We cannot know the future, scientific work is contested and topics such as climate change and immunisation programmes have high decision-stakes. As such, justification and application require an 'extended peer community': "Natural systems are recognized as dynamic and complex; those involving interactions with humanity are 'emergent', including properties of reflection and contradiction. The science appropriate to this new condition will be based on the assumptions of unpredictability, incomplete control and a plurality of legitimate perspectives" (Funtowicz and Ravetz 1993: 739). Facing up to the possibility of these relations is, as we have suggested, met equally with denial as with acceptance. Taking knowledge, in terms of its potential for economic growth, not only frames its relevance, but works to relieve those who participate in its realisation and application of a consideration of alternatives.

Wicked problems, just outcomes?

Against this background we can see an increasing emphasis not on growth, but urban sustainability. Symptoms of urban crisis include urban inequality and advanced marginality, characterised by: "mounting misery, stupendous affluence and festering street violence" (Wacquant 2008: 279). For many authors, deteriorating living conditions, civil unrest, unemployment, homelessness, economic insecurity and resource scarcity are all symptomatic of a general 'urban crisis' (Desmond 2016; Klak 1994; Pieterse 2008; Weaver 2016). Such characterisations draw attention to increasing *chronic* stresses that city administrations must manage and *acute* shocks, such as natural and humanitarian disasters, disease outbreaks, terrorist attacks or financial collapse. Whilst the term 'crisis' is often reserved for humanitarian disasters, the *Zero Draft of the New Urban Agenda* for Habitat III notes how population growth poses massive systemic challenges in relation to employment, housing, basic services and infrastructure: "the battle for sustainable urban development will be won or lost in cities … there is a need for a radical paradigm shift in the way cities and human settlements are planned, developed, governed and managed" (Habitat 2016: 1).

Cities benefit from density, agglomeration and proximity, characteristics which simultaneously create (often highly localised) problems including pollution and stress (Swyngedouw 2009). One key task for urban coalitions has been developing strategic solutions to urban sustainability problems, a quintessential epistemic mess (Bulkeley and Betsill 2005), whose causes and consequences are embedded within multiple layers of urban society. The governance of sustainable cities represents a 'wicked' issue whose solution is necessarily interdisciplinary, requiring multiple stakeholders' knowledge, skills and expertise (Polk 2015). Addressing urban sustainability problems requires capacity to integrate and manage a huge range of intersecting forms of global and local knowledge in order to develop appropriate policy responses, instruments and interventions (Moser 2013). 'Wicked' problems are different and may be seen as too complex and risky to embark upon, as well as problematic for those whose professional recognition rests upon established epistemic communities of practice.

The term 'wicked problem' was coined by Rittel and Webber in 1973. Through an examination of planning problems, they concluded that contemporary intelligence was insufficient to the complex task of planning across multiple domains, given the pluralities of interests and objectives involved. Whilst science is about 'taming', planning problems are getting wilder and more 'wicked' (1973: 160). Wicked problems have a number of characteristics including the absence of clear definitions and any sense of what is true/false or good/bad. Climate change is said to be a 'super wicked problem' (Levin et al. 2012) insofar as it is also characterised by: intense urgency; those addressing the problem also causing it; weak or nonexistent central authority and policy responses which irrationally discount the future. In this, we see Funtowitz and Ravetz's post-normal science rear its head. In a similar vein, others have written about 'messes', a term used by Russell Ackoff to characterise systems of problems which need to be addressed: "Managers are not confronted with problems that are independent of each other, but with dynamic situations that consist of complex systems of changing problems that interact with each other. I call such situations *messes*" (Ackoff 1979: 99). Complex problems have little consensus on how to solve them and often take place in contested and negotiated policy arenas. Roberts (2000) notes the relative merits of authoritative, competitive and collaborative strategies depending on levels of conflict present, the distribution of power among stakeholders and the degree to which power is contested. Yet we can also see that coproduction is a potential strategy for dealing with wicked problems and strategic messes and is distinctive in taking the question of expertise seriously. It fundamentally requires a reflexive disposition, alternative forms of urban governance and recognition that existing circuits of knowledge and expertise are limited and limiting.

A gap remains between policy discourses and more socialised forms of knowledge-sharing through open deliberation, understanding and populating alternative visions for the future. Whilst we see the popularity of texts on being a 'reflective practitioner' and the 'knowing-doing gap' in organisations (for example, see Pfeffer and Sutton 2000; Schön 1991), we see very little of taking these insights into a systematic, comparative process within and between cities in different countries where limitations, as well as strengths, and learning from alternative trajectories and values are honestly appraised. It is this gap that needs filling. Recognition of ambivalence and choice is ironed out by forms of knowledge and practices that separate the political and politics and place it within the symbolic power of the organisation of the urban political apparatus in the name of elites. Mutual understanding between different parties and how they are positioned in terms of the potential for creating alternative practices is displaced and the effects of that can erupt in struggles within civil society.

To counter this, calls for the 'just city' focus upon strategies that build coalitions of interest to focus on issues of equity (Fainstein 2010). To achieve this end, knowledge needs to be unbundled and rebundled (Perry et al. 2013) to prioritise synthesis, application and learning as much as the generation of new knowledge. It is a challenge to the imaginary whereby global excellence and competitive relevance lead academics, consultants and think tanks to peddle their models of reality as the reality of their models. Learning through shared know-how is precisely the kind of exchange between cities that should be encouraged to replace the dominant emphasis on one-size-fits-all solutions, drawing on an expanded concept and practice of urban expertise and evidence (McFarlane 2011). The search for just and environmentally sustainable futures requires organising cities in such a way as to connect knowledge about an area to the capacities and capabilities to make desired changes. That may be one which: "brings the multiple and disparate efforts of those fighting against unjust urban conditions into relief and relate their struggles to each other as part of a global orchestration improvised around the single tenor of justice" (Connolly and Steil 2009: 1).

Social scientific knowledge in action

There is a growing interest in the idea of 'deliberative' spaces (Davison et al. 2016), 'safer' spaces (May and Perry 2017), 'third spaces' (Comunian and Gilmore 2015) and 'third places' (Oldenburg 2000) linked to the idea of knowledge as commons (Hess and Ostrom 2007). If the alternatives we have discussed are to support more just urban transformations through facilitating more inclusive knowledge production, we need to consider how we practise as researchers. This does not presume a single model which can be replicated across contexts, but a commitment to a different way of working (May and Perry 2011). Much has been written about the *endogenous imperative* for new modes of knowledge production, in which the interesting areas of research are at the intersections of disciplines (Gibbons et al. 1994) and an *exogenous imperative* in which 'wicked issues', such as urban sustainability, inherently require different approaches to the production of knowledge (Polk 2015). However, less is said about a *reflexive imperative* to review the social organisation of knowledge within cities and the implications for academic practice – in other words, whose knowledge claims are being supported? Who benefits? (Agyeman and Evans 2004). As boundaries are moving and the practices we have criticised are also shaped and informed by those within universities, these contexts themselves need examination in terms of the content of what is produced, how and with whom?

New ways are needed to deal with societal challenges that ensure decisions taken today are robust enough for sustainable futures. Inclusion and participation should be recognised as core to the direction of cities. It is important to build not on the specialised knowledge of a few experts, but also the experience and knowledge of groups and communities in the city. That requires an acknowledgement that difference is not an impediment to knowledge for effective action to develop, but its precondition. A movement away from an irresponsible politics of possibility to a more dialogic approach is informed by causes that take account of complex environments. By seeking to constitute these collaborative practices, no claim is made that they represent solutions to preexisting problems, or that they are conducted without issues arising in terms of power, expectation and a capacity and preparedness to act in terms of their outcomes. What is being claimed is that we need to take the political climate and continuing issues seriously by building partnerships based on trust into practices and that takes time to achieve. We have argued that means changing the institutional expectations that weigh upon parties to these processes. In specialised divisions of labour, the fragmentation upon which neoliberalism relies so often sees declarative statements blend into categorical assertions leaving alternative forms of action to one side through a relief of responsibility to have any position other than that of the status quo. A clear casualty becomes the mutual understanding between different parties and how they are positioned in terms of the potential for creating alternative practices.

The process enables an understanding of forms of knowledge, including that which is 'tacit'. Whilst deployed in all sorts of ways in various fields of endeavour, it may be captured by the idea that: *"we can know more than we can tell"* (Polanyi 1983: 4. Original italics). The act of socialising knowledge continues apace in these formulations. Whatever the means through which we communicate about something, there is reliance upon its reception that completes its understanding. It is a gap to be bridged through: "intelligent effort on the part of the person to whom we want to tell what the word means" (Polanyi 1983: 6). This has the potential to break down that which saturates city-thinking: that is, the permanent possibility of a focus upon the future through a denial of present issues that affect the many, not the few who are lining their pockets through accumulation through dispossession (Banerjee-Guha 2010). It also means taking seriously the epistemic framing of so-called problem populations that serves to depoliticise issues (Pieterse 2008). As Harry Collins puts it at the start of his study into tacit and explicit knowledge: "tacit knowledge makes speakers fluent, lets scientists understand each other, is the crucial part of what teachers teach, makes bureaucratic life seem ordered, comprises the skill in most sports and other physical activities, puts the smile on the face of the *Mona Lisa* and, because we users bring the tacit knowledge to the interaction, turns computers from *idiots savants* into useful assistants" (2010: 1. Original italics).

Active intermediation and reflexive spaces

These forms of knowledge can be considered and mediated through a collaborative process of working with city officials and communities to exchange knowledge, learn and inform actions. Both the cultures of knowledge production and reception can become open to reflexive scrutiny and with that, the possibility for transformation. Knowledge can help us both a little and a lot. It can help a little in the sense that transformation is not a matter of theory, philosophy or knowledge and a great deal in the sense that it can: "destroy the rationalistic ideology, the illusion of omnipotence, the supremacy of the economic 'calculus'" (Castoriadis 1991: 197). Within a process of 'participative transformation' (Klev and Levin 2012), the exercise of thought and responsibility takes place alongside seeing reason and rationality as historical creations of our making. After all, we have changed many times in our history before and better possibilities remain open to us for how we organise our cities in a world faced with the depletion of natural resources alongside vast inequalities and injustice.

Consideration to more general and appropriate forms of organising urban research as a collaborative endeavour is needed. There is no model to be imported, but a framework of considerations through a process of comparative learning. Needs will vary between cities and there will be differences in the issues they encounter (what) and the capacity and capability to take action (how). Core to this work is its embeddedness in cities and the building of trust to ensure the viability and success of its development. Concerted action to achieve just, sustainable cities does require transformations in our societies. It requires effective organisation and the inclusion of those who are often excluded from the knowledge production process. For Michael Burawoy (2004) an intellectual division of labour is needed which differentiates between and transcends a policy social science that produces instrumental knowledge for a professional audience and a public one which produces reflexive knowledge for a critical audience. The challenge is to engage with multiple publics in multiple ways by connecting social science and civil society more systematically.

The relationship between knowledge, context and action is informed by these changing forces. Whilst often beset by 'devilish dichotomies' (Perry and May 2010), knowledge needs not just to be produced, but actively communicated and understood according to different contexts. The city is not just a unit of analysis, but a place in which knowledge is created in different places, disseminated in various ways, acted upon, denied and ignored. To this extent the challenge of urban sustainability is about bringing into being new ways of interacting between producers and receivers of research and organising those activities. The need for the integration of what is already known in cities is now greater than ever and to counter current trends, in the search for the new, we must not forget the past. Disparate knowledges can be integrated, seen alongside each other and re-contextualised. Sharing individual understandings can generate new social learning. Only then does it become possible to know when and how knowledge has had particular outcomes that are seen, by different parties, to have had benefits or contain potentials. Considerable effort is needed in order to learn from processes and there are no quick routes towards this end. This implies taking lessons from the past and not ignoring them in the name of slogans such as 'innovation' and 'enterprise'. It also means sharing an understanding of orientations and institutional positions, discussing their value as well as their limits to seeing. To tackle this means stressing the importance of understanding the relationship between content, context and consequence.

For the above purpose, mutual and cooperative achievement of understanding amongst collective participants is required. All parties must understand the meaning of communication requiring a 'public sphere', a discursive space outside the influence of elites where issues can be more freely discussed and defined in order to restrict elite power (Habermas 1989). To oppose hegemonic interests dictating public opinion and relations, social movements and public spaces are both needed to challenge the rise of consumerism and the stage management of the political process. When mobilising 'situated solidarities' in social movements and alternative forms of practice, recognition of interest is both unavoidable and necessary in order to bring about social change (Routledge and Driscol Derickson 2015). Here, our suggestion is that we draw upon recognition of being situated in a way that gives rise to certain values, but create and enlarge existing *mediated spheres* that provide the grounds for understanding of actions in a dynamic between existence and social scientific accounts. The emphasis is upon a process of generating intelligibility (Shotter 1993). The critical task for social scientists becomes that of boundary-spanning and sense-making between different realms: between science and society, justification and application, epistemic communities and communities of practice, endogenous and referential reflexivity and belonging and positioning.

Inspired by debates concerning the contextualisation of science and society and coproduction in research, different spaces for reflexive social science are being imagined. In complex social and political settings, reflexivity is needed to "manage disorderly thinking ... needing new boundary spaces as mediating institutions between different social worlds" (Durose and Richardson 2015: 45). Increasingly, there is demand for the development of the 'agora' as a social space in which science is debated and discussed, consisting of: "a highly articulate, well-educated population, the product of enlightened educational systems ... who face multiple publics and plural institutions" (Nowotony et al. 2001: 204–205). In this we also see echoes of Habermas' idea of a public sphere in terms of the deliberative ideal. That is not to fall into the idea we will reach ultimate consensus, nor to underestimate what is needed to reach this point.

The material terrain on which this takes place is of central importance. In this respect the search for just, sustainable futures requires organising cities in such a way as to connect knowledge and needs within cities to the capacities and capabilities to make desired changes and that, in turn, means taking democracy and the role of the citizen and communities of practice seriously. It means remembering that democracy: "is neither a form of government that enables oligarchies to rule in the name of the people, nor is it a form of society that governs the power of commodities. It is the action that constantly wrests the monopoly of public life from oligarchic governments, and the omnipotence over lives of the power of wealth. It is the power that, today more than ever, has to struggle against the confusion of these powers, rolled into one and the same law of domination" (Rancière 2006: 96).

Mediation is an active task, not a passive one in which so-called forms of nondirective facilitation becomes the ignoring of differences and values in the name of achieving outcomes that are not meaningful. 'Active intermediation' (May 2011; May and Perry 2017) is not a simple solution or model to be implemented, but a set of practices in the interstitial spaces between research and practice. It represents the active and constant "agonism" (Mouffe 2005) of engaged social scientific research: there is no state of resolution, rather a set of practices that inform the possibility of producing excellent-relevant knowledge. Active intermediation means working at the boundaries which inform the conduct, context and consequences of social scientific research and shape its transformative potential. As modes of knowledge production are changing with researchers involved in collaborative knowledge generation, it is not only the multidimensional reflexivity of the researcher that comes into play, but that of all knowledge producers in the process – and of how they interrelate. In our fragmented, fast-speed, time-poor, high-pressured societies, where policy proceeds at a startling pace in the absence of learning, collective spaces for reflection are needed even more. As epistemic permeability questions the boundaries between and within disciplines and the social world, the challenge is to design spaces for collectively producing knowledge in a reflexive ethos, without collapsing into group therapy, whilst maintaining concern to contribute to the possibilities of transformation of the world to which we belong.

Social scientific engagement with city officials to produce urban intelligence is not a simple process. For all parties it may mean an admission of ignorance or limits and not a celebration of expertise that is born of a distance from the contexts of action. Equally, context determining the content of knowledge is challenged through interactions with different groups that lead to relational reflections on practice and the process of sense-making. The danger of the content of 'expertise' being attributed in such a manner to confuse it with its consequence diminishes the democratic sphere of deliberation. Whilst not ruling out denial, interactions in the production of different forms of knowledge with those who are the translators of that knowledge at least reduces this likelihood and provides additional insight into the conditions that inform successful, inclusive outcomes.

By seeking to generate these practices on a more general scale, no claim is made that they represent simple solutions to preexisting problems, or that they are conducted without issues arising in terms of power, expectation and the capacity to achieve changes at varying scales of activity. What is being claimed is that we need to take the political climate and continuing issues seriously by building partnerships outside of the normal knowledge production process. That is a challenge to the short-termism that so often informs the evaluation of knowledge and to those who readily denigrate views according to their absence of 'realism'. We have argued that means changing the institutional expectations that weigh upon parties to these processes and that also means academics whose success is based upon what is assumed to be the production of 'new' knowledge. If the intention is to benefit different constituents in a city, the current situation is minimally unhelpful and maximally destructive.

John Dewey referred to 'experimental intelligence'. It can liberate and enable action to be more directed and less blinkered and free us from: "the bondage of the past, due to ignorance and accident hardened into custom" (Dewey 1957: 96). It is informed by a: "cooperative search for truth for the purpose of coping with real problems encountered in the course of action" (Joas 1993: 19). Dewey's emphasis upon the need for a pre-political basis of social cooperation introduces a corrective to the current one-sided politics where experts are mobilised to overcome the intransigences of the present through a selective view of the future. In this process and to return to our comments on proximity and distance, we cannot assume the existence of a relative autonomy to produce a critical social science for it is: "a historical conquest, endlessly having to be undertaken" (Bourdieu 2004: 47). As part of this there is a need to exercise an 'epistemological vigilance' over the blurring of the boundaries between everyday opinions and social scientific discourse (Bourdieu, Chamboredon and Passeron 1991) in order that what is grasped is: "both objective regularities and the process of internalization of objectivity" (Wacquant 1992: 13). The reason is not: "to discourage scientific ambition, but to help make it more realistic. By helping the progress of science and thus the growth of knowledge about the social world, *reflexivity makes possible a more responsible politics*, both inside and outside of academia" (Bourdieu in Bourdieu and Wacquant 1992: 194. Original italics).

To inform the production of such a culture, there is a tension between the production of truth and an excavation of classificatory practices that frame the ways of seeing the world we have discussed. A condition of entry and success in research fields can be a suspension of the necessities of life in order that contemplation becomes an end in itself and where failure to do so, is easily individualised as a matter of character, divorced from context. A critical commitment to understand the relations between classificatory practices and the socio-economic conditions that prevail is informed by these dynamics, whereby the idea of distance marks out the distinction of scientific work. That same distance also allows the collapse of knowledge as it becomes implicated in relations of dominance in the knowledge economy. Matters of language are important for this work. Writing about the media and the conservative revolution, Bourdieu notes: "Even words are fashioned so as to prevent our speaking about the world such as it is" (2008: 331). It is an analysis of the construction of these 'necessities' in terms of their causes, justifications and consequences that informs critique. That opens up a space for the excavation of alternatives in collaboration with urban populations that encapsulates values that are excluded, ignored and dismissed through the desire to acquire knowledge assets that are assumed to be solutions to problems – as defined by particular frames of interpretation provided by the doxosophers of the knowledge economy.

Summary: Mobilising social science to inform possibility

Those writing in the traditions of critical theory have taken us so far in understanding issues relating to the production of social scientific knowledge, reflexivity and societal transformation and the subject (May and Perry 2017). Any success of that practice is based upon a set of judgements concerning the insights that it generates into the human condition, how those inform actions and contribute to improvements in quality of life. Therefore, it is normative in orientation. If we seek the basis for criticism in the autonomy of the free individual untrammelled by the process of rationalisation, this may easily become an abstraction and nothing more than a duplication of prevailing ideology as how can any individual be separated from the social relations in which they are immersed? The idea that facts are more important than issues of value is a selective history of scientific justification and endeavour and in this study we have seen how: "Science informs values and actions which in turn motivate science, so one is in effect dealing with fact-value and theory-practice helices here" (Bhaskar 1986: 172).

Whilst it is a confusion to take the content of a critical-emancipatory social science automatically into its consequence for subsequent actions, the peculiar effects of the relations charted between policy, politics and process easily sees alternative visions being castigated as unrealistic. Essentially, it is the attribution to knowledge of its potential to fulfil value as given by narrow, economic criteria concerned with prediction, based upon individual preference. That needs to change. The direction of energy in terms of the attainment of money and the idea of the subject in terms of consumption and exchange is informed by the 'law of value'. In relation to other domains, we speak of 'values' (Graeber 2001): "Value theory, then, is about how desire becomes social. It is about how our actions become meaningful by being reflected back at us in the form of representations – ultimately, of those very actions – that seem to be their aim and origin. And this is about how different conceptions of 'society' are constantly being thrown up, like shadows on a wall, as a necessary part of that process" (Graeber 2011: 109). The work that goes into ensuring those different conceptions do not emerge from the shadows of the knowledge economy is considerable and when those are seen, they are attributed with individualistic self-interested exchange or dismissed as contextual interests divorced from necessities.

All of our practices can become compartmentalised within frames, or ways of seeing urban issues. We need to enlarge our engagements with others in order to produce alternatives. Without that in place, neoliberalism will continue to exert an influence that is not sustainable in relation to both natural resource depletion and social equity. To approach these challenges a dialectical relation between thinking and doing can be built into collaborative practices: to practise without thought is to be blinkered and to think without practising is to be stilted. To break down the dichotomies that do not promote understanding, but inform misunderstanding, a distinction between 'knowing how' and 'knowing that' may be embodied in active intermediation. This recognises that: "Intelligent practice is not a step-child of theory. On the contrary, theorizing is one practice amongst others and is itself intelligently or stupidly conducted" (Ryle 2000: 27). When we describe people as 'shrewd' or 'prudent' or otherwise, we are not imputing a knowledge to them, but refer to their ability to do things: "Theorists have been so preoccupied with the task of investigating the nature, the source, and the credential of the theories that we adopt that they have for the most part ignored the question what it is for someone to know how to perform tasks" (Ryle 2000: 28). This does not bracket critique. After all, in the case of cities, politicians and officials frequently regard themselves as people dealing with realities and all too often we have heard the idea of those who do not understand this self-evidence as being without relevance. The knowledge produced for versions of the economy, separated from the social, is equally irrelevant, but the difference is the sheer amount of effort that goes into the current circuits of attributed value.

A core component of change is an alternative relationship between university and city. That shapes and forms the possibilities to engage with localities that is dependent on institutional position, strategic mission and the internal structures and cultures that value different forms of work. If universities are at the heart of the knowledge economy and the knowledge economy is urban, then urban researchers must pay heed to how they are increasingly implicated as political actors in, rather than purely critics of, territorial projects. Without this, the ability to constructively critique what are often loosely articulated and inadequately theorised new urban visions in the knowledge society is then limited, not only by the potential benefits of silence, but by a complicity in the project of creation, along with the complex sets of relationships between those that practise and those that fund research. Researchers must reflect not only on how the world has changed, but on how perspectives and tools of analysis must also alter to recognise and make visible the 'background assumptions' (Gouldner 1971) that are held concerning epistemological foundations (Walker and Wong 2004).

The ideas of expertise we have considered constitute a celebration of knowledge within a limited sphere of activity. To overcome this requires newer divisions of labour and being willing to admit of ignorance, not just celebrate expertise and yet being confident enough to engage with others. Academia is not set up for that and current trends place unrealistic burdens upon science in general through expectations which it cannot live up to. The world is richer than acts of representation allow and this drives the need for engagement. Learning is a two-way process and it is something that communities, including those within research contexts, can inform and improve. The need for new ideas and the integration of what is already known is now greater than ever. In the search for the new, we must not forget the past. Disparate knowledges can be integrated, seen alongside each other and re-contextualised. Sharing individual understandings can generate new social learning. Only then does it become possible to know when and how knowledge has had particular outcomes that are seen, by different parties, to have had benefits or contain potentials.

Considerable effort is needed in order to learn from imaginative and effective processes and there are no quick routes towards this end. This implies a willingness to learn from the past and share an understanding of orientations according to working in different contexts and what is valuable and what are the limits of those places. This speaks to the role of academia in bringing about urban transformations, through critique, engagement and reconstruction of possibilities for action, rather than through the application of a narrow impact-led agenda, via technology transfer, commercialisation and patenting (Benneworth et al. 2015). What is at stake is the opportunity to make good the promise of knowledge-based change with widespread benefits for all and overcome the dichotomous tensions between excellence and relevance, competition and collaboration, elite advantage and social cohesion, that perpetuate contemporary discourses. In placing greater value upon a broader understanding of the contribution of a range of knowledges to socio-economic-political, environmental and cultural development, the possibility can emerge for a real 'agora' to be forged.

We have recognised that these possibilities are mediated through the politics of the global-local scale, organisational and professional rationales and the framing of ideas and practices in hierarchies of knowledge. A concern with coercion and consent means that we all risk participating in the maintenance of hegemony, despite our efforts to support more transformative and emancipatory change. In the relationship between consciousness and reality, we can seek ways of playing a role in the construction of counter-hegemonic thought patterns that embrace a difficult, messy and contentious space. There is no substitute for continual efforts that are aimed at coherent, consistent, coordinated and well-communicated understandings between parties. Such work is not an annoying distraction, but a necessary precondition for facing contemporary challenges. Creating such spaces is needed for all parties in order to imagine, learn and act for more just and sustainable futures beyond the promise and politics of the knowledge economy.

References

Ackoff, R.L. (1979), 'The future of operational research is past', *Journal of the Operational Research Society*, 30 (2): 93–104.

Adam, B. (1995), *Timewatch: The Social Analysis of Time*, Cambridge: Polity.

Agyeman, J. and Evans, B. (2004), 'Just sustainability: the emerging discourse of environmental justice in Britain?', *The Geographic Journal*, 170 (2): 155–164.

Andersen, H.T. and Atkinson, R. (eds.) (2013), *The Production and Use of Urban Knowledge: European Experiences*, Dordrecht: Springer.

Banerjee-Guha, S. (2010), 'Revisiting accumulation by dispossession: neoliberalising Mumbai', in Banerjee-Guha, S. (ed.) *Accumulation by Dispossession: Transformative Cities in the New Global Order*, London: Sage.

Banerjee-Guha, S. (ed.) (2010), *Accumulation by Dispossession: Transformative Cities in the New Global Order*, London: Sage.

Bauman, Z. (2014), *What Use is Sociology? Conversations with Michael Hviid Jacobsen and Keith Tester*, Cambridge: Polity.

Beck, U. (1992), *Risk Society: Towards a New Modernity*, London: Sage.

Beck, U. (2006), 'Living in the world risk society', *Economy and Society*, 35 (3): 329–345.

Beck, U., Giddens, A. and Lash, S. (1994), *Reflexive Modernization: Politics, Tradition and Aesthetics in the Modern Social Order*, Cambridge: Polity.

Benneworth, P., Miao, J.T. and Phelps, N.A. (2015), 'Old and new lessons for technopoles', in Miao, J.T., Benneworth, P. and Phelps, N. (eds.) (2015), *Making 21st Century Knowledge Complexes: Technopoles of the World 20 Years After*, London: Routledge, pp. 275–295.

Berlin, I. (1979 [1969]), *Four Essays on Liberty*, Oxford: Oxford University Press.

Bhaskar, R. (1986), *Scientific Realism and Human Emancipation*, London: Verso.

Boltanski, L. and Chiapello, E. (2005), *The New Spirit of Capitalism*, translated by Elliott, G., London: Verso.

Bourdieu, P. (2000), *Pascalian Meditations*, translated by Nice, R., Cambridge: Polity.

Bourdieu, P. (2004), *Science of Science and Reflexivity*, translated by Nice, R., Cambridge: Polity.

Bourdieu, P. (2005), *The Social Structures of the Economy*, translated by Turner, C., Cambridge: Polity.

Bourdieu, P. (2008), *Political Interventions: Social Science and Political Action*, texts selected and introduced by Poupeau, F. and Discepolo, T., translated by Fernbach, D., London: Verso.

Bourdieu, P. and Wacquant, L.J. (1992), *An Invitation to Reflexive Sociology*, Cambridge: Polity.

Bourdieu, P., Chamboredon, J-C. and Passeron, J-C. (1991), *The Craft of Sociology: Epistemological Preliminaries*, edited by Krais, B., translated by Nice, R., New York: Walter de Gruyter.

Bulkeley, H. and Betsill, M.M. (2005), *Cities and Climate Change: Urban Sustainability and Global Environmental Governance*, Hove: Psychology Press.

Burawoy, M. (2004), 'For public sociology', *American Sociological Review*, 70 (1): 4–28.

Castoriadis, C. (1991), *Philosophy, Politics, Autonomy: Essays in Political Philosophy*, edited by Curtis, D.A., Oxford: Oxford University Press.

Chiapello, E. (2014), 'Capitalism and Its Criticisms', in du Gay, P. and Morgan, G. (eds.) *New Spirits of Capitalism: Crises, Justifications, and Dynamics*, Oxford: Oxford University Press.

Cohen, S. (2001), *States of Denial: Knowing about Atrocities and Suffering*, Cambridge: Polity.

Collins, H. (2010), *Tacit and Explicit Knowledge*, Chicago: University of Chicago Press.

Comunian, R. and Gilmore, A. (2015), *Beyond the Creative Campus: Reflections on the Evolving Relationship Between Higher Education and the Creative Economy*, Kings College London, http://www.creative-campus.org.uk/final-report---beyond-the-creative-campus.html (accessed May 2017).

Connolly, J. and Steil, J. (2009), 'Introduction: finding justice in the city', in Marcuse, P., Connolly, J., Novy, J., Olivo, I., Potter, C. and Steil, J. (eds.) *Searching for the Just City: Debates in Urban Theory and Practice*, Routledge, pp. 1–16.

Conti, A. (2005), *Metropolitan Proletarian Research*, http://www.ecn.org/valkohaalarit/english/conti.htm (accessed May 2017).

Crouch, C. (2011), *The Strange Non-Death of Neoliberalism*, Cambridge: Polity.

Davison, A., Patel, Z. and Greyling, S. (2016), 'Tackling wicked problems and tricky transitions: change and continuity in Cape Town's environmental policy landscape', *Local Environment: The International Journal of Justice and Sustainability*, 21 (9): 1063–1081.

de la Mothe, J. (2001), 'Knowledge, politics and governance', in de la Mothe, J. (ed.) *Science, Technology and Governance*, London and New York: Continuum.

de la Mothe, J. (ed.) (2001), *Science, Technology and Governance*, London and New York: Continuum.

Deleuze, G. and Guattari, F. (1984 [1972]), *Anti-Oedipus: Capitalism and Schizophrenia*, translated by Hurley, R., Seem, M. and Lane, H., preface by Foucault, M., London: Athlone.

Desmond, M. (2016), *Evicted: Poverty and Profit in the American City*, New York: Penguin.

Dewey, J. (1957), *Reconstruction in Philosophy*, enlarged edition, Boston: Beacon Press.

Dreyfuss, R., Zimmerman, D.L. and First, H. (eds.) (2001), *Expanding the Boundaries of Intellectual Property*, Oxford: Oxford University Press.

du Gay, P. and Morgan, G. (eds.) (2014), *New Spirits of Capitalism: Crises, Justifications, and Dynamics*, Oxford: Oxford University Press.

Durose, C. and Richardson, L. (2015), *Designing Public Policy Through Coproduction: Theory, Practice and Change*, Bristol: Policy.

Fainstein, S.S. (2010), *The Just City*, Ithaca, New York: Cornell University Press.

Forst, R. (2014 [2007]), *The Right to Justification*, translated by Flynn, J., New York: Columbia University Press.

Fuller, S. (2000), *The Governance of Science: Ideology and the Future of the Open Society*, Buckingham: Open University Press.

Funtowicz, S.O. and Ravetz, J.R. (1993), 'Science for the post normal age', in Westra, L. and Lemons, J. (eds.) *Perspectives on Ecological Integrity*, Netherlands: Springer, pp. 739–755.

Gibbons, M., Limoges, C., Nowotny, H., Schwartaman, S., Scott, P. and Trow, M. (1994), *The New Production of Knowledge: The Dynamics of Science and Research in Contemporary Societies*, London: Sage.

Gibson-Graham, J.K., Cameron, J. and Healy, S. (2013), *Take Back the Economy: An Ethical Guide for Transforming our Communities*, Minneapolis: University of Minnesota Press.

Giddens, A. (2009), *The Politics of Climate Change*, Cambridge: Polity.

Gouldner, A. (1971), *The Coming Crisis of Western Sociology*, London: Heinemann.

Graeber, D. (2001), *Toward an Anthropological Theory of Value: The False Coin of Our Own Dreams*, New York: Palgrave.

Graeber, D. (2011), *Revolutions in Reverse: Essays on Politics, Violence, Art, and Imagination*, London: Minor Compositions.

Graeber, D. (2015), *The Utopia of Rules: On Technology, Stupidity, and the Secret Joys of Bureaucracy*, London: Melville House.

Habermas, J. (1989), *The Structural Transformation of the Public Sphere*, translated by Berger, T. and Lawrence, F., Cambridge, Mass: MIT Press.

Habermas, J. (2006), *Time of Transitions*, edited and translated by Cronin, C. and Pensky, M., Cambridge: Polity.

Habitat (2016), *Zero Draft of the New Urban Agenda*, United Nations Conference on Housing and Sustainable Urban Development, Quito, May 2016.

Harvey, M. and McMeekin, A. (2007), *Public or Private Economies of Knowledge? Turbulence in the Biological Sciences*, Cheltenham, UK: Edward Elgar.

Hay, C. and Payne, A. (2015), *Civic Capitalism*, Cambridge: Polity Press.

Hess, C. and Ostrom, E. (eds.) (2007), *Understanding Knowledge as a Commons: From Theory to Practice*, MIT Press.

Honneth, A. (2007), *Disrespect: The Normative Foundations of Critical Theory*, Cambridge: Polity.

Irwin, A. and Michael, M. (2003), *Science, Social Theory and Public Knowledge*, Maidenhead, Berkshire: Open University Press/McGraw-Hill.

Jasanoff, S. (2004), 'The idiom of coproduction', in Jasanoff, S. (ed.) *States of Knowledge: The Co-production of Science and Social Order*, London: Routledge.

Jasanoff, S. (ed.) (2004), *States of Knowledge: The Co-production of Science and Social Order*, London: Routledge.

Joas, H. (1993), *Pragmatism and Social Theory*, Chicago: University of Chicago Press.

Kennett, P. (ed.) (2004), *A Handbook of Comparative Social Policy*, Cheltenham, UK: Edward Elgar.

Klak, T. (1994), 'Havana and Kingston: mass media images and empirical observations of two Caribbean cities in crisis', *Urban Geography*, 15 (4): 318–344.

Klev, R. and Levin, M. (2012), *Participative Transformation: Learning and Development in Practising Change*, Aldershot: Gower.

Knorr-Cetina, K. (1999), *Epistemic Cultures: How the Sciences Make Knowledge*, Harvard: Harvard University Press.

Koch, M. (2012), *Capitalism and Climate Change: Theoretical Discussion, Historical Development and Policy Responses*, Basingstoke, Hampshire: Palgrave Macmillan.

Latour, B. (1993), *We Have Never Been Modern*, translated by Porter, C., London: Harvester Wheatsheaf.

Latour, B. (2004a), *Politics of Nature: How to Bring the Sciences into Democracy*, Cambridge, MA: Harvard University Press.

Latour, B. (2004b), 'Why has critique run out of steam? From matters of fact to matters of concern', *Critical Inquiry*, 30(2): 225–248.

Lefort, C. (1986), *The Political Forms of Modern Society: Bureaucracy, Democracy, Totalitarianism*, edited and introduced by Thompson, J.B., Cambridge, Mass: MIT Press.

Levin, K., Cashore, B., Bernstein, S. and Auld, G. (2012), 'Overcoming the tragedy of super wicked problems: constraining our future selves to ameliorate global climate change', *Policy Science*, 45 (2): 123–152.

Marcuse, P., Connolly, J., Novy, J., Olivo, I., Potter, C. and Steil, J. (eds.) (2009), *Searching for the Just City: Debates in Urban Theory and Practice*, Routledge.

Marquand, D. (2004), *Decline of the Public: The Hollowing Out of Citizenship*, Cambridge: Polity.

May, T. (2011), 'Urban knowledge arenas: dynamics, tensions and potentials', *International Journal of Knowledge-Based Development*, 2 (2): 132–147.

May, T. and Perry, B. (2011), 'Urban research in the knowledge economy: content, context and outlook', *Built Environment*, 37 (3): 352–368.

May, T. and Perry, B. (2013), 'Universities, reflexivity and critique: uneasy parallels in practice', *Policy Futures In Education*, 11 (5): 505–514.

May, T. and Perry, B. (2017), *Reflexivity: The Essential Guide*, London: Sage.

May, T. with Perry, B. (2011), *Social Research and Reflexivity: Content, Consequences and Context*, London: Sage.

McFarlane, C. (2011), *Learning the City: Knowledge and Translocal Assemblage*, Oxford: Wiley-Blackwell.

Miao, J.T., Benneworth, P. and Phelps, N. (eds.) (2015), *Making 21st Century Knowledge Complexes: Technopoles of the World 20 Years After*, London: Routledge.

Milne, S. (2012), *The Revenge of History: The Battle for the Twenty-First Century*, London: Verso.

Mirowski, P. (2014), *Never Let a Serious Crisis Go to Waste: How Neoliberalism Survived the Financial Meltdown*, London: Verso.

Morgan, G. (1983), 'Knowledge, uncertainty and choice', in Morgan, G. (ed.) *Beyond Method: Strategies for Social Research*, Sage, p. 383.

Morgan, G. (ed.) (1983), *Beyond Method: Strategies for Social Research*, Sage.

Moser, P. (2013), 'Integrating urban knowledge', in Anderson, H.T. and Atkinson, R. (eds.) *Production and Use of Urban Knowledge*, Netherlands: Springer, pp. 17–34.

Mouffe, C. (2005), *On the Political*, London: Routledge.

Noveck, B.S. (2015), *Smart Citizens, Smarter State: The Technologies of Expertise and the Future of Governing*, Cambridge, Mass: Harvard University Press.

Nowotny, H., Scott, P., and Gibbons, M. (2001), *Re-thinking Science: Knowledge and the Public in an Age of Uncertainty*, Cambridge: Polity.

O'Connor, J. (1987), *The Meaning of Crisis: A Theoretical Introduction*, Oxford: Blackwell.

O'Neill, J. (2007), *Markets, Deliberation and Environment*, London: Routledge.

Oldenburg, R. (2000), *Celebrating the Third Place: Inspiring Stories about the 'Great Good Places' at the Heart of Our Communities*, New York, NY: Marlowe and Company.

Ostrom, E. (2015 [1990]), *Governing the Commons: The Evolution of Institutions for Collective Action*, Cambridge: Cambridge University Press.

Perry, B. and May, T. (2010), 'Urban knowledge exchange: devilish dichotomies and active intermediation', *International Journal of Knowledge-Based Development*, 1 (1–2): 6–24.

Perry, B., May, T., Marvin, S. and Hodson, M. (2013), 'Rethinking sustainable knowledge-based urbanism through active intermediation: what knowledge and how?', in Andersen, H.T. and Atkinson, R. (eds.) *The Production and Use of Urban Knowledge: European Experiences*, Dordrecht: Springer, pp. 151–167.

Pfeffer, J. and Sutton, R.I. (2000), *The Knowing-Doing Gap: How Smart Companies Turn Knowledge into Action*, Boston, Mass: Harvard Business School Press.

Pieterse, E. (2008), *City Futures: Confronting the Crisis of Urban Development*, London: Zed Books.

Polanyi, M. (1983 [1966]), *The Tactic Dimension*, Gloucester, Mass: Peter Smith.

Polk, M. (ed.) (2015), *Co-producing Knowledge for Sustainable Cities: Joining Forces for Change*, Abingdon: Routledge.

Rancière, J. (2006), *Hatred of Democracy*, translated by Corcoran, S., London: Verso.

Rancière, J. (2010), *Chronicles of Consensual Times*, Bloomsbury Publishing.

Rittel, H.W.J. and Webber, M.M. (1973), Dilemmas in a general theory of planning, *Policy Sciences*, 4 (2): 155–169.

Ritzer, G. (2015), *The McDonaldization of Society*, 8th revised edition, Thousand Oaks, California: Sage.

Roberts, N. (2000), 'Wicked problems and network approaches to resolution', *International Public Management Review*, 1 (1): 1–19.

Routledge, P. and Driscol Derickson, K. (2015), 'Situated solidarities and the practice of scholar-activism', *Environment and Planning D: Society and Space*, 33 (3): 391–407.

Ryle, G. (2000 [1949]), *The Concept of Mind*, Harmondsworth: Penguin.

Scambler, G. (2002), *Health and Social Change: A Critical Theory*, http://www.mheducation. co.uk/openup/chapters/0335204791.pdf (accessed May 2017).

Schön, D. (1991 [1983]), *The Reflective Practitioner*. London: Ashgate.

Shotter, J. (1993), *Cultural Politics of Everyday Life: Social Constructionism, Rhetoric and Knowing of the Third Kind*, Buckingham: Open University Press.

Stehr, N. (ed.) (2004), *The Governance of Knowledge*, London: Transaction.

Strydom, P. (2000), *Discourse and Knowledge: The Making of Enlightenment Sociology*, Liverpool: Liverpool University Press.

Strydom, P. (2002), *Risk, Environment and Society*, Buckingham: Open University Press.

Swyngedouw, E. (2009), 'The antinomies of the postpolitical city: in search of a democratic politics of environmental production', *International Journal of Urban and Regional Research*, 33 (3): 601–620.

Virilio, P. (1986), *Speed and Politics: An Essay on Dromology*, originally published in 1977, translated by Polizzotti, M., New York: Semiotext(e).

Wacquant, L. (1992), 'The structure and logic of Bourdieu's sociology', in Bourdieu, P. and Wacquant, L.J., *An Invitation to Reflexive Sociology*, Cambridge: Polity.

Wacquant, L. (2008), *Urban Outcasts: A Comparative Sociology of Advanced Marginality*, Cambridge: Polity.

Walker, A. and Wong, C.K. (2004), 'The ethnocentric construction of the welfare state', in Kennett, P., *A Handbook of Comparative Social Policy*, Cheltenham, UK: Edward Elgar, pp. 116–130.

Weaver, T. (2016), 'Urban crisis: the genealogy of a concept', *Urban Studies*, 54 (9): 2039–2055.

Westra, L. and Lemons, J. (eds.) (1993), *Perspectives on Ecological Integrity*, Netherlands: Springer.

INDEX